I0699764

# WHEN KNOWING COMES

A NOVEL BY

## KELLY GREEN

*Boise*

This is a work of fiction. Names, characters, organizations, places, events, and incidents are either products of the author's imagination or are used fictitiously. See Preface for additional information.

Text copyright © 2022, 2023 Safe Passage Press LLC

All rights reserved.

No part of this book may be reproduced or stored in a retrieval system, or transmitted in any form or by any means, electronic, mechanical, photocopying recording, or otherwise, and may not be used for training, developing, or educating any type of artificial intelligence, without express written permission of the publisher.

Published by Safe Passage Press LLC, Boise, Idaho

www.ReadKellyGreen.com

ISBN: 979-8-9876584-1-3 (paperback)
ISBN: 979-8-9876584-0-6 (hardback)
ISBN: 979-8-9876584-2-0 (e-book)

Cover design and image by Luísa Dias.

Printed in the United States of America.

First edition.

# Content Disclosure

This novel is only for adults and includes scenes of sexual violence against children (the National Sexual Assault Hotline provides free, confidential help 24/7, call 800-656-4673) and suicide (the Suicide & Crisis Lifeline also provides free, confidential help 24/7, call 988).

# Preface

The original idea for this novel goes back decades, to when I learned a thing about a person I care about and was reading Pat Conroy's The *Prince of Tides* at the same time. But then something else happened, and then something else happened, and again. Finally, in 2018, as I sat reading yet another comprehensive report about the sexual victimization of our youth, I became overwhelmed to the point of getting up off my ass to finish the story in the pages that follow.

You may identify with the experiences in this story, but this is not about you or any particular person. The people, youth association and soccer clubs in this story are completely fictional despite their generic-sounding names. If you see any similarity to your life, your experience, or your organization, that is because—sadly—your story is not unique. The experiences reflected here have happened to thousands or possibly millions of people. If you doubt that statement, I invite you to review the over 80,000 sex abuse survivor claims filed in the Boy Scouts of America bankruptcy. The commonalities among stories are as astounding as they are disturbing.Unfortunately, that is only one example.

This book may trigger unwelcome memories for some. And to be clear, the memory may not be a mental recollection, but may manifest itself physically through tension, sleeplessness, or other maladies. So, while your brain may tell you that you're fine as you navigate this story, your body may tell you something different. Listen to your body and stop reading if you need to do that. Reach out to the resources provided.

My hope is that survivors will find validation here, not more pain. Your experience was real, your feelings are valid, and shared by many. You are not alone. The same is true for the secondary victims: the spouses, the parents, the children and siblings, the organizations, and the communities. Your pain is also real, and valid, and you are a survivor, too.

Finally, please be aware that proceeds from the sale of this novel will be donated to not-for-profit organizations dedicated to the prevention of child sexual abuse.

Imagine a world where avoidable childhood
trauma has been successfully eradicated.

*For all survivors, especially Dad.*

"It can't be true, ... [b]ecause if it *is* true, and it *is* this bad, then everyone knows. If they knew, they'd stop it, right?"

Rachael Denhollander, *What is a Girl Worth? My story of breaking the silence and exposing the truth about Larry Nassar and USA Gymnastics*

*One*

# THE BOY
# 1972

Most who had visited the pristine California lakes as children cherished their summer memories of frolicking in the water surrounded by dark groves of towering pines. Some kept sentimental keepsakes of those good times, like carefully whittled sticks, arrowheads, small stones, or pinecones. Yet a few people inexplicably clung to their summer mementos while retaining no childhood memory of their origin, perhaps in the misguided hope that the memory might return.

On one late summer day, a treasure-hunting deep-sea diver expertly adjusted the flex hoses connecting his bubble-shaped helmet to the ship above. He jerked and waddled in the puffed-up diving suit, pushing himself down further and further. The unexplored lake depths muted all the world's sounds. The shrill of parents arguing, the threats of schoolyard bullies, shrieks of anger and pain; dense quiet replaced all real-life sounds in the underwater wilderness. The burbling hoses, his lifelines, and blooping bubbles from his mouth provided the only sound.

Ten thousand years ago, a Spanish sea gallop… gallon… a Spanish sea ship had crashed upon the rocks in rough winter seas and had spilled its treasure along the bottom of this ocean-lake. The world-famous diver undertook the dangerous mission of recovering lost golden doubloons. Upon reaching the bottom, he thrust his heavily gloved hand into the muck, sifting through it until he felt a solid object. At first, the object slipped through his glove-encumbered fingers, but he didn't give up. After several attempts, he captured the golden nugget—for surely that's what it must be—and trapped it in his palm. The tightly gripped nugget promised endless wealth. He was rich. Or maybe it was magic. Maybe it was a magic golden nugget, just like one of Jack's beans.

With the nugget secure in his fist, the diver surfaced. Carefully, he peeled back his slim fingers, allowing the sunlight to illuminate his treasure. He stared wide-eyed at the bit of gold-flecked crumbly granite because there could be no doubt. Not California fool's gold, but a magic golden rock. Only it wasn't the same as a magic bean, not like Jack's bean at all. He realized it was a rather unique magic as an effervescent wisp rose from the rock, expanded, and stretched into an impenetrable bubble that surrounded not only the rock but its holder. It was a magic shield, a *secret* magic shield. The only person who could ever see the shield was the Boy holding it and nobody would ever know. Nothing could hurt the Boy now that he possessed the secret magic rock.

Looking up, the secretly shielded Boy saw the naked Man shouting and waving the boys back to the cabin. Reluctantly, the Boy accepted the end of swim time. Clutching his secret defensive weapon, he dog paddled toward the beckoning naked Man. The three, also-naked, prepubescent boys laughed and shivered as they stepped out of the remote mountain lake onto the rocky shore. The fragrant but unkind pines threw down infinite needles that pierced their bare feet. But boys are tough. Exhilarated by their daring escapades, they bounced about the shore—as boys do—and ignored the needles' prick. Their laughter rose through the air, past treetops, but didn't reach the ears of any spirit concerned for their wellbeing.

The Boy had never before swum naked, much less reveled in nakedness. The titillating adventure of icy wetness against bare skin energized his little body until freedom replaced shame. His growing confidence, edged with nudity's invigoration, sparked endless imaginative adventures. And why not? The two other boys were doing it. Besides, everybody knows cowboys swim naked. Cavemen swim naked. Real Men swim naked. *I'm no pussy.* The small, quiet Boy held his chin up and pranced to his summoner, empowered by the revelations of his self-discovery.

The dripping Boy made his way to the Man who was offering a promise of warmth, a brightly colored terrycloth towel. After tossing old bath towels to the other boys–the tallest and the second tallest–the Man wrapped the Boy–the smallest–snug in the biggest, thickest beach towel, holding him close, safe, with strong though wrinkled hands. Remnants of warmth from the receding sun, combined with the warm towel and attention, comforted the Boy.

The Man was no longer completely naked, having slipped on, but not laced, his waffle-stompers. Without socks, the waffle-stompers dwarfed his ankles, and capped the bottom of his hairy legs. Lake water dripped from the oil of his thin, slicked-back hair and diverted at his eyebrows to leave tracks on his checks. Even his gray mustache held tiny droplets, evidence of a failed attempt to wipe his face. But the Boy only noticed the smile under the mustache, welcoming and kind.

"This is our secret," the Man said. He winked at the Boy, pulling him into the conspiracy, an invitation to independence. "Anyway, most adults wouldn't understand."

"Yeah, never tell or you'll be a rat," one boy said. That boy, the oldest and tallest, and a veteran of lake cabin escapades, looked to the Man for affirmation and the Man smiled back his reward.

The Boy nodded. "I never swam naked before. That was fun," he said.

"You betcha," the Man said to the Boy while tucking him tighter into the towel. "No pussies here."

The boys all laughed, mutually relieved they weren't pussies, but were well on their way to manhood.

"Now, who's hungry?" the Man asked.

The unrehearsed choir responded: "I am! I am!"

"Last one there's a rotten egg!"

Like bouncing towel burritos, the swaddled boys blasted past the pebbles, sticks, and pine needles scattered on the lakeshore to the cabin. In late summer, after school had started, there was unlikely to be anyone else near the isolated forest lake. Nobody would see three wet-headed, towel-wrapped boys and one naked, gray-haired man make this short trek. Any potential observer might momentarily think it odd but would quickly dismiss any concern as unfounded since most people would consider acceptable the event, normal even. Skinny-dipping at the lake was a tradition revered, emulated, and passed on through generations. An elderly gentleman spending the weekend with a group of young boys at his lake cabin was itself a tradition. Lucky was the boy invited to take part.

Back at the cabin, the Man instructed the toweled boys to put on their pajamas. No sense in getting dressed just to have to put your pajamas on later. Once everyone was dry and pajama'ed, with full tummies, the Man lit a small fire in the ramshackle fireplace. The cabin had a large living room full of big-boy toys, a new stereo and speakers, a couple of pinball machines, and a foosball table. Best of all, the Man allowed outdoor behavior indoors, so the boys chased each other around, shouting.

"I can beat all of you!" said the tallest, oldest boy. He jumped up, thumped his chest, ran to the foosball table—its plastic handles cracked from years of rugged but playful use—and positioned himself for an epic battle.

"No way, Dude! I kicked your ass last time. Watch me do it again," the second tallest, second oldest boy shouted. And he grabbed the handles on the opposing side. Each boy began the mad dash, grasping and spinning the handles so the threaded soccer players smacked the ball with their wooden paddle feet. The warmth generated by active, youthful bodies added to the fire's warmth.

"Score!"

"You suck!"

Clacking, shouting, laughter, and bustling noises filled the room. As the Man watched him, the Boy quietly watched the more rambunctious children with a shy smile. The Boy was still the newcomer, not yet finding his own groove. When another boy shouted a game-induced profanity, the Boy turned pink and looked down at his fidgeting feet.

"Hey," the Man called out to the Boy, "help me find some tunes to spin." The Man sat on the floor next to a long stack of vinyl albums. When he saw the enormous music selection, the Boy's blue eyes widened. The Man smiled, patting the floor next to him. "Sit here. What do you like?"

"Uh, I don't know," the Boy replied. He sat next to the Man and together they thumbed through the large cardboard album covers. Their hands touched briefly while awkwardly reaching for the same stack. But the Boy remained lost in excitement over the musical smorgasbord. He couldn't contain a pleased gasp at the Man's collection, which was up to date with pop music—everything from Al Green to Led Zeppelin. He had been expecting old fart music like the stuff his dad listened to, maybe Sinatra or something.

With another gasp, the Boy pulled out his chosen album and spouted as many words as he had during the entire trip to that point. "You have the Jackson 5! I can't believe you have the Jackson 5! I love this!"

The Man laughed as he demonstrated how to balance the vinyl disc on the player and set the needle on the swing arm to start automatically. He stood behind the Boy, placing his hands on the Boy's arms. The Boy didn't shrug, didn't flinch.

"Careful not to scratch the records with the needle. There you go, like that. Good job." The Man delivered the compliment with a genuine smile.

Bubblegum funk-pop pumped up the party. Shouting over the speaker's volume, the foosball competitors slammed the paddles. His parents didn't let him listen to music like this, black music. He couldn't watch *Soul Train* at home, but now and then could sneak views at his friends' houses. Intuitively but timidly, his body moved in time to the beat. He considered trying dance moves he'd seen on *Soul Train*, but decided against it. The other boys remained absorbed in foosball but might laugh if they noticed. He wasn't ready to take that chance.

"Hey guys, watch this!" The Man grabbed a Budweiser can and yanked off the aluminum pull tab. He sucked down the entire beer in one breath, sputtering and laughing, foam bits spraying down his shirt. "Oh yeah, baby!" he announced, laughing as he reached for another can.

"I want one!" the tallest, oldest boy said.

"Me too!" said the second tallest, second oldest boy.

The Boy's parents would not have approved of the beer and glossy sex magazines that followed, but the other boys welcomed the shocking contraband without reservation. The Boy struggled with the choice presented—between getting in trouble or being cool—but the allure of coolness won out, and the Boy tried his first sip of alcohol, scrunching up his face as bitterness assaulted his mouth.

With a thump on the Boy's back, the Man said, "Atta-boy! Look at you, becoming a man." The other boys cheered, accepting the Boy into the clan. The Boy swallowed hard, the beer bubbles flaming inside his nose, and looked up into the Man's eyes with admiration. Disgusting beer stink lingered in his mouth, but everything would be okay because the Boy had found a place where he belonged.

*****

Eventually, the night became quiet. Just off the kitchen in a closet-sized room, the Boy climbed alone into the queen-sized bed, such a big bed for a tiny room. Since there were no linens, he crawled into the two zipped-together sleeping bags tossed onto the bare mattress. Warm, safe sleep pulled at the Boy's happily exhausted body. If not for the three-quarter moon hung like a lit potato just outside the window, the Boy would be blinded in darkness. The buzzing of a single mosquito sang to the Boy who dozed to the melody.

A muted thump of something falling jostled the Boy from his almost sleep. He looked up to see the Man in the open doorway picking up something from the floor. The thing's shape was familiar, but obscured. A relaxed smile breaking his face, the Boy greeted the Man who stepped inside and closed the door.

With each creak of the closing door, the magic golden nugget resting on the adjacent nightstand emitted another shimmering wisp, their density increasing exponentially. The wisps twisted and spread, first as a giant umbrella, then the massive wings of a beneficent angel. The white-feathered wings opened wide and tucked the Boy into their breadth like a mother eagle settling onto her nested eggs before morphing into a giant storage tank with welded steel walls encircling the Boy. A huge padlock secured the tank so bad things couldn't get in. The Boy floated above the bed, alone in the steel tank, without emotion, without feeling, like drifting in space. All was quiet and safe inside the tank. Nothing happened inside the tank.

Later, the Boy didn't hear the Man leave, didn't hear the door close, didn't hear anything. The safety tank faded away, and the night was silent. The grunts and groans had been faint, as though coming from a different dimension. He felt—but didn't feel—the wet stickiness between his legs, the drips of sweat on his back. His body stiffened as he watched the mosquito crawl up along the tacky green wallpaper, slowly making its way to the ceiling. The blood sucker's long spindly legs tentatively touched one spot after another before committing to its next unhurried move. The crisscross weave of the wallpaper's texture mesmerized the Boy, and he became lost in the comfortingly consistent pattern of pale green. There was nothing, no sleeping bags, no Man, no Boy, nothing except the mosquito and the wallpaper.

If a mosquito was human-boy-sized, crawling on the ceiling would be like dangling above Earth from outer space. The Boy was the mosquito, flying around searching for escape, but not finding any exit. He viewed freedom through the window amid the night-darkened green of pine trees. He looked at the green walls and the green plaid lining inside the sleeping bags. So much green. *Everything is green.*

*Two*

# TRAINING
# 1998

Heather Elbridge swung her mom-car, a newish Grand Cherokee, into the parking lot slightly too fast—not fast like an out-of-control-control, reckless kind of fast, but fast like a stressed-out,over-worked, mom-who's-late-for-soccer-practice-pick-up, kind of fast. Her peripheral vision caught the boys finishing up last laps as she pulled in over the center line between two compact parking spots and jammed the transmission into park. Thankfully, practice was also running late.

*Not practice, "training,"* she reminded herself. Her eleven-year-old son, Atticus, affectionately called Ace, had been accepted on this new high-level, competitive U-12 team that didn't practice, they "*trained.*" *Practice* was for amateur child athletes.

This new soccer club, the FC Strikers, did not suffer amateurs. In fact, the club owned their own field and clubhouse, a large residence that at some point had been somebody's farmhouse. The club had remodeled to add administrative offices, meeting rooms, and locker rooms with showers. Over the years, the club had diligently maintained, improved, and expanded the old farmhouse. Next to the house stood a large barn, obviously original to the old farm, where the club stored various soccer gear and maintenance equipment for the fields. Heather figured the water cost alone for so many grass fields had to be expensive, not to mention the cost of the underlying land. High-end residential developments had overtaken the area a few years ago and surrounded the old farmhouse and fields. Meaning, no doubt, this land was worth a lot of money.

Ahead on the grass, Heather spied the group of soccer moms gathered in the abundant shade of a black oak tree. Yes, all women, all moms. Later in the season, the dads would attend games and maybe some training sessions. Early in the season, however, it was always the moms.

At the head of the group, Heather recognized Team Mom, who managed the parents, coercing them into obeying the coaches who otherwise couldn't be bothered with trivial family needs. Communication with soccer families was beneath the coaching staff and top club administrators, except in those cases of family wealth, connection, or talent. The female staff and team moms organized all the boring housekeeping details. Soccer-World work distribution assigned all menial and clerical jobs to women. Moms ruled mundane team organization—like who brings the water bottles—while men dominated all the important decisions.

The huddled soccer moms quietly listened to Team Mom rather than socializing freely in smaller groups. Judging by their rapt attention, something important was going down. Heather resigned herself to joining the gaggle for the potential reward of useful information. She glanced in the rearview mirror at her youngest child, Lisa, who just turned eight and would enter the third grade in a couple of weeks when school started. Lisa seemed to be occupied humming some little ditty to herself and coloring rainbow unicorns in a tattered coloring book.

*I'll listen for just a minute and then return to Lisa*, she thought. *Lisa will be ok.*

She did a quick check in the visor mirror and wiped the flour off her cheek. It had been a busy day at her bakery, training new staff how to make croissants—the best croissants in California, at least in her opinion.

"Sweetie, I'm going to say 'Hi' to the ladies over by that tree." She pointed to make sure Lisa knew where. "It's ok if you need to get me, but don't climb into the front seat because I'm leaving the car running. Do you understand?" Heather asked uncertainly. She couldn't turn the car off and shut the doors. Everyone knew about the danger of leaving any living thing, especially children, in a locked car during late summer. The best solution was to force Lisa to come along. But leaving her alone for a minute seemed a small, acceptable risk.

Lisa nodded her head *yes* without interrupting her humming and without looking up.

"What do you do if someone you don't know asks you to unlock the car?" Heather asked.

"I know, I know, Mommy, don't talk to strangers." Lisa's sweet voice repeated the memorized answer to this frequent question. "Strangers are dangerous and can hurt me, so I have to stay away from strangers." She had learned all about *Stranger Danger* in school. The school district aspired to protect children from molestation by teaching them about the danger strangers represented. Like most parents generally, Heather agreed with—and was relieved by—that curriculum.

Like most parents of young girls, Heather worried about her daughter growing up in a world where girls were targets of abuse. She was determined to educate Lisa well about protecting herself. Lisa loved gymnastics, but Heather fully intended to push martial arts studies soon. Every female should master self-defense. Maybe someday abusers, and not women, would be responsible for preventing abuse. An ideal world would not require self-defense. In the meantime, Heather's daughter would learn every self-protection skill possible, whether or not she wanted to.

Satisfied with Lisa's correct answer, Heather shut and locked the car door, leaving Lisa inside alone, *only a minute*. As she walked over to the clustered women, Heather tried and failed to remember Team Mom's name, who she always thought of as Soccer Mom Barbie. Although a perfect moniker, Heather remembered Team Mom was not named Barbie. Team Mom was everything a typical Barbie image invokes: slim, bleached blonde hair, fake boobs, and muscular legs from teaching Pilates classes five days a week. And she had the bubbly personality you would expect to complete the package. *Stop that*, Heather thought firmly, reprimanding herself for her harsh judgment of a person who was also genuinely caring and self-sacrificing. Team Mom always had a hug ready. She also had the empathy to know when a hug was needed and the wisdom to know when it was inappropriate, even when needed. Heather vowed to stop judging Team Mom and all the other less Barbie-like soccer moms. It being time to let go of stress, work stress, Lisa-alone-in-the-car stress, the-world-is-fucked stress, all the stress, she promised to keep her focus positive. She stood straight, dropped her shoulders, and intentionally relaxed her facial muscles into a natural smile as she approached the group.

"Hi Heather, come join us!" sang out Team Mom in her happy voice. "Everyone, this is Heather, Ace's mom. Ace is the new talent who joined FC Strikers."

A swift buzz of greetings followed this brief introduction, but Team Mom cut them short. "Heather, you're just in time. We are talking about having a get-together soon so we can laminate player cards, maybe over coffee."

"Or wine—" another female voice interjected, followed by more giggles.

"Wouldn't that be fun?" Team Mom welcomed the suggestion.

Heather choked down a groan she hoped was undetected by the better moms who were excited about the prospect of laminated player cards, whatever that was.

"That sounds great." Heather lied with a smile of amusement at this new Soccer-World absurdity, though she hoped Team Mom would read it as one of friendliness.

The impromptu planning of the laminated-player-card party continued as Heather let her focus shift to the boys on the field. The boys had finished the last run and Coach Sean had the group in a circle around his feet, gulping from their water bottles. Heather was glad Ace made it to Coach Sean Geoghan's team. Not only was Sean the most winning coach in the area—with several state titles to his name—but he was also wildly popular with the players and their families. Getting invited to join an elite team was a prestigious accomplishment in Soccer-World. A child should enjoy a strong sense of accomplishment at least once in their life, before adulthood provided multiple opportunities to wallow in failure. So why not enjoy small successes while they seemed important?

Heather watched the boys who circled around Coach Sean in matching training gear, matching backpacks at their feet, absorbing every word dropped by Sean, little faces tilted upward in rapt attention. Later in the season, the boys would listen less and less while they pulled off their shin guards in the cool grass. With the season just starting, the boys were practically bursting with images of heroic success, of winning the season's grand prize, the State Cup. Coach Sean had not yet made final decisions on position assignments or tournament invitations.

Ace was also paying close attention to the lecture, as Heather knew he would. Heather also knew, with some pride, that Ace absorbed the bubbling happiness from the surrounding boys. It was his nature. The other kids' sweaty and flushed faces revealed their tiredness from the physicality of a challenging practice, *training*.

A dark-skinned kid with adorable dimples and long curly hair sat next to a pale-skinned, blue-eyed Ace, elbow-jabbed him, and giggled. The new boy's face shone with easy laughter; he had a face comfortable in friendship, the type of face that made you feel like he'd been a friend since forever. Ace placed his hands on his stomach as the boys shared a silent, secret giggle. Heather observed the connection, relieved her introverted son had made a friend with a cheerful kid .

Even from some distance, Heather automatically liked the new dark-skinned kid. His friendly, upbeat aura radiated about him and sailed across the field to her. Ace's expression, usually so serious, appeared at once invigorated and relaxed. She sensed an extraordinary commonality between her son and his new friend that dissolved their ethnic differences and she hoped they would enjoy spending more time together. The rest of her family could put up with Soccer-World weirdness for that outcome.

Ace had embraced the opportunity to take his soccer play to a higher level. Heather was confident Ace would step up to meet the challenge. All the teachers loved Ace, an obedient and quiet boy who took learning with a seriousness not typical of the raucous boys under their daily care. Heather sometimes wondered whether Ace was overlooked because he didn't cause any trouble. She doubted teachers would look back on their careers and fondly remember Ace as a favorite student. More likely, the memories of Ace would blend into the memory of hundreds of other good kids, also forgotten as individuals. This didn't sadden her one bit because she knew her son would come into his own one day, in his own time.

Coach Sean looked up at the group of women, stood tall, and trotted over, while the boys—who were in no hurry to be embarrassed by their moms—followed slowly in a single line like lambs through a chute. In his typical attire of expensive, branded athletic gear, Coach

Sean looked like the world-class coach the club touted. The distance across the field did nothing to dim his bright twinkling blue eyes, but he wasn't looking at the women who were waiting for him. His attention remained focused on herding the boys forward. He didn't seem excited or even interested in meeting the women.

The Strikers had brought Coach Sean over from Ireland. He had previously played at some fancy English club before his career coaching youth soccer. Heather didn't remember the name, but it sounded impressive, Liverpool or Manchester or something like that. She was sure that, whatever his background, it was less important than everyone made it out to be. Sometimes, perception is reality. Still, you couldn't argue with success. The Strikers were renowned for playing at the highest competitive level of youth soccer in California. Sean's arrival added even more prestige, which also brought more money to the club.

The soccer moms fussed and giggled as Coach Sean approached, but he ignored the flirtatious attention. Instead, he held himself awkwardly among the women, unusual for such a good-looking man.

*He's not ignoring them; he's oblivious to their attraction*, Heather thought as she watched him. Not once did he make eye contact or wink at the twittering soccer moms. Nor did he toss his head in an arrogant demonstration of his prowess. Typically, the Alpha-types basked in all the feminine attention they could attract. Yet Coach Sean was oblivious if not shy, definitely not Alpha. No toxic masculinity here. In fact, he seemed almost childlike, sweet. She had heard rumors he was unmarried, which seemed unusual for a devout Catholic his age, that she guessed to be his early thirties.

When the crowd quieted in anticipation, he greeted everyone with a warm, bright smile, and slightly exaggerated Irish brogue. "Hello, ladies."

The "ladies" twittered again in response. Heather rolled her eyes at this, but only in her mind because she didn't want to start off on the wrong foot. His awkwardness was the sole reason she could see that some woman wouldn't have already snagged this man. He didn't seem gay. In fact, he didn't exude any sexual vibe, only excitement like a child on Christmas morning. She forced herself to shut down that train of thought and listen.

"… and by now you should all know that playing at a competitive level means mandatory participation in certain elite tournaments that are out of town. There will be travel and travel expenses. You'll have to help your athlete deal with missing school and making up assignments. This club gets invitations to take part in the most prestigious, most competitive tournaments in the Western United States. This is a big deal. You should be proud of your athlete, proud of his talent and dedication. We will get you dates and other info later, after the decisions are made. Susie always does a brilliant job of organizing the travel. If you have questions, be sure to contact Susie. She takes great care of the team and everyone." Coach Sean beamed at the ladies.

*Susie! I have to remember that: Susie, Susie, Susie,* thought Heather. She glanced at Team Mom Susie, who seemed flustered by the well-deserved compliment.

"Ok, everyone, we will see you at the next practice," Susie said. "Please remember to wear your white trainers and please double-check that you've grabbed your own backpack. We've had problems with mixed-up backpacks before and it's a hassle." Heather marveled at Susie's organization and attentiveness to detail as the team mom spurted additional reminders.

*Damn, stereotyping again, stop it!* Heather admonished herself again for underestimating a woman who had just proved her intelligence. *I have to stop making negative assumptions about women, even the Barbies.* Susie looked up and smiled at Heather as though reading her thoughts. Heather smiled back and wondered if they would, or could, ever become friends.

As the talk broke up, Ace came up to his mom, physically exhausted and as happy as she had ever seen him. Coach Sean was right; this was a big deal. She smiled at her son and reached out to him, but hesitated. Maybe it was too uncool for a mom to put her arm around her son. She shook that thought aside and did it anyway. Ace would have to deal with the social ramifications of his mother's embarrassing affection. But in a surprise move, he snuggled next to her for an instant and smiled, still her little boy who loved cuddling affection. Well, sometimes anyway. The moment was only that—a moment before Ace nudged her away to walk independently.

She was proud of him, but even more importantly, his happiness mostly reassured her he might be prepared for the harsh world. She wanted her son to understand strength does not require excluding affection, and he could have both, unlike her husband, Ace's dad.

Maybe she was doing parenting right. She tousled his light brown, curly hair—just like his dad's—and resisted the urge to pick him up in a big bear hug and smother his face with kisses. He was so big now she couldn't pick him up anymore, anyway.

"I'm proud of you, Ace," she said.

He shrugged and turned, but not before she saw his smile.

Before they could walk to the car, Sean called out to Ace, who, with his mom, immediately stopped, turned, and snapped to attention. Behind Coach Sean tagged along a younger man, or boy, maybe in his late teens or early twenties. She would later learn that he was Sean's nephew, JJ, who had moved from Ireland to America to live with his uncle for some reason or another that made sense in their family. Other than the bright blue eyes, the two were quite different. JJ didn't look like a kid who played any sport, even soccer. A too-small head, with red hair and freckles, topped his gangly body.

"Hey Buddy, I don't think I've had the chance to meet your Ma," Coach Sean trilled.

Heather, who missed her window for escape, looked back at him and smiled. "Hello, I'm Heather, Ace's mom."

"Well, I'm glad that you're here, so I can tell you what a brilliant talent your son is. We're chuffed to have him on the team. We're expecting great things from this athlete," Sean said as he rested his hand lightly on Ace's shoulder.

"Thanks, Coach. I know he shares that excitement. Ace is a hard worker. We're proud to support his athletic career any way we can." Heather wasn't typically obsequious, but she understood fawning was expected.

The club expected unquestioning parental obedience to its authority, no matter how immature or misguided. She had been warned the Strikers' administration was a group of overly testosteroned narcissists who cherished the club's success with all the vigor of men who had failed to achieve much success anywhere else in their lives. She also knew all the other elite athletic clubs operated the same way, and blind loyalty was included in the admission price everywhere.

"I can see that he's a hard worker," Sean replied with a nod. "Good, because there's lots of work ahead. Since he started at a lower level, he'll need to catch up on a few skills. Usually, early in the season, my nephew

JJ and I run extra training for boys that need a bit of a boost. I haven't decided yet who to invite but would consider Ace if he is interested in stepping up his game. You guys talk about that and let me know."

With that, Sean tousled Ace's hair, the same way Heather had done a minute ago, as Ace looked up at her with pleading eyes. The hair thing seemed excessively intimate, but Heather understood there must be trust between a coach and players. Perhaps that was his way of developing trust. She put it out of her mind.

An urgent honking from the parking lot broke the moment: *Lisa!* Equally anxious and embarrassed, Heather knew she had to get back to Lisa immediately. Heather mumbled goodbye and ran toward the car as another mom pulled Sean away, wanting his attention. Atticus followed his mom and ran to his sister, cheerfully waving at her sitting in the driver's seat, gripping the car's wheel. Lisa was fine, just bored and needing attention. Yet another potential catastrophe of a hectic life averted.

On the drive home, Heather mulled over this series of new experiences from the last ten minutes as the usually quiet Ace happily chattered away about his various soccer successes. This was a new journey for them both, for the whole family, and she wasn't sure what to make of it yet. Every time she thought she was ridiculously over-committed, something else threw itself in her lap, year after year. She snuck a glance at Ace as he cracked a soccer joke she didn't get, but she smiled anyway.

Time would tell with soccer, but Ace was happy, and now she needed to get everyone home to wrestle with different alligators. She tightened her mouth and thought about her husband, Steve. The distance between them had grown, which she attributed to his stress. Her instinct screamed at her, and screamed again, *that's not it. Something serious is wrong with Steve.* But logic provided no other explanation. Still, her inner voice insisted *my family is at risk.* Her attempts to reach Steve had proved pathetic. But she resolved to try again that very night.

# Three

# AN EVENING AT HOME
# 1998

Home now, with the dinner dishes and children put away, Heather Elbridge found herself exhausted and ready for bed. But she stuck to her resolution for another try tonight. She had time to make herself pretty because Steve was downstairs drinking, and he wouldn't come upstairs for a while. She had brushed her teeth, showered, perfumed, and moisturized. Getting pretty wasn't the hardest part. The hardest part was shopping for something sexy, particularly trying on different clothes, peeling off her jeans in the closet-sized dressing room, just to put them back on and try again, and again. The absolute worst part was the dressing room mirrors, but that evil was unavoidable.

At home, Heather could avoid her reflection in the mirrored closet door, and so she did. She tried to remember the time in her life when she felt sexy. That was before kids. Even then, there were only moments. She had always been critical of her body, but there was less to criticize those days. Now she had bits of gray at her temples, thankfully blending in with her much darker, but still natural blonde hair. Her lack of athleticism became more obvious with age. Sporadic aerobics classes at the gym kept unacceptable pudginess away, but her legs had seen better days. Her life's path had not given her the option of becoming a pilates instructor like Soccer Mom Barbie. Heather was once cute-and-petite and had owned it, but that had vanished, replaced by short-and-dumpy, which she found much harder to own.

With a deep breath, she sat on the floor, her back to the closet mirrors. She crossed her legs, palms up on her knees, closed her eyes, and forced her mind into the submission of silence, the thought of breath her primary focus. Even after several decent attempts, she couldn't silence her chattering mind. She tried a different tactic, bending her mind to the new silk on her freshly showered skin, itself softened by after-shower lotion. The intricate lace trim was not soothing, but not scratchy either. She thought the fabric's blush pink complimented her pale complexion. Perhaps red or black would've been sexier, but she didn't look good in those colors. She didn't look great in pink either, but it was the least worst color at the lingerie store.

Comfortable now and focused, she went deeper into the sensation of the fabric on her skin, expanding the feeling through her body like a warm, slow current. As her senses explored the silk, her mind envisioned herself as a runway model, long legs sashaying across the platform while onlookers admired her sleek new lingerie with *oohs* and *ahhs*. Steve watched her from the imaginary crowd and he wanted her again, like he did when they were younger. He leapt onto the stage, but drunkenly stumbled into her and they both went down hard.

*Damn.* The wrongness of that mental picture jolted her unexpectedly and crashed her meditation. She had avoided thinking about Steve's drinking because thinking about it made it real. Her inner voice nagged again. *Something's wrong with Steve. Alcohol is the symptom, not the problem.* With a determined breath, she banished that thought after a brief but bloody mental battle and no progress toward understanding.

*One more time.* Refusing to give in yet, she forced herself back to breath work. Another deep inhale… She tried hard to accept herself at that moment. Yet instead of finding her inner sexy, she once again felt like a frumpy, middle-aged woman who looked silly in a fancy, floofy nightie meant for a younger, tighter body. She should acknowledge her insecurity, be aware of its presence as it floated past. But she didn't want to. She wanted to shove it away, pound on it with her fists, and scream at it.

*Okay, enough of this*, she thought. After one last breath, she got up from the floor, avoiding eye contact with herself in the mirror, to finish her evening hygiene rituals.

Primped and polished, she climbed into the unmade bed to wait for him. She considered putting on makeup, maybe concealing the blotches on her face, the dark circles under her eyes. But no, that would be stupid. Not only was it bad for the skin, but he wouldn't notice. If they made love, it would be with lights off. He doesn't like sex with the lights on. If he isn't interested, the light will be off anyway for sleep. So, either way, he won't see the blotchy skin and dark circles. Or maybe he wouldn't notice just because he never noticed.

That's when she heard his footsteps on the stairs. Not too much longer after that, her husband stumbled down the hall and toward the bedroom in his usual tighty-whiteys and T-shirt. Unlike herself, Steve had been athletic in his younger days and had stayed fit and firm. Her eyes wandered to his long, muscular legs, so sexy. Yet his adorable brown hair, casually tousled, framed a face that had seen adversity. While his body did not show his age, hardship lined his face. The sun had sucked away his youth in the days when sunscreen was for wimps. Steve had never been a wimp. Now his skin was rough beyond the help of any exfoliant, no matter how well advertised. Recently his facial lines deepened with his mood. Lovemaking had the power to turn around the darkest moods, but whatever haunted him had the stronger pull.

Her focus pulled back to his deep blue eyes as he lingered in the doorway with his hand hovering over the light switch.

"You ready for lights out?" he asked.

"Yes."

Without speaking again, he flipped the switch, and the room went dark. She watched his dark form glide to his side of the bed, pull back the covers, and swing those beautiful legs underneath. Unexpectedly, he lingered over her for a minute and gently kissed her on the mouth. He pulled back a bit and looked her in the eyes, stroked her bare, no-makeup cheek. *Maybe he noticed.*

Then, another sweet surprise: he murmured lowly but clearly, "You are everything to me. I love you very much." She absolutely believed the truth of his words, despite the smell of alcohol on his breath.

His tender affection made her feel sexy in the silly nightie. Her arousal trickled down her legs to her polished toenails until her feet twitched under the covers. She smiled at him and kissed him again with a teeny bit more passion. She was careful not to be *too* passionate because, as he had told her many times, he didn't like it when she initiated sex. The line to walk was that he notice her sexiness without noticing she was trying to seduce him. To avoid turning him off, she had to conform her behavior to an ever-expanding list of detailed, confusing rules.

She wanted to press her body against his, take off his T-shirt, and put her hands under the waistband of his underwear to feel his bare skin. Her skin hungered for the touch of his. But that would be a mistake. It was all she could do to keep herself from squirming in this state of arousal. That might be a giveaway, too. If he knew she wanted it, it would turn him off. Rejection would follow. She must keep her skin-hunger in check. She forced her body into stillness and hoped something would spark. Perhaps the stars would align favorably tonight and the fire, his fire, would light.

They couldn't keep their hands off each other when they first met. She was still in college, and he was finishing up law school, both so young. They had met at a night on the town with friends at the periphery of each other's friend circle. Her memory of that night was a brightly colored whirlwind of laughing and light. And sex—crazy, fun, sloppy sex. She had thought her uncharacteristic promiscuity was a silly mistake. Now it was a treasured and increasingly distant memory of their once-steamy attraction.

In the beginning, they had been close physically, not shy about the public displays of affection. He showed his desire for her with his eyes, with his hands, with his flirting. The fading of their sexual intensity wasn't the confusing part. Loss of intimacy was the most confusing part. The more he fell in love with her, the less physically intimate he became. As love grew, sex disappeared. For him, sex and love were incompatible elements, like vinegar and oil separating after every shake of the flask. Heather's attraction grew with the growth of emotional intimacy. *Is life so unfair that men and women are so different?* She struggled to understand but failed.

Rather than seriously considering that the reasons might have nothing to do with her, Heather figured she was too old, unattractive to him. Childbirth and time had taken their toll on her body, which would never be the same. It wasn't a lack of self-esteem that drove her conclusion. On the contrary, she knew he could be sexually stimulated. Just not by her. She found the pornographic magazines he had sometimes hid between the mattresses. She knew he drank at strip clubs with the boys. Since he obviously hadn't outgrown sex, she concluded the problem must have been her. Hard, cold logic informed her conclusion.

He eased back to his side of the bed without returning her smile and pulled the covers up around him, to settle in for a good night's sleep.

That meant *no*. Once again, it wouldn't happen tonight. The rejection was sharp, like a blade across her tongue scraping off her taste buds and depriving her of life's flavor.

She rolled onto her side and lifted her hand to stroke his back, but her hand did not connect. She longed to touch him, but her body remembered his reactions from multiple previous attempts. He would stiffen, maybe even snap at her for her audacity. His contradictions confused her; tender touches, handholding, hugging were welcome, but sexual touches were unacceptable.

She wondered what went wrong this time and pressed herself deeper in the bed, shrouding herself with the blankets so he would not hear the coming sobs. She thought a better wife would understand, maybe even be relieved her spouse didn't want sex. Maybe her feelings were wrong, inappropriate, shameful. Maybe she was a terrible person. She instinctively reacted to the sense of her own immorality by pulling her legs to her belly, making herself small and tight as she trembled and choked on her despair.

This he noticed. His eyes opened, staring at the dark, bare wall straight ahead. He should hold her close, soothe her tears away. He wanted to make love to her, except for the fact he didn't. Her pain was a betrayal to him. She should love him without making physical, sexual demands. All her requests for sex were a breach of trust, a broken promise of love. This he felt as deeply as he felt the contradictory desire to reach for her, pull her close to him. His emotional closeness to her needed to stay physically at arm's length.

*That is how it should be*, he thought. *No, that isn't how it should be. I can't think about this now.*

He still considered her cute-and-petite. She was still the love of his life, the woman who had turned him upside down when they met in college, who had stuck with him through law school, and who had given birth to his children. He saw the woman he yearned to nurture and grow old with. She triggered a tenderness he didn't allow anyone else to see, not even her, not really. As she struggled with her self-image, he struggled with showing love. His love was there, it was deep, but he must protect it from the cruel world, bury it and never allow the light in, as though it were a fragile thing that might forever break if discovered.

He stared harder at the wall and noticed a slight crack in the paint. He forced his attention on that meandering crack, following it from where it started at the floorboards to a point where it seemed to fade away into nothingness near the ceiling. The crack in the wall pulled his mind away and his body followed, sinking into a slightly tipsy sleep.

*****

Steve's scream woke Heather up. It wasn't a thundering scream of terror, but a muffled scream, muted by sleep. *He's dreaming he can't call for help*, she thought as she looked at his face. His body was stiff, twitching, but neither that nor the scream was enough to rouse him. She considered waking him up to save him from the nightmare. The sound of another muffled scream confirmed she should. She snuggled close to him and told him it was ok. She brushed her cheek up against his, whispering in his ear.

"Everything's ok. You're home and I'm here. You're dreaming."

He snuggled into her, soothed by her closeness and soft voice. The stiffness and twitching stopped. His eyes opened and looked back into hers. She used to wake to his nightmares only rarely, but with his increasing stress the sleep disruption had become nearly commonplace.

"Everything is ok," she said. She brushed her lips against his cheek.

"Thanks, Babe. I love you." With a grunt, he pulled the covers up and turned his back to her.

She reached one finger toward him and stopped. Touching him would prove his physical presence, assure her she wasn't imagining him, that she wasn't dreaming. The touch of his skin might fill the void—if only a little—giving her a taste of how it would feel to touch him all over, mingle her body with his. Yet somehow it would also feel like stealing, taking something from him that didn't belong to her and never would. She pulled back her hand and tucked it close to her chest.

She longed to touch the person who hid behind the barricades he had built, the person she loved. His stiff adherence to rules, to routine, to duty, was a self-imposed barrier and while he might feel safe hiding inside his fortified self, she knew it was more a prison than a stronghold.

*How can I bring him back into the world, my world, our world? What can I do?* Her thoughts faded, replaced by sleep. Tomorrow would start another long day, and they both needed to sleep.

*Four*

# The New Law

# 2019

## Sunday, October 13

Yo's small, fuzzy ears stood at attention as she lifted her quivering nose. A soft high-pitched note—not quite a whine and not quite a yawn—escaped her smiling mouth and her fluffy golden tail thunked on the floor under Ace's desk. The front door at Elbridge & Garcia, LLP, slammed shut, followed by the sound of feet running down the hall. Only one person slammed the door like that, and Yo—short for Yolanda — knew exactly who it was. Ace's law partner, Lupe, had returned from her workout break and rushed into his office, bringing a fervent emotional surge. Her emotions created a psychic wave that was sometimes overwhelming, at least for empaths. Ace scratched Yo's head, not just because she expected it, but also because the touch of her fur helped quiet his hyperactive mirror neurons. With practiced effort, he tempered his reaction to Lupe's enthusiasm. Not that he didn't love floating on her exhilarating emotional waves. He was the problem, not her. His heightened sensitivity overreacted, overwhelming him. With Yo's help, he managed his responses with focused if sometimes forced, calm.

When Lupe entered his office and after she tripped over the threshold—again—he turned his overworked eyes from his stacked papers to look at her. Yo was already dancing about Lupe's knees, wagging, and sniffing, enthusiastically processing all the aromatic data about Lupe's recent activities. Ace took in all the contradictions that were Lupe; with her slim neck and legs, she appeared lithe and graceful as a ballerina but was quite clumsy and often raucous. Her unblemished skin appeared soft, but underneath the softness was steel. Ace had often wondered if her skin was as luscious as it looked but restrained his impulse to touch her in the way necessary to find out. Pony-tailed and sweaty, Lupe looked like she had run the entire two miles from the gym, but Ace knew she had driven and then ran the short distance from the parking lot because a true California native believes driving is always the better option. A musky note laced her slightly floral, slightly spicy scent, making her smell even more delicious than usual, but enjoying that brought him to dangerous, unprofessional territory. He allowed himself to soak in her unfailing positivity, which carried the vibe of good news, and her smile spread to his face.

"They did it, Ace. They changed the law," she said. She pumped her arm, water bottle in hand, and bounced on her toes as she hollered. "Did you hear that world? They did it!" Her bright brown eyes flashed and her face—make-up free—shone. Yo joined the celebration by jumping about, for no other reason than the pure joy of celebrating, so Lupe bent over to treat her with loving scratches about her scruffy neck.

"Lupe, calm down. What are you talking about?" Ace asked.

"It was on the radio. Governor Newsom signed it. They changed the law so sex abuse survivors can sue on old claims. It's about effing time."

The impenetrable lead box—hidden these many years—churned in his gut, making its weight known as the demons stirred within it. Each twist and turn released a whisper of the toxic lead entombing the demons. Ace's smile disappeared. He gasped, then forced himself into silence, but her words tumbled out unabated. She hadn't noticed, yet. How could she when she didn't know?

"Come on, Ace. We won't have to turn the older survivors away anymore. Now, when they're grown up and have the courage to fight back, the law won't stop them." Lupe eyed his slumped shoulders and raised her eyebrows as though asking a question.

Ace knew she didn't understand. There was no way for her to know. He crunched his teeth on his pen, ignoring the red ink dribbling onto his fingers, and failed to suppress the bitterness in his voice. "You think that will change anything?"

"Sure, it will. Now we can go after those *pendejos*."

Lupe's youthful enthusiasm, infectious as it was, still didn't get a rise from Ace. She frowned.

"What's wrong?" she asked.

"You mean besides the tsunami of lawsuits over destroyed lives, destroyed children? A lawsuit won't fix lives." In frustration, he raised his voice more than he intended.

"Come on, Ace. Don't be that way. This is a great opportunity for my law practice, helping survivors of sexual assault. It's what I always wanted to do. You knew that when I came on board here."

It was true. She had leveraged her brilliance to graduate from law school at the top of her class, law review editor, the works. Tired of solitary practice and impressed by her ambition, Ace had recruited her right out of law school. He had believed that he'd be able successfully to shut down his attraction to her, but so far he mostly failed. She had joined on the promise of pursuing her dream to find justice for sex abuse survivors. He considered that ambition distasteful, but the price of recruiting a star-quality law partner. That was the deal, but he thought—he hoped—she'd drop that dream in the face of harsh reality. He had underestimated her determination, but worse, he'd forgotten the lead-encased demons and the shame now seeping back into his bones. Also underestimated was Lupe's ongoing challenge to his hidden feelings. He dropped his pen and stared at her; his icy voice covered the pain with hardness. "I don't like it."

"What the hell, Ace? Do we have a problem? I've always wanted to do this work, to help survivors. Now I can do more and you're acting like... like... I don't know. What the hell?" She stood now, feet firmly planted with hands on her hips, defiant yet confused.

"Yeah, I know..." Ace averted his eyes, his words clipped.

"Wow," Lupe became uncharacteristically quiet for a moment before speaking in a softer voice. "Is everything ok with you? Are you stressed about that brief due tomorrow?"

"I'm sorry, Lupe. I think it's a bad idea. Litigation solves nothing for people. It just opens old wounds, re-traumatizes the traumatized. Do you really want to get involved in that?"

"Yes. Survivors are entitled to justice. I will get that for them." Lupe stiffened, indignant.

"No, you can't, because there is no justice. No justice for something like that, just pain."

Her eyes opened with disbelief. "Wow, Mr. Negative. How did you get so cynical?" she asked. Ace provided no explanation, so she stuck her chin out and continued. "Ok, then. Clarification—clients can get the best our system can do. They can get accountability, public acknowledgment." She squarely met Ace's hard stare. "*Money.*"

Ace blinked and turned away. "I've got to finish this brief."

"It's time, Ace. It's beyond time. Boy Scouts, churches, universities, they've all been caught, forced to do the needful. It's not too late anymore. We can make a difference in the world."

"Lupe, please." Ace looked down at his papers, shoulders slumped in defeat. He had partnered with Lupe because she was a master of combining resolve with strength, so he knew he wouldn't win the argument. Maybe if he explained it to her, told her what had happened, she would understand. But he wasn't ready for that. He thought he'd vanquished the demons, trapped and buried them in the leaden box, but periodically they challenged their confinement, like now, churning again in his gut, awake and seeking escape.

"I'm going to do this. *We* are going to do this." Lupe stared him down giving him a chance to answer. When he didn't, she stomped out of his office, shutting his door with a shake of her thick brown ponytail.

*She wants me to do those cases with her*, Ace thought. *She never shies away from a fight.* Ace admired Lupe's idealism, a trait he didn't share. He knew from hard experience that litigation makes life worse, not better. Fighting for justice is expensive and painful. Justice itself was ever elusive. Moisture collected around his collar which had become tight. The office wasn't air conditioned on weekends, but that hadn't stopped him from spending multiple hours in the heat. Usually, he was working too hard to notice, but today even the morning heat seemed unbearable.

Ace turned back to the appellate brief but couldn't focus. Would this client find justice? What could compensate his client after years of battle, tens of thousands of dollars in legal fees, months of sleepless nights, and the unspeakable stress of depositions and motions? And that was just the legal side of the problem. *Why would I put anyone through that? Why would I put myself through that?*

But it wasn't his decision to make, not entirely.

Ace's friend Robbie had a right to know and should hear it from Ace, not some news channel. If he didn't tell Robbie maybe the whole thing would blow over, but that was doubtful. Ace tapped his leaking pen in sync with the clock's second hand as he stared at the fifty-page, double-spaced brief in front of him but he couldn't focus. Instead, he turned his gaze to the framed picture of him and his dad, taken when Ace was eleven years old. Ace, in his team uniform, was holding a soccer ball under one arm and beaming after a game won, his dad's arm looped around his shoulder in a protective embrace. His dad, wearing a business suit, sported a rare but genuine smile. Not to be left out, Robbie, also uniformed, had photo bombed the picture, making a characteristically goofy face at the camera.

*What would Dad have done?*

The answer to his self-imposed question was obvious but unwelcome. Dad had been a staunch believer in Justice and the American Way, even naming his son Atticus after a supposed literary legal hero. Dad would have taken up his sword without fear to slay the evil behemoth, just like Lupe.

*But Dad was courageous for other people, not for himself. And I'm no legal hero, despite my namesake.*

Ace again tapped his leaky pen on his brief in contemplation, but the damn thing nearly exploded, and a sticky puddle of red ink seeped into the paper then spread across his fingers. The key to Ace's conundrum was his lifelong friend Robbie, who would doubtless find out even if Ace didn't mention it.

Yo sat quietly at Ace's feet, then laid her head in his lap with her kind, liquid eyes staring up at him. He leaned over and buried his face in her golden fluff, absorbing the purity of her feelings: joy without judgment. Yo believed he could do anything, even the horrible right thing.

Ace sighed and sat up. "All right then, Yo, let's go see Robbie."

*****

"Fucking AAYA. Fucking youth soccer." Robbie slammed his coffee so hard it splashed and burned his beefy hand.

"Sorry I ruined breakfast," Ace said. Ace's hopes of avoiding an emotional outburst were unreasonably optimistic and predictably short-lived. He swallowed the angry air Robbie had expelled before remembering to center himself. He focused on pulling in the cool morning air lightly scented by the withering jasmine blooms hanging over Robbie's shady terrace; it was a welcome change from the stifling hot office.

"No worries, Love," Robbie's breakfast companion and boyfriend Tony said. Tony folded and placed his newspaper on the glass-topped table between the orange juice and half-eaten omelet. Ever the consummate host, he softly patted Ace's hand before filling an empty glass for his guest. "Would you like some champagne in that?" Tony asked quietly. Without waiting for a response, Tony strode off toward the kitchen fridge, having apparently decided for the group that mimosas were required. Yo, who was always off duty at Robbie's, trotted after him, hoping to score a treat from the best treat room in the house. Ace appreciated Tony's attention to others, a trait common in dogs but rare in humans, and one you'd expect from a massage therapist or a barista. Tony was both.

Tony, who also happened to be a stellar croissant baker, worked in the coffee shop and bakery owned by Ace's mom Heather. His talent was unteachable—taste so sensitive that he knew how much butter the dough needed, and he knew when the butter had exceeded its shelf life. Heather had introduced Tony to Robbie because she'd spotted a smart match. She was right.

"All that was so long ago, isn't it too late to sue?" Robbie asked after Tony went off to the kitchen.

"That's what I'm telling you. California changed the law, so you can sue now if you want, but I don't think you should," Ace said, switching his focus back to Robbie.

"Wow. Tough decision."

"Not really, just forget it. I felt conflicted about even telling you. Maybe I shouldn't have said anything."

"No. I'm glad you did. That was the right thing."

"It's better that you just leave it. Forget about it and move on. You have a good thing now with Tony, live for that." Ace met Robbie's eyes with hope.

"Sure." Robbie stood, walked to the edge of the condo's balcony, leaned against the rail, and looked across the parking lot to the city park not far away. He chomped on a local delicacy—a sticky biscuit and cinnamon roll combo—while staring silently into the autumn colors, where several squirrels rushed about their business preparing for winter. Ace was saddened but not surprised to see Robbie processing his feelings through hunger.

Ace was startled, however, when Robbie's face hardened. It was a rare sight, and Robbie's silence even rarer. But true to his mercurial nature—just like his mom—both Robbie's frown and his silence quickly flittered away. His eyes sparked with that twinkle that always preceded a smile and this time a devious smile followed causing his dimples to reappear.

"No," Robbie said. He adopted a mock boxer's stance, bouncing on his toes and punching his fists in the air in front of his ample belly. "I'mma fuck those fuckers up. I'mma—"

"Language!" Tony admonished. He had just arrived with a newly opened fizzy bottle. Tony laughed and with a flip of his California surfer-boy blond hair, wiggled away to pour the champagne.

"Are you ready for a fight, Tony? We're gonna eff the effing eff out of the effing eff-wads. Can I say effing—" Robbie's voice broke as he doubled over in a coughing fit.

"Oh my God, Robbie." Tony flashed to Robbie's side, and kneeling, asked, "Are you ok? Can you breathe?"

As he slumped into his chair, Robbie held up a limp hand and nodded while trying to recover his voice.

"Robbie…?" Ace finished the question with his stare.

Robbie shook his head. "No, Ace. I'm fine." He contradicted this confirmation with a contradicting cough.

"Robbie…?" Ace asked again, his stare intensified.

Robbie cleared his throat and croaked another confirmation. "I'm fine." He sipped water from the cup handed him by Tony, who was looking more alarmed.

"When is the last time you saw your cardiologist?" Ace asked.

"Damn it, Ace, not now."

"Wait, what? Cardiologist?" Sure enough, Tony was even more alarmed.

Nobody answered Tony. Ace, who had assumed that Tony already knew, gulped his mimosa, avoiding Tony's questioning gaze. Robbie should have told him.

"Tony, I'll tell you later, I promise." Robbie clutched Tony's hand.

Tony kissed Robbie on the forehead and mumbled something that Ace didn't hear, but it seemed like a reluctant acceptance, with maybe an *I love you* thrown in.

Ace stood to leave. "We can talk about the lawsuit later. You should rest."

"Ace, I want it. I want to fight." Robbie's resolve came through loud and clear even though his voice had not fully recovered.

"Why?"

"Because they won't admit what they did. They never did and they still don't. Even if I sue, maybe they never will. But I can't help but wonder what an apology would feel like. I want it, I want to rub their nose in it." Robbie said.

Tony leaned in to top off their orange juice glasses with bubbly. "Your feelings are valid, Love, whether they admit it or not. What happened to you was real. I believe you, Ace believes you. It doesn't matter what they say now."

"I love you and your psycho-babble," Robbie winked at Tony.

"You can't control what they do," Tony continued, "you only need validation from yourself because you'll never see that—or an apology— from them. It's time to forgive yourself. You did nothing wrong."

"I know, but I still want an apology. Maybe if I sue them, I can get that. At least maybe I can get acknowledgment it happened, that it destroyed my life, my family, and Ace…" Robbie shifted his gaze to Ace.

"Tony's right. I've moved on, Robbie. You should, too," Ace said, staring back, knowing it was a lie. Ace felt Robbie's optimistic resolve and knew what was coming before Robbie said a word. Usually, Robbie's can-do attitude elevated Ace's mood. But not this time.

"You're just like your dad. Haven't you learned that it's impossible to hide from it? If you try to shut it out, it will rot and fester and then bite you in the ass that much harder." With every objection Ace raised, Robbie strengthened his resolve.

How could Ace possibly explain the devastation—the stress—of litigation? Even when you win, you lose. They would face triggers, and triggers, and more triggers. The memories will torture and taunt them until it all rushes back in living color, like yesterday, like today. Ace's self-told lie that he had moved on—gotten over it—risked exposure. Ace's own feelings pushed out Robbie's; dread replaced determination. Yo snuggled her head against Ace to comfort him, but even her efforts couldn't prevent the toxic lead box in his gut from creaking open.

*Five*

# THE FIRST GAME
# 1998

*A**nd here we go, our introduction to the adult craziness of competitive youth sports*, Steve Elbridge thought on the sidelines at the season's first game.

Before he could finish his thought, like a shot, Lisa was off and running to join the not-playing-soccer-today siblings who chased the younger, not-playing-soccer-today siblings around the grassy patch next to the parking lot.

"Lisa, stay where we can see you," Heather shouted.

Without looking back, Lisa waved an acknowledgment of the soon-to-be-ignored instruction.

*Well, at least they are making the best of their mandatory attendance. Lisa will fit right in with that bunch*, he thought. Her purple tennis shoes—which lit up on every accelerating footfall—amused him and he allowed himself to smile.

This late summer day was as clear and pleasant as most in Northern California, maybe a little on the warm side. Baseball caps, sunglasses, and ponytails dotted the sidelines, plus one floppy straw hat you might expect to see on a cruise ship, or the beach, with bleach-blonde hair artfully flowing underneath. That would be Team Mom—what's-her-name—who overdressed for the occasion in her wedge heel sandals and short, summery dress. Steve's eyes ran down her trim legs with admiration. *She must be the one Heather called Soccer-Mom Barbie*, he thought. *When you have legs like that, why not?* A small group of soccer moms bubbled together, surrounding her in the center and basking in this social opportunity.

The game captivated the other sidelined parents, soccer dads and the less bubbly soccer moms, who all wore more conventional soccer-parent-styled clothes with nice shorts and t-shirts, logo athletic gear that displayed an understated wealth. Steve, still not convinced the club was the right fit for his son, looked down the sidelines to assess the men. *They seem attentive and well-dressed*, he thought with approval. He had noticed the parking lot was full of late-model luxury cars when they had arrived, to his mind a sign of minimal adequate success. Steve might have pulled Ace out of the FC Strikers that day if the lot had overflowed with beaters. Popular opinion about the club, which was overwhelmingly positive, would not sway him. He would be careful, if slow, about making his own determination. Since the club experience was new, absolute confidence in his final judgment was paramount. Then again, Steve was careful about every commitment. Soccer was no different.

Even without complete introductions, Steve could tell which parents belonged to the FC Strikers and which parents belonged to the other team. Each family stood opposite their kid's team on the other side of the field. The centerline bisecting the field continued invisibly through the spectator sidelines, marking a clear division. The separation helped to keep the all-too-frequent hostility between sides under control. Sometimes, an uninformed fan, frequently a grandparent, would sit on the wrong side. A quiet intruder who didn't cheer might be tolerated, but the vocal ones would find themselves isolated as people moved away. Staying on your own kid's side, you could cheer without restraint. Also, you might overhear snippets of conversations between outbursts. Rumors started on less.

A large man with a bodybuilder's physique and light blonde, cropped hair stepped up, grabbed Team Mom by the elbow, and swung her around to look into his unremarkable blue eyes. Her bubbly demeanor dissipated when she turned and faced him with a frown. Steve couldn't hear the words, but whatever the discussion, it must have been serious. In complete contrast to Team Mom, the man's pale face held no kindness.

Heather jabbed Steve lightly with her elbow. "That's her husband," she said. "He's always like that. Their kid is Josh, the big blond defensive back."

Steve nodded and turned his gaze to the field to see the solid, German-looking kid, Josh—the largest kid on the team—at center back.

Heather squeezed his hand, standing tall on her toes to whisper in his ear because the club's founder, Agostinho Santos, approached with his wife, Gabriela. Steve looked up with a jolt. The approaching man appeared to be Black; not that Steve was prejudiced or anything. He wasn't sure how to convey he wasn't prejudiced. *I thought he was Latino or Hispanic or something. Mrs. Santos looks Hispanic. Maybe he's both Black and Hispanic. Is Santos a Spanish or maybe an Italian name? Is African-Brazilian a thing?* Nearly everyone in Steve's professional life was White, nearly everyone in his neighborhood was White, and because of that, he was looking forward to making a new friend who wasn't white. Another bonus was that Hispanics typically love soccer. It was a little weird he wasn't sure how to act, so he shifted uncomfortably.

Gus and Gabi were originally from Brazil, and thus Latino and not Hispanic, as Heather would later clarify. Brazilians speak Portuguese, not Spanish. Rumors were that Gus came from a wealthy family. Steve thought that must have been true because Gus didn't seem to work outside the club and children's sports couldn't be lucrative. In a collared polo shirt with the FC Strikers club logo, crisp jeans with an expensive-looking embossed leather belt, and Teva sport sandals without socks, Gus was a good-looking man, gray at the temples, fit, if a little chubby and a little short, but still earned Steve's approval. The Tevas didn't quite go with the outfit, but maybe that was a Brazilian thing. More likely, it was a California thing.

Mrs. Santos, Gabi, was by Gus's side, a step behind as they approached. She was a beautiful woman, with large light brown eyes and dark hair perfectly coifed in long wavy curls. Tall and slim, she looked young, the result of her unrelenting battle with time. Clearly, Mrs. Santos was no stranger to the beauty salon, a fact betrayed by her meticulously manicured red nails that matched her lipstick. Steve guessed there had been a few successful visits to the plastic surgeon as well. Gabi was the only woman within sight wearing high-heeled shoes. Her embellished jeans fit tightly, showing off her well-tended physique, the dots of sequins sparkling in the sun. Her tight, collared shirt with the team logo matched her husband's shirt. You couldn't guess by looking at her she was the mother of four boys.

Gus walked right up to Steve with no sign of intimidation—yet another bonus to Steve's mind—and offered his hand with a genuine smile.

"Hello, I am Gus Santos. This is my wife, Gabi. Our boy out there is Roberto," he announced loudly, with a slight accent. Gus pointed to Robbie, who was the kid with dark brown hair and long legs he must have inherited from his mother.

"Steve Elbridge. This is my wife, Heather. We are Atticus's parents." Steve replied formally, dropping Heather's hand to accept the handshake. "Looks like Coach has your boy at starting forward." A fact that didn't surprise Steve, who didn't disapprove of some nepotism—in fact, he thought that was as it should be. If Steve had sustained the brain damage required to run a kids' soccer club, his kid would be the starting forward, too. In fact, Robbie had earned the position by becoming a top scorer in the state. Sadly, the assumed nepotism would follow him through his time at the Strikers.

"Oh yes, Robbie likes to put the round in the square thing!" Gus laughed with a shake of his belly and without reservation.

Steve frowned, but then laughed once he understood the joke. He approved of Gus, even though Gus was talkative, something Steve was not.

"Coach is going to try Atticus out in different spots to see what works best. We're not sure where he'll end up. I think he's just happy about the chance to play. That's Atticus coming in now." Steve pointed to the field.

The men both looked at Ace, one of the smaller kids on the field, his hair bouncing in his face, as he ran onto the pitch. He subbed in at right wing when the whistle blew to start play. The opposing player, using both hands, pulled the ball behind his head for the throw-in to his teammate. In his first official play with the Strikers, Ace shouldered that kid to the ground, stole the ball, and sped it forward along the sideline. Ace spotted Robbie ahead, one step back from an offside position, and made the aggressive pass forward. Robbie dashed past the defender, caught the pass, and took the ball to the net. The opposing goalkeeper faced Robbie with no help from his defense. Robbie faked a shot, causing the keeper to commit in the wrong direction. He then hammered the round thing into the square thing, putting the Strikers ahead 1 - 0.

"Yay, Robbie! Way to go! Good game!" The Striker parents cheered for Robbie with a positive shout-out or two for Ace. Yet the exuberant shouts from the Strikers' sideline were matched by the disgruntled shouts of Arsenal parents on the other side of the midfield line.

"Foul! Illegal tackle! What the fuck!" Opposing fans believed Ace fouled their player, who was dramatizing a fake injury on the turf.

"Offside! No Goal! No Goal!" The same fans insisted Ace's pass to Robbie was an illegal offside; it wasn't. Additional demeaning and vulgar insults bellowed from the sidelines rewarded the volunteer service of the teenage referee who did not call a foul. The rivalry between the Strikers club and the Arsenal club was fierce.

Gus ignored the flood of negativity with good humor as he looked over at Steve and commented with a big smile, "Looks like our boys are an outstanding combo. I hope we see a lot more of that."

Steve smiled back pride in his son. The friendly spirit enhanced Steve's deliberative process about the club's qualities. He approved of parental encouragement, particularly from well-heeled parents. With one hand resting over his middle, he sipped at the collective joy before setting all positive emotions aside to admire from a distance, since connecting with other people was risky. He might be safe in a moment of connection, but would not risk allowing the connection to deepen.

When the noise quieted a bit, Gus said to Steve, "Hey, talk to Coach about Ace coming to the San Diego tournament. Looks to me like your boy is plenty talented enough to make the cut."

"Well, Atticus would be excited to go, probably, but I don't know…" Steve hesitated. He looked down at the grass under his feet and dug the toe of his shoe into the turf as he considered the prospect. Something didn't feel right, but he couldn't articulate any reason.

"He'll love it. It's so fun for the kids. You should get Ace some extra training. Coach Sean and his nephew JJ run some private coaching on the side you could get in on. I'll put in a word with Sean if your son is interested." Gus rambled on, oblivious to Steve's discomfort.

"Oh, and definitely do futsal this winter," Gabriela piped in unexpectedly with genuine, if excessive, enthusiasm, and with a strong accent of indeterminate origin. "Futsal is so fun for the kids when is too icky for outside. Very popular in Brazil."

"Absolutely!" Gus exclaimed, throwing up his hands in emphasis. "We love futsal, the kids love futsal, everyone loves futsal."

Insightful as always, Gabi caught the confused looks on the faces of Steve and Heather and explained, "Futsal is an indoor sport the kids play on basketball courts in America. The ball is a little smaller, heavier, makes the kids work harder on foot skills. Foot skills are very important. Is a great way to keep up their touches between seasons." Gabi didn't look like a soccer pro, but she sure spoke like one.

Gus beamed and nodded.

"We've already spoken to Atticus about the requirement for tournaments. He has been excited about that, hoping to get invited to San Diego. I'll talk to Coach about getting in some extra training on the side. Putting in some extra hard work never hurts anyone. Thank you," Steve replied with a little less stiffness in his voice.

Steve turned his head to the field in time to see Atticus make a critical mistake. Instead of working overlaps on the sideline, Ace passed the ball to the center field. The pass went directly to an opposing player who ran up the middle toward the Strikers' net. Steve winced. The Strikers' big blond center-back Josh stepped up to stop the progress, taking back possession for the Strikers. Though he was relieved Ace's miscalculation hadn't resulted in an opposition score, the glaring mistake still agitated Steve. While Steve appreciated the solace, he liked compliments substantially more.

"No worries, friend," Gus said. "New players always take extra time to get into it, you know. Your boy will be fine. Hey, a group of us are getting together for beers at a sports bar to watch Manchester play Liverpool after the kids' game next week. Are you in?" Gus asked Steve. "I mean both you guys, of course, but it will probably be all men…" Gus stammered and cast a sideways glance at Heather.

"Oh, that's ok, I have a million things to do next Saturday anyway," Heather said. "But you should go, Steve, unless you have to work."

Steve nodded his acceptance with a smile. "Sure. That sounds great."

"Coach Sean played for Liverpool, even though he is originally from Ireland," Gus explained. "So, he's a big fan and drags the rest of us along to help cheer on his old team. It's not bad, for European football anyway," Gus said with a loud guffaw. Gus was aware Brazil wasn't the birthplace of all things soccer, but it should be.

Steve caught the implied reference and joined the laughter. "Well, in that case, I better be there, but Lord help us all when Liverpool plays

Brazil!" Steve tried to joke, but only revealed his ignorance about world football teams. National teams don't play league teams. Gus was ok with the ignorance. Most Americans didn't get it, but football was growing in popularity, particularly after the US women won the FIFA Women's world cup a few years back.

*Only in America do women bring national attention to a man's sport*, Gus thought, smiling at the unique phenomenon in this unique country. *Although only an American woman would rip off her jersey and run around in a sports bra on live international television*. He reminisced with good humor and his smile broadened.

A couple of vapid soccer moms arrived, surrounded Mrs. Santos, and spouting compliments interrupted the discussion.

"Your hair is ridiculously gorgeous."

"Oh my god, I love it."

They pulled Gabi away for a chat about hairstyles and salons. Poker-faced, Steve thought Gabi's hair looked old-fashioned and overdone, and he was sure Heather would agree.

Steve wasn't surprised Heather avoided the women's discussion, since Heather was not one for shallow small talk, particularly on girly topics. He could not imagine himself in love with a woman taken with such frivolity. Rather, Steve noted with approval that Heather had completely turned her attention to the game. She was actively encouraging the team, shouting out what a good job each boy had done. *As though they were little kids. There will be no dissuading women from babying their little boys*, he thought. Reflecting further, Steve decided extra attention was good for boys, but was most appropriate when provided by mothers rather than fathers. He felt a brief gush of renewed love and smiled at Heather for attending to his son's need for encouragement.

The game ended with a cheer; the Strikers won with a final score of 1-0. As the boys from each team lined up for the post-game hand slaps, an abbreviated version of handshakes, Steve's phone rang. He looked down at the screen and saw the name of a client, an important one who respected his lawyer enough that he wouldn't be calling after hours on a private cell phone unless something was urgent.

"I have to take this call," Steve said to Heather, even though he would rather ignore it. With a stress ball churning in his belly, Steve dashed away to find a quieter place to talk and found a shady tree a short distance away where he could still see the field. His client, it turned out, was upset about the shenanigans of some parties in a corporate merger Steve was handling. As he watched the young athletes from a distance, Steve assured the client the matter would be handled.

"I'm sure the documents are wrong, the dates are wrong," the client said. "Can't we just take care of that date problem? You know… Nobody would notice…"

"You know we can't do that," Steve said. Because this was an important client, Steve chose his next words carefully and articulated them softly. "It'd be a false representation. Technically, it could be fraud. The company could get sued."

"Damn it, Steve. You're our lawyer, so you're supposed to do what we want. Our company pays your firm a lot of money. How would it look if we had to pull our business? Think about what you are saying."

Steve's chest tightened with a flash of pain. *The firm needs this client; we might fail without that steady work, the steady revenue.* His hand flew to his chest, and he gasped before responding with clipped words.

"I understand. Maybe there is another way—"

"You do whatever you need to do, so this works out in our favor. Do you understand that?"

"Ok, I'll find a solution." *There is no way I'd do something that unethical,* Steve thought, looking about furtively to confirm no listeners lurked nearby before turning his gaze to the field. He watched the boys with the phone in one hand and rubbed out the pain in his arm with the other.

The hand slaps finished, the boys lined up facing their team's spectator sideline, ready to make the traditional run across to show thanks to their parents. Their little, sweaty faces beamed in the sunlight, glowing with the happiness of winning. Despite the game's demanding physical work, the boys were as bouncy and active as though fresh, bolting across the field with high-pitched victory shouts. Steve's eyes found Atticus in the group and watched as his son ran over to his mother, giving her a high-five.

Atticus searched the crowd and Steve realized with some regret that he was looking for his dad. Steve prioritized his work, providing for the family, and saving for college. But he felt a twinge of envy for women who could connect with children without sacrificing family security. He envied any parent who didn't have to take phone calls for work. It occurred to Steve he also envied moms who babied their sons or hugged them affectionately with no one thinking that was weird.

Steve turned his back to the field to immerse himself in the phone call. This client needed his attention, and that paid the bills. He should have time later to connect with Atticus.

"Look, let me think through some options. I'll get back to you," Steve said with finality.

"Fine."

By the time he finished the phone call, most parents and players had left. He turned and walked back to the field, one hand still resting on his middle. A handful of parents remained, hurrying their kids to pack up. The day was young enough that some parents might yet accomplish something productive. Steve spotted his family across the field, on the Strikers' side. Heather and Atticus were speaking with Coach Sean, or rather Coach Sean was speaking while Heather and Atticus nodded and smiled. Lisa was halfheartedly practicing cartwheels nearby, one of her favored activities. At least it was exercise.

Steve walked up in time to hear Coach talking about the play between Robbie and Atticus, clearly impressed with the duo who had scored the game-winning goal. The man crouched down to make eye contact with Atticus with one hand on the boy's shoulder. Atticus was beaming in response to the compliments and attention lavished upon him. Steve stepped up to introduce himself. Extending his hand, he said, "Hello Coach, I'm Atticus's father. Good game out there today."

"Ya, the boys were brilliant. Ace is a promising athlete. He's a brilliant addition to the team and has tons of potential," Coach Sean replied, standing up to accept Steve's hand. "I spoke with your wife Heather before about Ace joining a group of us for some extra training. My nephew JJ is going to college here for his year abroad in America. He's my brother's son from Ireland and is running a clinic to help the kids improve foot skills." Coach Sean pointed over at JJ, who was awkwardly sitting on the grass at Robbie's feet, working out a nasty knot in the shoelaces of one of Robbie's cleats.

Steve appraised JJ, who had a tattoo of a cross on the side of his neck below his ear, usually hidden under the scruff of long, red hair. *Ugh, why your neck?* Steve tightened his lips into a frown. Goth-light and gangly, JJ didn't seem to belong on a soccer field. *And why are you tying that kid's cleats? Children this age should be responsible enough to keep their own cleats tied.* But on reflection, the team's star player was getting special attention, as expected in the adult sports world, to Steve's mind. Special treatment for coddled athletes would obviously start at the youth level. His frown deepened with his consternation.

Coach Sean said, "Of course, JJ's doing this under my supervision. We want the boys to get as many touches on the ball as possible. Do you think Ace might join us for some extra training?"

Steve didn't answer immediately to deliberate the situation before he replied, "Yes, I think we can make that happen." He looked over at Atticus, whose anxious expression immediately morphed into a gigantic smile. The tightness in Steve's shoulders released when he realized this was the right decision because it made his son happy. He smiled back at Atticus.

"Excellent. Susie can get you all the information you need." Sean said. He winked at Atticus and patted him affectionately on the back.

Steve grabbed his head. It felt like it had exploded as though slammed into a cinderblock wall.

He tightened his jaw and ground his molars. He was angry, raging hot furious. Sometimes this happened to him, and he didn't know why. Then it was gone, just like that. It was as though he disappeared, then reappeared in a blink. Steve looked around to confirm nobody had noticed what happened to him. Thankfully, nobody had detected his overreaction to nothing. Or if they did, they saved Steve the embarrassment by hiding it. Before he could think about it further, Coach Sean was gone. The moment passed and Steve didn't know what had just happened.

Heather gathered up Lisa and the family made their way back to the car together. Lisa and Heather held hands; Steve and Atticus walked side by side without touching.

# Six

# Telling The Parents

# 2019

With Lupe and Yo at his side, Ace burst through the front door of the Santos family home without knocking and walked in as he had done for over twenty years. And just like always, Gabi greeted him, standing tall in her designer stilettos with flawless coiffure and makeup. Overflowing with warmth, a Santos family trait shared with her husband and son, her smile filled him with instant sunshine. Ace kissed her on the cheek and in a surprise move, he didn't kiss her other cheek but snatched her into a big bear hug. Gabi giggled.

"Ace, honey, the hair, the hair… please." As if her sticky, heavily sprayed coiffure—a relic from the seventies—could be disturbed by anything less than a nuclear explosion.

But everyone knew she loved the attention.

Robbie came around the corner to join the group just as Gabi said something incomprehensible to Lupe in Portuguese. Ace turned pink because even though he didn't understand the words, he knew Gabi relished the matchmaker role and had just nudged Lupe toward romance, marriage, or something along those lines. Gabi had frequently hinted that Lupe and Ace should build more than a professional relationship. Once again, Gabi's unfailing ability to read people was spot on.

"*Mãe*, please. Just because you understand Spanish doesn't mean Lupe understands Portuguese. English, please," Robbie said. Even as an adult, his parents' over-the-top personalities made him feel awkward, and he failed to hide the embarrassment in his voice.

Lupe laughed. "It's ok. I'd respond in Spanish if I'd understood." Lupe and Gabi kissed alternate cheeks with genuine affection.

Yo sat at attention by Ace's heal, obediently manning her post through the neck scratches administered by Gabi who cooed at her in Portuguese. Unlike Lupe, Yo seemed to understand.

Gabi ushered the group into the adjacent living room, where Gus was lounging in a tasteful mid-century designer armchair with his bare feet resting on the cool, gray tile floor. Ace strode up to Gus, his second father, with his hand ready for a firm handshake, but Gus rose and accented the usual bear hug with a back slap. After more greetings and small talk, the group settled in to address the serious business of the day.

Lupe cleared her throat, and everyone turned their attention to her.

"I know that Ace and Robbie have told you about Robbie's decision to sue the Association for…" Lupe stopped to ponder the flooring, and then looked up again before she continued, "… for what happened to him with the Strikers." Poker-faced, she held her chin so steady that her usually bouncy brown ponytail stilled.

Silence: the winter sun shone through the picture window overlooking the backyard and softened the cold tile floor before fading into evening. As if in solidarity with the moment, the neighborhood was uncharacteristically quiet, no children skateboarding in the street, no dogs barking in the distance, nothing. Each person in the room grappled with the shared awkwardness, yet each person was determined to suffer through the discussion because that's what families do for each other, particularly in tough times. The shared love dwarfed the shared awkwardness.

Ace sank his hands into Yo's neck and pulled her calm through his fingertips, the calm that steadied his demons and allowed him to function with a clear head. He nodded at Lupe to continue. She would have more challenging conversations to face in her legal career, particularly in her chosen field of expertise, and he believed in her.

"Ace asked me to talk to you because this is my area of expertise more than his, and Roberto wanted us to come talk to you guys because, obviously, this affects you. So, this gives you a chance to ask questions if you have any," Lupe said. She paused for a breath, centered herself and continued. "Look, litigation is usually ugly. This lawsuit will be particularly ugly because of the deeply personal and intimate nature of what happened. We expect the Association to be nasty, to attack not only Roberto but his family, including you guys."

Gus and Gabi nodded as though they understood, but the younger people in the room knew they were clueless. Lupe looked straight at Robbie, her eyes asking for his help.

Robbie met her gaze, sighed, then turned his head to Gus and spoke. "Dad, they are going to blame you," Robbie said. His voice was soft, almost pleading, but his eyes pierced straight into his dad's.

Gus hung his head in response to his son's words and then slammed his open palm on his thigh. "They should blame me! How did I not protect you? I should have protected my child."

Gabi, who had been momentarily distracted by her cell phone, snapped to attention. The discussion was old, but the anguish remained fresh. Twenty years had not diminished the guilt.

"*Papai*, please…" Robbie pleaded. He tapped his fingernails on the wooden armchair. If there were another way, Robbie would protect his dad from testifying. But Lupe was right, the Association would do everything possible to make Gus look bad. Robbie's childhood efforts to protect his parents by hiding his abuse, and lying about it, had magnified the problem to the point he could no longer protect them.

"My son, how can you forgive me? I cannot forgive myself…"

Gus's heavy breathing filled the silence. Gabi pulled her chair closer to her husband, her big brown eyes shimmering, her shiny new smartphone and its social infinity forgotten. She brushed her lips against his cheek and rested her hand on top of his.

"*Pai*, it's ok, really it's not your fault," Robbie said.

"But if I protected you, maybe you would be different. You know… maybe you would have turned out differently if it didn't happen, if I had been a better father," Gus said.

Robbie rolled his eyes. Everyone knew Gus was not referring to Robbie's obesity. Although in a different reality, Robbie probably wouldn't have weight problems. He might even have been a world-class soccer player or at least Division-1 college. As it was, Robbie's athletic glory days had been wrecked by the time he turned twelve. That's when Robbie turned from an A-student to a D-student, from a funny kid to an angry kid, when his life's opportunities began slipping away. Yet Robbie's scholastic struggles weren't Gus's point, either.

"Please don't bring that up, *Papai*. That has nothing to do with it." Robbie's voice hardened.

Lupe looked at Gus and her eyes widened as though she couldn't believe where the discussion was headed. She placed a reassuring hand on Robbie's shoulder.

"Yes, yes, of course, it's the reason. That doesn't run in our family. Nobody else in the family has that… is like… you know. It must be the reason. It's my fault," Gus said adamantly.

"Damn it, Dad! Stop! Just stop!"

"But—"

"No! Stop it!" Robbie started yelling in Portuguese.

Gus uncharacteristically whimpered back in Portuguese.

Gabi cringed. Her face lifted and froze with her mouth dropped open.

Ace made a face at Lupe, a face that said *You wanted this. Deal with it.*

Lupe took control. She stood and spoke firmly. "Stop it. *Silencio.*" She waited a beat before continuing. "All right, let's get it together, everyone. Calm down. Nobody blames anyone for anything. That's not what this is about, and it certainly is not about Roberto being gay. You must understand that before we go to trial. Roberto's sexuality is irrelevant to this case."

Heads nodded and feet shuffled as each person worked to control their emotions.

"*Bueno.* Mr. Santos, you will be a witness, and maybe Mrs. Santos, too. The Association will say that what happened to Roberto was your fault because you were terrible parents who cared more about the Strikers' reputation and getting money donations than you did about the children. I'm sorry to say that they will point the finger directly at you, Mr. Santos, but that will almost certainly happen."

Gus stared at the floor and looked like he was about to cry, but Gabi's face hardened, and she mumbled something in Portuguese.

Lupe continued, "We decided on a strategy called pulling the thread. That means we will hit the issue head-on to dilute its impact."

Ace interjected. "That doesn't mean that you guys are bad parents because you're not. You guys are good, loving parents; it's just what they will say. Don't buy into the Association's defense story. Not only might your attitude weaken our case, but it just isn't true. Stay focused on the truth: you guys are good, loving parents. Robbie and I believe that, and you must, too. Please don't doubt yourself."

"Exactly," Lupe said. "We have reviewed everything from the legal viewpoint, and you have done nothing wrong. Could you have done something better? Sure, we all could, but that just makes you human. What happened to Roberto wasn't your fault. We need you to be strong."

"I don't blame you guys," Robbie said. "Really, I blame the Association." He knew he had to placate his parents for the lawsuit to succeed, but he couldn't help but wonder: *What if Dad had protected me? Why didn't my papai protect me?* Robbie wouldn't—couldn't—ask his father these questions, not only out of respect but also to avoid laying unnecessary guilt. Gus labored enough with self-imposed guilt. Robbie would load the burden on himself, but not his father.

Gus sighed loudly and lifting his head, turned toward his youngest son and nodded. Robbie's mouth softened with relief at his dad's acknowledgment. It wasn't really a lie after all, and it made his parents feel better. *So worth it.*

Ace and Robbie looked at each other, and Ace nodded his understanding. He knew exactly what Robbie was doing.

"But why sue? I still don't understand why," Gabi said.

With the room calmed, Lupe sat back down and fingered her earring. "Suing is Robbie's decision. It's his legal right and we all need to stand by him. *All* of us." Her eyes shifted to Ace, who said nothing but dug his fingers deeper into Yo's neck fur.

"But your heart, Roberto. Is already so stressful. You don't need more stress," Gabi said in a soft voice.

Ace had already lectured Robbie on this point, so Robbie avoided the daggers from Ace's eyes to answer his mom.

"*Mãe*, I'm strong. I promise. I can do this," Robbie said.

Ace shook his head and grunted.

Robbie turned to confront him. "Damn it, Ace. So what? Yes, this will be hard, but I refuse to die with no apology."

"Wait, you are dying?" Gus asked, looking confused and worried.

"I'm going to be ok, *Papai*. I promise I'm not going to die. But yeah, to Ace's point, the doc said my heart is weak. I'm getting better. Tony is a big comfort to me and is helping me through this."

Gus and Gabi both reddened at the mention of Tony. Robbie's parents had not rejected Tony, but didn't know how to accept the man either. It made for some uncomfortable family gatherings.

"Ace, do you think Roberto should have this lawsuit?" Gabi asked. Her eyes leaked concern and her mouth settled in an uncharacteristic frown, but she also analyzed Ace's face like she could read his mind.

"What I think doesn't matter," Ace said. "It's Robbie's decision."

"But you're our lawyer. You tell us," she said, indignant.

Lupe and Ace made eye contact with a mutual sigh. Neither wanted to explain the incomprehensible nuances of conflict-of-interest rules for legal representation under the American justice system.

Lupe took the challenge. "No, we are both Robbie's lawyers, not yours. We can't be both at the same time. Technically, it's a conflict-of-interest."

Gabi appeared unconvinced. "Okay, but you will still tell us what is best to do."

Ace and Lupe sighed in unison, but Gabi wasn't giving up. "Why do we have to do this lawsuit? I don't understand," she said.

"It's my decision, *Mãe*, and I want to do this. Ace tried to talk me out of it, if you must know, but I'm doing it anyway," Robbie said. "They deserve to pay for what happened to me. I want them to apologize."

"But I apologize to you, Roberto," Gus said. "It's not enough, I know, but…"

"It's not about that. I'm determined to hold the Association accountable. And not because I'm dying. Because I'm. Not. Going. To. Die." Robbie tried to make a joke with his last point, by standing up and shaking his bottom as if to a beat, but the joke fell flat with the humans. Yo responded to the fun tone in Robbie's voice by lifting her head to him and wagging her tail, but nobody laughed except Gabi, who grabbed the first opportunity to exit the darkness.

"Of course not. Enough of this serious talk." Gabi stood and kissed Robbie on the cheek. "Now, you all stay for dinner. We have Indian takeout. Not from America Indians, but, you know, India Indians. Is delicious." She strode to the kitchen, and everyone knew she would not allow them to leave until food was served. Robbie followed to help, taking advantage of a convenient escape. Yo looked up at Ace, who signaled her release so she could follow them to the best treat room in the house.

When Gabi and Robbie cleared the room, Ace spoke to Gus in a low voice. "You aren't ready for this, are you?"

Gus shook his head.

"You are going to be fine. You can do it. But they will ask you lots of hard questions. Be clear and honest," Ace said. "That's it. And no matter what happens, Robbie loves you."

"I'm sorry, Ace. Tell me what to say. Please, just tell me," Gus said.

"No," Lupe interjected, "what you will say is the truth. We can't tell you what to say. That's not how it works."

Gus nodded.

"What I can tell you is how to act. You've got to get over yourself. This is not about you." Ever the victim advocate, Lupe took Gus by the shoulders, willing the older man to look at her. "You will do this for Roberto. This was not your fault, do you understand?" If her strength of will couldn't convince him, nothing would.

Gus nodded, still looking down.

"Look at me. You must not accept blame, and you certainly cannot do that on the witness stand. You *will be* strong for Roberto."

Gus didn't respond, so Lupe continued in a softer voice. "I can spend more time with you to get you ready. I can't tell you what to say, but we can practice what it's like to testify in a courtroom. Would you like that?"

Gus nodded.

"Not a problem. We'll get something set up right away," Lupe said.

Gus tilted his eyes upward to Ace, cheeks drawn, and his bushy eyebrows pressed together. "Yes, I will do that. What about you, Ace? Are you ready?"

"I kind of tried to talk Robbie out of it, but he really wants this. You can try too, but Lupe's right. It's his decision," Ace said, avoiding the personal question.

Gus nodded again, but Ace spotted a glimmer of an idea forming. *Maybe Gus will talk him out of it. Good.*

The glimmer didn't get past Lupe, who glared at them with hands on her hips. "The two of you will not pressure Robbie. You will support him and make this as stress-free as possible. *Entiendes?*"

This time, both men nodded.

"But really, what about you, Ace?" Gus tried parental mode again. "Not the law stuff, but how do you *feel* about this?"

Ace forced himself not to look at Lupe when he answered, because he knew the answer would surprise her. He didn't want Lupe to know anything about his past, but he felt conflicted because he wanted the encouragement and support Gus offered. If he admitted his feelings to Gus, he'd have to first admit them to himself, and that might feel like failure, but he took the chance. "I can't help thinking about my dad. The thoughts won't go away and I'm scared, *Papai*, really scared." Ace had reverted to using the Portuguese word for "father" that he had adopted in childhood from Robbie, but rarely used anymore.

"You are afraid of living through the horror again, or if not living through it, feeling it all again," Gus said.

"Yeah, that's a bit dramatic, but something like that. I'll stand by Robbie, but I'm scared." Ace feared facing the demons he had locked safely away years ago, he feared losing, he feared proving himself right that the entire legal system was bullshit. He also feared he wasn't strong enough, wasn't good enough to handle the task asked of him. Worst of all perhaps, he was afraid of failure, of losing and letting everyone down.

"Roberto knows. He would not make this decision if he thought it would hurt you."

"I know." Ace's dad had raised him never to admit weakness, but he felt safe revealing his childhood fears to Gus, who had stepped up to be a sort-of adopted father figure. For the first time, Ace realized that his dad, Steve, must have been afraid, too. He had always thought his dad just didn't have any demons, but that couldn't be true. *Dad hid his torment the same way I do. Would he be proud of me now?*

Gus stood and patted Ace on the shoulder before heading to the kitchen. "Let's eat," he said.

Ace caught Lupe looking at him and could practically see smoke coming out of her ears as her massive brainpower kicked into gear to solve the puzzles just presented her. He knew he'd have some explaining to do later, definitely later.

*Why does everyone but the guilty bear the burden of this mess? Why do the survivors have to do all the work?* Ace thought. He grabbed his head, trying to squeeze out the paradox of justice and injustice, but it followed him into the kitchen and joined him for dinner.

# Seven

# AT THE BANK
# 1998

Mr. and Mrs. Santos, overdressed by California standards, strode through the lavish office park as though traversing an alien planet. The local bank branch—nestled in lushly landscaped terrain, with small grassy hills and lacy shade trees—was typical in suburban Northern California but nearly nonexistent in São Paulo, Brazil. Most offices were nondescript, since this complex was designed for professional work, not for aimless public wanderings. The one-story, flat-roofed buildings had offices for accountants, lawyers, and tech startups, all tastefully distanced between meandering paths. However, the office park also held a coffee shop, an office supply outlet, and a local branch of a bank that provided basic services to businesses. This branch focused on services to high-wealth individuals and commercial enterprises.

Gus endeavored to portray an image of casual success, so he wore an expensive blue suit, shiny shoes, and a fancy belt, but no tie, his notion of casual success. As always, the couple was well-groomed. Mrs. Santos caught the eye of both men and women in the bank as she and her husband entered. Her flashy style matched her flashy smile, and she lit up the room as they entered.

*Always with the grand entrance. She still has it,* Gus thought, beaming. Gabi's regal bearing rarely went unseen and, even after all their years together, Gus still noticed.

The bank employees were eager to assist this good-looking—and rich-looking—couple. A bank employee, recognizing his clients and wanting to get the jump on his fellow associates—also his competitors—rushed over to greet the Santoses. The banker wore a suit and tie, looking like the recent business school graduate he was. His first proper job was as a relationship manager at the bank, which allowed him to network with lots of wealthy locals.

"Good morning, Mr. and Mrs. Santos. We have all the loan paperwork ready to review and sign. Please follow me, this way." The young banker led the Santoses to a small glass-walled conference room, where several papers were neatly laid out. Disposable pens with the bank's logo stood in pencil cups nearby. Eager to make the best impression on these clients, the banker pointed out the credenza where fresh coffee and ice water had been carefully arranged.

Gabriela eyed the coffee, always ready for a caffeine boost.

"I'd love some coffee," she stated with a radiant smile. She floated to the credenza for the coffee as the men eased into the blue leather conference room chairs. Although she seemed uninterested, Gus knew she listened sharply. He had caught her surreptitious glances at the banker and would ask her assessment privately later.

"Congratulations on the success of the Strikers," the banker said. "Every family around wants to get their boys on your team. You should be very proud."

Gus basked in the compliments. "We worked very hard, Gabi and me, and the boys. Soccer is very important in our *família*."

"Obviously so, and such talent, too," the banker nodded obsequiously. "Everyone is really impressed with the continuing success of the club; not only have you raised it up to local and regional prominence, but you're getting national attention as well. I saw that piece about the club on ESPN. Congratulations!" The banker made eye contact with Gus to show his really super genuine genuineness.

Gus responded with a small nod, underplaying his rush of pride and missing the disingenuousness of the flattery.

The banker shifted to a business-like tone. "Now, you'll recall that the type of loan the Strikers applied for is known as an 'income-stated loan.' Do you have questions about that before we go on?"

Gus shook his head; he remembered nothing about income-something loans, and he didn't care.

"Well," the banker explained, "under current underwriting standards—that means requirements for loan approvals—we can make loans based upon the worth of the real property pledged as collateral and statements of income." He sized up his customers. Gus maintained eye contact, but tapped his fingers rapidly on the tabletop.

The banker continued, "For the Strikers, this means that we can loan funds against the real estate owned by the club if the financial statements show a steady source of income the club makes, but we don't need additional proof that you actually make the income that you say you do. You only need to tell us honestly what you are making."

Gus interrupted. "But you didn't ask us to prove how much money we make. I don't understand." The banker had already told Gus they didn't need to prove the FC Strikers made any money, but Gus was incredulous. Just because the property was valuable didn't mean the club would have enough cash for payments. "We can't make payments with chunks of grass," he added. Gus squeezed his bushy eyebrows together because this made little sense to him. He just didn't see a reason the loan made sense to the bank. *Why do they not care whether I have money coming in to make payments? These Americans are crazy. This money is so easy.*

"It's true. Banks don't need *proof* anymore to make real estate loans. Less paperwork makes the loans get through faster. We've been able to help lots of clients get loans like this. You only have to prove the property is valuable and —"

"Yes, yes, the property is quite valuable. When do we get the money?" Bored with the discussion, Gus cut off the banker again.

"Our community is really lucky to have the resource of those fields. Given all the developments being built, developers would easily snap that land up. The price of real estate has really skyrocketed at that location, which means a lot of businesses are thriving. Good times for everyone." The banker's voice rose in his excitement over the mutually assured prosperity of income-stated loans.

Gus glared and spoke slowly and patiently, as though English was the banker's second language. "When do we get the money?"

The banker fidgeted and looked down. "Well, there is one other thing that the bank needs from you." He stopped and took a breath. "I think we talked about this. You remember me telling you about the guaranty agreements, right?" He waited uncomfortably and continued when Gus didn't respond. "Well, that means you and the missus agree if anything goes wrong and the loan isn't getting paid, then you guys will make the payments personally. I have to make sure you understand that part."

"No. The club will pay the loan."

"Of course, it will. The guaranty agreement is just in case, for some unknown reason, that doesn't happen. It's a standard bank requirement that somebody else agrees to be responsible for the money. Really, it's just a belt and suspenders type of thing."

Gus frowned and his eyebrows pinched as he looked down at his hands to consider this inconvenient truth. If they ever had to pay back the loan, it would bankrupt his family. Going to Gabi's *papai* for money would be a mortifying admission of his failure as a man, as a provider for his wife and boys. Then again, surely the bank was more interested in recovering the property than in chasing the Santos family for the money. Not only that, but this money would give him the chance to provide for his family the way they all deserved.

Gus considered explaining the financials to Gabi. *She's not interested in the details of this money, he thought, but she will catch every nuance of this banker's character. She will know if he's lying or dishonest.* Gabi smiled at him with her eyes as she slurped her coffee. *Meu Deus, I love this woman. I will get this money and shower her with the best of everything.*

"We understand," Gus replied for both of them.

"Good, good. Let's go through these papers, then. This first document is called a Deed of Trust. That's the mortgage paper on the property. The second document here is the Promissory Note. That's the paper promise to pay back the loan. Would you like more time to read through the documentation, make sure everything's correct? I can leave you for a few minutes to discuss. All of this is in typical legal language, so if you have questions, I would be happy to translate into regular English, explain what all this stuff really means," the banker added helpfully.

"No, I think we are ready to sign everything. Just show us where to do that," Gus said. A slick red convertible passing outside the window caught his eye, the driver's shiny long hair billowing behind her. Their next stop was the car dealership. He was eager to see Gabi behind the wheel of a flashy sports car, like the woman in the convertible but—for reasons Gus couldn't fathom—she wanted a Lincoln Navigator, basically a monster truck. He hoped that once she test drove the sports car, she would change her mind.

"Sure thing, your signature goes here as the President of the Strikers, Agostinho dos Santos, and your wife's signature is below as the Treasurer," the banker instructed, flipping through the pages to point out the professionally typed signature blocks.

"There's no '*dos*' anymore. We changed that when we became American citizens. We are now just Santos. So just Agostinho and Gabriela Santos," Gus corrected patiently. This mistake came up periodically.

"Ah, ok, we'll get that signature block changed then." The banker signaled his assistant to come and take the papers. After giving her instructions for the correction, he turned his attention back to Gus. "Since there are no other officers of the organization, no other signatures are required. We have reviewed all your corporate documentation, and everything is in order. You have done a really good job of keeping the club organized."

Gus didn't value a compliment on being organized, which seemed to him a pointless attribute. However, any compliment is better than a complaint, and he had done a magnificent job with everything. He had deserved the coming rewards.

After more chit-chat and empty compliments from the banker, the assistant came back with the corrected papers.

"And here, this is the personal Continuing Guaranty Agreement," the banker said, setting aside a three-page document on the table. "You will both sign this paper as individuals, not as the club. This is the *personal* agreement."

As the Santoses fumbled through putting their signatures on the paperwork with the notary, the banker mentioned, "You know if the club is ever interested in expanding its board of directors, I could put you in touch with lawyers, accountants, or other professionals that might really help you out." The young banker was eager to please, and he knew customers typically appreciate the networking opportunities offered by their banker's contacts list.

Gus had previously considered off-loading some administrative responsibility to others who would be glad to serve. The problem with an expanded board of directors was control. Once the door is open to others, they might push their own different ideas and different agendas. Gus might have to share power. In his view, that wasn't an acceptable solution to avoid a little paperwork.

Worse, an active board might interfere with Gus getting this money and might impose restrictions on how he spent it. Since he built the club, Gus felt entitled to spend the money it generated however he wanted. He earned it. The club had everything it needed, including a founder who could maintain the proper image of wealth required to attract wealthy donors. The Santoses lived in the right neighborhood, drove the right cars, took the right vacations, all as expected. Wealthy people expect to associate with other wealthy people.

While disinclined to share his authority, Gus understood the potential benefits of placing some well-connected people, powerful people, on the board. Also, he wouldn't reject a valid networking opportunity; more parents with money means more kids with money, which basically means more money. This was not a straightforward decision. Compromise, perhaps? There must be a way to take advantage of networking opportunities without the resultant burden of financial oversight. Gus would noodle through that conundrum later. And he'd ask Gabi about it since her talent was reading people.

"You know, I might just take you up on that," Gus replied. "We have legal issues come up sometimes. It might be useful to have a lawyer around. My wife has done an outstanding job with the books, so I don't see the need for an accountant." Gus smiled at Gabi who had no training in bookkeeping or accounting and did nothing but sign what Gus told her to sign.

"Certainly," the banker beamed, happy to be of service. "Now, here are your copies. Funds should be available to draw down into the club's account by tomorrow. It's always a pleasure to help a valuable community organization. We appreciate you chose us as your financial partner. Please contact me any time you need anything, for the club, or for your personal banking needs." The banker handed Mrs. Santos a logo embossed folder of papers with his business card paper-clipped to the top. He grasped her fingertips for a feminine handshake and thanked her as an obvious afterthought.

As always, Gabi had made Gus proud. She had been perfect: shapely legs crossed at the conference table, signing the papers when and as instructed, and saying nothing unless serving her husband his coffee. Gus squeezed the banker's hand with a firm shake and a smile. *Now we get our reward, her reward.*

One step outside the bank's door, Gabi transformed from the sophisticated corporate wife to a giggly little girl, bouncing up and down on her toes. *A real man keeps his wife happy; happy wife, happy life,* Gus thought, pleased with himself for being a good husband as he gave her hand a gentle squeeze. Her touch held all the sensuality of their youth. He thought back to earlier times, back to São Paulo, where they grew up together.

*I have kept my promise to her father.*

*Eight*

# THE PROMISE

# 1972

## SÃO PAULO, BRAZIL

Agostinho dos Santos sat stiffly on the upholstered settee in the foyer where the Marinho family housekeeper had directed him to sit. While his body was there, his mind was on The Beautiful Game. With his back straight, he kicked softly at a pretend soccer ball on the polished stone floor. He ran the imaginary ball along the outside of his foot, then pulled it in the opposite direction with the other side of his foot, gently, gently. Again.

Agostinho had worn the same Brazilian yellow jersey with blue shorts during the game two years earlier—in 1970—when he was fifteen years old. Even though his family had shared the event crowded around the old black and white television, in his memory, the Mexican stadium had been an ocean of vibrant colors, dominated by Brazilian green, yellow, and blue. The crowd roared in his mind as Agostinho— imagining himself as his hero, Roberto Rivelino—got a foot on the throw-in from his Brazilian teammate. With one swift, flawless touch, Agostinho passed the ball with a tall arc to Pelé, who was outside the goalkeeper's box. The lone Italian defender and Pelé jumped in unison, but it was Pelé who got his head on the ball. And of course, Pelé did what Pelé does and scored the opening goal. The Beautiful Game. Agostinho's real soccer ball was in his crumpled backpack, dumped on the floor next to him.

*Control, gentle touches, control, again,* he thought, as his foot practiced the move over and over. He was determined to master his hero's signature move, the *elastico*. Mental training—including muscle memory, and discipline—was always important and his only option while he waited. His alternative option was listening to the muffled yelling from down the hall. His turn would come, and he would deal with it then. Until then, *elastico*. *Control, gentle touches, control, again.*

The hair on Agostinho's neck stood up in response to another frosty draft from the air conditioner. How strange to grow up in a warm city just to surround yourself with fake cold air. He tried to ignore the lavish—if gaudy—décor in the Marinho house. Not that such grandeur was commonplace for him, quite the opposite. Agostinho's family lived in a more modest middle-class apartment in a stable, middle-class neighborhood in São Paulo.

His eyes floated to a framed, hand-painted portrait of the Marinho family, no doubt the work of a famous artist, probably Brazilian. A very young Gabriela sat on her father's lap in the center surrounded by her two older sisters and her mother, standing in a semi-circle and facing the artist. Sr. Marinho's hand rested protectively on little Gabriela's shoulder; obviously, she was his favorite, his baby. Multiple other portraits and framed photographs filled the foyer, memorializing a long line of wealthy Marinhos with their horses, sailboats, and fancy cars.

A small, ancient-looking statuette of an African warrior, cast in darkened bronze, stood proudly under the enormous portrait. Agostinho didn't have to wonder how or why the Marinho family would come to own African artifacts, but he did wonder about the art's origins and the original owners it had been stolen from. The mismatched scale of each piece unintentionally echoed the racial power dynamics in Brazil that Agostinho didn't want to think about.

Every centimeter of the Marinho home displayed ostentatious wealth. Every painted portrait was mounted in a gilded frame, causing glints to light the shadows. A large porcelain vase dominated the foyer and the fragrance from its fresh sprays of vibrant pink orchids filled the air. Every surface was hand polished to a bright gleam; their finishes screaming at him: *She may never be happy without money.*

So, he ignored all of it. The 1970 FIFA World Cup Final and the *elastico* sharpened his mental discipline on the other great love of his life, football.

An oversized door with intricate carvings in the dark wood flew open from the end of the hall. The yelling was suddenly not muffled.

The loud voices spilled out the door and echoed against the vaulted ceiling. Gabriela stomped out, her wet and puffy face shouting profanities in Portuguese at her father. *Our child will be strong and beautiful like his mãe*, Agostinho thought. *I love that she is brave, standing up to her father. No matter what her father says, I will love her forever.*

"Gabriela, please, please listen to your *papai*. He does what's best for the family, for all of us. You must listen to him, please *Cordeirinho*." Another feminine face, also wet and puffy, not yelling but crying, emerged behind Gabriela: her mother. The mother begged the headstrong daughter to obey her father, and her voice softened but still quivered as she used Gabriela's childhood nickname, *Cordeirinho*—little lamb—but Gabriela was having none of it.

Age aside, the women looked the same: one a slightly younger version of the other. Both women wore red lipstick smudged with tears. Both had clear, light skin with high cheekbones, and light brown eyes contrasted with dark hair. It would be obvious to any observer they were related, sisters perhaps, since the older woman looked younger than her age. Their behavior, however, was markedly different. To Gabriela's confident, articulate anger, her mother displayed distressed desperation.

The mother reached out for Gabriela's hand, but Gabriela defiantly turned her back. Her golden hooped earrings bounced as she turned, and her eyes flashed at Agostinho. The fire he saw in them was not a trick of light but reflected Gabi's core, and if possible, he loved her even more. Without another word, she quickly turned again and stomped her stacked platform sandals up the sweeping staircase. True to her nature Gabriela wore bold colors, with brash gold and brown stripes and she looked like a fashion model storming down a runway instead of storming up the stairs.

*She doesn't want me to see her crying*, he thought. *I don't care what he said to make her so angry. I will make things right with her.*

Her mother, wearing similar earthy colors but substantially subdued in tone, followed Gabriela up the stairs, still pleading, still crying until the women disappeared somewhere into the rooms above. The yelling and carrying-on once again became muffled. The room at the end of the hall, however, became quiet. Although the ornate door was ajar, Agostinho couldn't see into the room. All he saw was a thin wisp of cigar smoke wafting through the opening. He didn't need to look inside to know it was the patriarch's study, the study of Gabriela's *pai*. He also knew Gabriela's father was in there, waiting for him.

Agostinho's feet stopped kicking. He no longer thought about football. The outburst had jolted him back to the mansion, back into Gabriela's house. Eventually, the entire house became quiet, and he was still sitting there. As the moments passed, he wondered if he had been forgotten. *No, the bastardo is making me wait*, he thought. *I will not be weakened by his tricks. I love her.* Determined to get this over with, Agostinho stood with a swell of his chest. Nobody came. He took a tentative step down the hall, then hesitated. Maybe he should wait after all? No, he should show the man his bravery; he should go.

Agostinho stood taller and straighter, then strode across the foyer, down to the end of the hall. The sound of each footstep echoed in Agostinho's ears, and the hall suddenly seemed longer than it had been earlier.

Agostinho nudged open the door, stepped inside, and announced himself: "Agostinho dos Santos, *Senhor.*"

The patriarch, once handsome but now rather piggish, sat behind an enormous mahogany desk and smoked a cigar. His large jowl drooped below the point of his chin as he blew out thick smoke. The flash of Sr. Marinho's small diamond ring, worn on the pudgy pinky finger of his right hand, caught Agostinho's eye, who then noticed a simple gold wedding band on the man's left ring finger. The red velvet smoking jacket he wore was tight around the belly and looked like something from the 1940s. *It's so old. He is so old*, Agostinho thought.

Cigar smoke filled the wood-paneled room, but Agostinho still caught a faint whiff of Gabriela's jasmine and musk-scented perfume. He couldn't identify the brand, but he was sure it was expensive and must have been heavily applied. Typical. The pigman glared at Agostinho with his narrowed, deep brown eyes.

*Gabriela clearly did not get her good looks here*, Agostinho thought. *Although she has his lips. He is a pig with lips.* Agostinho, who looked for the humor in everything, sucked the inside of his cheeks to keep from laughing. He stood waiting for *Senhor* Marinho to ask him to sit, but that didn't happen, so he sat down in a burgundy tufted leather chair without being invited.

"*Olá, Senhor.*" Agostinho spoke tentatively.

"Well, what do you have to say for yourself?" The patriarch had no need for pleasantries. Before Agostinho could answer, Sr. Marinho slammed his hand on the table and exploded. "Damn it. My daughter is too good for you, you are where you do not belong. Your father works for *me*. He works on the  shop floors, for God's sake. And now, now look what you have done. Well, what do you have to say for yourself?" He repeated as though he had given Agostinho sufficient time to respond before. This time, he waited for Agostinho's answer.

*This old pig man knows nothing of love,* Agostinho thought.

"Your daughter and I, we are in love, *Senhor.*"

"So, you will marry her then? You, who claim to love her, would allow her to marry beneath her place. You have no education, no money, nothing. Your family belongs in the *favela*, the city's slums, and you come to my house and claim love for *my* daughter."

"I am not… my family is not from the *favela, Senhor.* My father is a good man." Agostinho stiffened at the insult and spoke forcefully. "I come from a hard-working Brazilian *família.*" Agostinho knew the man judged him unfairly for his dark skin. Perhaps if his skin were lighter, he would be more acceptable. Even though Brazil was home to immigrants from all over the world, from Japan to Italy, racism against the dark-skinned, particularly those with African ancestry, persisted. "My *família* is *Brazilian,*" Agostinho repeated himself to emphasize his nationality over his ethnicity. His background was not wealthy like the Marinhos, but respectable and solidly middle-class. He was ready to defend his own name and the honor of his family to this pompous pigman.

Sr. Marinho grunted in disapproval, and repeated his question, slowly and with emphasis. "Well, what do you have to say for yourself?"

"If she will have me, I will marry her. I ask your permission and your approval."

"Ha. That child will do as she will, or so she says. My *pai* would have disowned her, thrown her out on her ass for carrying a *bastardo.* I will be more generous. You will marry her, yes, because *I say so.*" He threw Agostinho a pointed glare, pressing his dominance.

*Yes, pigman, you think you are such an important man, but you are pigman,* Agostinho fumed. *You think you have control of this decision.*

*If you say no, I marry her anyway. But I let you think you are the big man, so that we will have your blessing.* Agostinho glared back before realizing he had won. The pigman had just consented to the wedding.

"Yes, sir." He replied through softened lips, trying to sound compliant. He was victorious…maybe.

"You have endangered the soul of my *cordeirinho*. You will both confess your sins, repent, and marry in the church. There will be no discussion about this."

"Yes, sir."

"Gabriela, she wants a big wedding like her sister. She will not have this. You and she have shamed our family name. I will be witness and your *pai* will be witness. The *mamães* insist on attending and we will respect their feminine sensibilities. The priest will conduct the ceremony at the altar, but we will have the church empty. Nobody will know. We will do this immediately."

*Seriously?* thought Agostinho. *"Feminine sensibilities," what the hell is that? No wonder Gabi rebels against the pigman. I will never be this way with my woman.* Agostinho unilaterally decided to raise a modern family where women are equal and strong. Consultation with his future wife on that point was unnecessary. And since he was winning, calling out Sr. Marinho's asinine patriarchy became avoidable, so Agostinho stayed conciliatory.

"Yes, Sir."

"Good, that is settled, then." His voice became hard. "And the last thing is not a compromise, but my *cordeirinho* will do as her *pai* directs." Sr. Marinho sized up how Agostinho would take this last bit of news before continuing. "I will allow Gabriela to keep her connection with her *mãe*. *Senhora* Marinho will make me miserable if I do not allow this and as her husband, I will keep her happy, within reason. But you will both leave; you will move to America and no longer engage with the Marinho family or benefit from the Marinho name. You are exiled. My family name will not bear this shame."

Agostinho's mouth gaped open and his bushy eyebrows squeezed together. He did not expect this at all. Given the Marinho patriarch's reputation and the reputation of the Marinho patriarchs before him, Agostinho expected he would be thrown out of the palace, his *pai* fired from his job, his family attacked, driven away. Gabriela might be taken away for a secret abortion or an extended trip to have the child in secrecy before returning to São Paulo. *But America… that is why Gabriela was crying. That is why she was so mad.*

And then because he had to know, "… and my *pai*?"

Sr. Marinho grunted again. "He is a good worker, your *pai*. I hope you are as good. He will keep his job, but he and *Brasil* will lose a son."

Another surprise. The pigman was no pigman after all. Agostinho had misjudged. He looked the patriarch deeply and directly in the eyes and understood. Agostinho saw softness in the man's eyes, contrasting the harshness of his voice. *This man revers the honor of his family; he loves his daughter and wants to protect both. He will not destroy my father, or my family because he is modern. I was wrong about him because he is a good man. If my skin were lighter or my family richer, he might even allow us to marry and stay despite our mistake.*

"The lawyers are making the arrangements. I have investments in America, and because of that, you will become American. The child will be born American. My daughter and grandchild will have a modest home, but you will support your family and not expect money from me." Sr. Marinho flicked the ash of his cigar and rolled the tip around in the ashtray as though unsure what to do with it. "They say there is marvelous opportunity in America for *morenos*. The *Americanos* give away money to anyone with half a brain. You can make a good start there."

Agostinho nodded his agreement, though he wasn't sure what he would do in America. He didn't even speak English yet.

"Yes, sir. Is that all?"

"Yes, you are dismissed. You will be contacted about the arrangements." The old man turned back to his stack of papers.

Agostinho slowly rose to leave, still stunned by the unexpected turn of events from the day. He laid his hand on the door frame, paused, and turned back to face Sr. Marinho.

"*Senhor*, I love her, and I will care for her forever. You have my promise I will make her happy. I will give her everything. She will never want." Without waiting for a response, he turned and left the room. He did not see the sad, hopeful look Sr. Marinho gave him as he walked out.

# Nine

# ONE OFFER-TWO VOWS
# MID-2020

"Are you nervous about this?" Tony smiled and squeezed Robbie's large, damp hand.

"I'm nervous about the courthouse. It's just weird, the happiest day of our life at the same place we'll face off against… them." Robbie stared at the yellowing beige, two-story building, an embarrassment in architecture that looked like a giant, discarded cereal box tossed onto its back, flimsy and dull. How could one of the wealthiest areas in the world lack enough civic pride to allow this eyesore to represent its justice system? "Maybe we should get married someplace nicer."

"We can do that, love, but not until the pandemic is over. Today is just for us, just for the legal part. Then we'll have a real wedding with everybody there." Tony popped a tiny, pursed-lip kiss on Robbie's hand.

Robbie considered what the wedding would be like with all the Brazilian relatives in attendance. As children, Robbie's nuclear family had traveled to São Paulo to visit family living there, but infrequently, so they weren't close. Although Robbie would've appreciated having Brazilian grandparents, aunts, uncles, and cousins at his wedding, he accepted that couldn't happen. A big Brazilian wedding would've been awesome, but the São Paulo family was even more old-fashioned and out-of-touch than Gus and Gabi. The American Santoses hid Robbie's homosexuality from the family in Brazil. And although Robbie wanted more connection with his Brazilian family, they might never know about the love of his life, Tony.

Thus, his lifetime achievement of coming out was marred by the inconvenience of family honor, tradition, his heritage, not to mention the pandemic. Another reason Robbie and Tony had settled for a quick pandemic wedding was to avoid being alone during the quarantine-like lockdown. *Accept the things you cannot change…*

"Ya, I guess…" Robbie said. "Anyway, where the hell is Ace? It's not like him to be late."

"He's not late. We're early, Love."

"Whatever." Robbie, not accustomed to wearing a suit and tie, pulled at his collar as the rising heat from the blacktop parking lot magnified his discomfort. As a fifth-grade teacher, Robbie not only never wore a suit, and he didn't even own one. The few suits he kept from his post-university years didn't fit anymore. During the pandemic, they did nearly all their shopping online, but suits require a good fitting. Buying the suit was its own trial; every dressing room had mirrored his obesity. The well-meaning department store sales staff, ever-patient, said nothing. When one suit was too tight, they would scurry off with an encouraging word about another available option in inventory.

Tony had helped him through the ordeal with affectionate tolerance. They had gone to the local mall together to pick something out. Tony had tried to hold hands, nuzzle as they walked, but that was impossible. They had gone to buy a suit, not be harassed by chronically disaffected teenagers with nothing better to do than bully passers-by. Homosexuals holding hands were easy prey. As it was, the teenagers had glared, ready to pounce at the slightest provocation. A squeeze of the hand would give them cause. But Tony's mere presence had given Robbie strength. He knew he was loved.

The dreaded shopping venture—which seemed to take forever—had been a resounding success. Robbie surprised himself with how good he looked, which was not always an easy accomplishment for large people. He thought about how looking good in a suit came so naturally for Ace, who was just like his dad Steve, or at least how Robbie remembered him. As a child, Robbie had looked up to Steve as the model of Americana, the perfect white dad with the perfect white job, and perfectly good-looking with the perfect white family. Of course, as a child, Robbie had not understood the inherent and unrelenting pressure of perfection.

*What does Ace remember about his dad?* Robbie wondered. He knew that the lawsuit would be hard on Ace, but secretly that was one reason Robbie was so determined to move forward. He worried about his friend, worried that Ace had never dealt with the past and that it festered inside him like rotting garbage. Ace refused to talk about it, as though it had never happened.

*This lawsuit will heal us both when we win,* Robbie thought, *but what if we lose? What would happen to me? What would happen to Ace? Maybe he'll crawl so far into a hole it'll kill him.*

And of course, as if knowing that Robbie was thinking about him, Ace showed up right at that moment.

"Hey guys, you ready for the big commit?" Ace said with a grin.

"Yes! Yes! Yes!" Tony jumped up and down on his toes, failing to contain his excitement.

*He bounces just like mom. Oh my God, am I marrying my mom?* Robbie laughed at himself. Knocked back into the joy of the moment, he held up a ring box and said, "Got the rings right here."

"Ok, but we have a minute and I need to talk to you guys about something. I got a call from a lawyer for the Association. They got the lawsuit we filed, and they want to talk settlement before they spend too much time fighting. Is now ok to talk or do you want to wait?"

"No, let's get that out of the way. Is that okay with you, Tony?"

Tony nodded. "Sure, Ace. What did they say?"

"They will pay you one million dollars over ten years to dismiss the lawsuit."

Silence.

Finally, Robbie spoke. "There's something else, though, isn't there? What is it?"

"You have to sign a non-disclosure, non-disparagement, and non-cooperation agreement. They also want me to agree not to sue them again for other clients."

"In English, Ace, please."

"They want you to shut up, not to make the rest of your story public. You would be silenced. That's nondisclosure. Non-disparagement—you won't say anything bad about them, like on social media, or anywhere. Non-cooperation—you won't help anyone else sue them."

"They can't do that!" Tony said.

"Well, yes, they can," Ace said. "I told you guys the system is fucked up."

"But the story is already out, the press knows, the lawsuit is public. So, it's already disclosed, isn't it?" Robbie asked.

"Not everything. The existence of the lawsuit and the original documents we filed is publicly available information, but there's still a lot unknown that would come out in the trial." Ace's eyes met Robbie's, and they both knew exactly what had been private up to this point, and what would stay private if the trial stopped. "Nobody has testified. Your dad hasn't had to testify. If we never go to trial, Gus won't be cross-examined. So, they won't be able to ask about Coach Sean. They won't cross-examine Gus about taking Strikers' money."

"What about the non-cooperation part? Does that go to Lupe, too?"

Ace shifted his weight and stuttered. "Well…uh…yeah, it does."

"So, what'll that do to her career? This is what she wants to do, so it'll be bad for her professionally, right?"

Ace looked at his shoes and nodded.

"Damn it, Ace. You didn't even tell her, I'll bet. You're throwing Lupe under the bus here." Robbie widened his stance, locked his knees, and placed his hands on his hips, jutting out his chin with the accusation.

"No, I won't do that. I'm hoping we can negotiate an exception for her. I swear, I'll get them to drop that part." Ace stared right back at Robbie, with a challenge in his voice.

"Hmmm, I know how you feel about her. You can't hide that from me no more than I could hide something like that from you."

"Look, let's not talk about that right now. I'll try to get out of it. What about the rest of the deal? This is a good time to get out. You can avoid putting your dad on the stand. You can avoid having to tell the world all the nasty details."

"I know. It's not that. An apology is what I want. I want validation. I want them to admit that they hurt me, that I really was hurt, and it wasn't my fault. It wasn't my parents' fault."

"It's a decent amount. Help start your family like you guys want." Ace turned the focus back to Robbie. Robbie and Tony had been talking about adopting kids. But with Robbie as a public-school teacher and Tony a barista, baker, and massage therapist, the couple had modest means. The settlement wouldn't give them a lavish lifestyle in Northern California, but they could save for kids' college, have a nice home, and cars that were paid for. They would be more comfortable with the settlement money.

"Fuck them. One hundred thousand dollars a year for ten years. Fuck them. That doesn't do shit," Robbie said, growing increasingly agitated.

"Shhh, it's ok love. Ace knows it's not about the money for us," Tony said.

Robbie said nothing, so Ace continued, "Money would probably be the only thing you would ever get, if you even get that, but we could ask for more. I think they might come up."

"How much is enough to make them stop, make them pay attention, make them protect kids? Can you tell me a number? How much?"

"No. That number is bigger than what's on the table. Do you want to try for more?"

"Damn it, Ace. I don't want money. I want it to stop."

"They've already implemented some protections because of you. You did that. We could push for more protections."

"It's not enough."

"What would be enough?"

Robbie shook his head. Nothing, nothing would be enough.

"You wouldn't have to testify," Ace added, changing the focus. "You could maintain some privacy. The details aren't out there yet."

Robbie gulped. *This could be over*, he thought. *I could keep a semblance of dignity*. But that momentary salvation would offer a mere fleeting respite for Robbie. *No, it will never be truly over.* Settling would do nothing for other children. Then again, other children weren't there having their lives shredded publicly. Settling would do nothing for Ace, who was fighting not only for Robbie but for something else. But again, Ace wouldn't have his life shredded in front of the entire world, either. The Elbridge family's suffering would remain secret. Robbie asked, "What about you? What is justice for you, Ace?"

Ace narrowed his eyes. When he spoke, his words were cold and hard, like concrete. "Damn it, Robbie. Take the deal. Let's get out of this. Let's stop the pain already."

"Is this about you now, Ace?" Robbie's cheeks heated. "Was this always about you?"

"There is no justice; it doesn't exist. Yeah, I admit it. I want out. We could lose. How much more will it hurt if we lose?"

"So, you're afraid now? Afraid of losing? You don't believe in justice now?"

"Damn it, Robbie. Why don't you get it? There-is-no-justice. It's a made-up thing. You will never get that, never. Flawed humans in a flawed society created a flawed system of justice in a flawed, hate-filled country. It won't stop. If we win, it won't stop. Nothing we can do will make it stop," Ace spoke fast as he paced and stared at the ground.

"If you mean nothing will change the past, you're right. The rest is a bunch of shit."

"The world's problems aren't yours, Robbie. You can't help everyone. You can be finished, move on. Accept the inhumanity, accept the failure of justice, and just move on."

"Maybe you should take your own advice, Ace," Robbie said, then continued, "But you're wrong. I will never be done with this. Whether or not we brought the lawsuit, whether or not we win, it will always be there, deep inside. You, of all people, know that because it's the same for you."

Ace stopped pacing and stood staring at the ground. Even without Ace's empathic intuition, Robbie felt Ace's pain. Their pain twisted together, one event pretzeled with the other, tying them together in an infinite woven loop. Ace took a breath and finally spoke. "Yeah, I know."

"Of course you do," Robbie said. He stood directly in front of Ace. "We will not lose. We are going to force them to admit what happened. There is no way in hell I am—we are—agreeing to be confidential. I want to rub their faces in the shit stain they made of my life and yours."

Ace looked up into Robbie's face but didn't look convinced.

"There is justice, Ace. God exists. Love exists. You must see that. You will win," Robbie said.

"Robbie, how can you say that after everything?"

"You are stronger than you know, Ace. I know that deep down, you are a believer. You can't hide from me either. I know you."

The men went silent. Robbie was naturally open to people, outgoing, but he knew Ace was not. Ace wouldn't let people get too close. He was just like his dad, quiet, serious. Robbie knew he was one of the few people that could speak to Ace this way, one of the few people standing ready to hold Ace up through troubled times.

"They'll blame your dad for not protecting you and they'll blame Coach Sean," Ace finally said.

"They'll bring up Coach Sean?"

"Of course, they'll bring up Coach Sean."

"Yeah, of course they will," Robbie nodded reluctantly.

"They're going to ask Gus what he knew and when he knew it."

"Fine, Dad's ready. Everyone knows soccer is financially corrupt. Nobody cares."

"If they attack your dad, it'll be vicious."

*Assholes*, thought Robbie. *My suffering, Ace's suffering, isn't enough blood for them? Now they attack my family, my papai.* Robbie held his head up, looked Ace straight in the eye, and grinned broadly. "Fuck the Association."

Despite himself, Ace smiled back. "Ok, I'll tell them *no deal.* Your dad will get on the stand and testify about the money, about Sean."

"Damn straight. Let's roll."

"Ooo, I love your strong manly talk," Tony said with a chuckle while leaning in close to Robbie and bringing them all back to the seriousness and joy of the moment.

With that, they pulled up their n95s and marched into the courthouse, ready for vows.

*Ten*

# ANOTHER GAME
# 1998

Coach Sean analyzed the kinesthetics of growing bodies as he watched the boys play. Adolescence creates such magnificent disparities among children. Many of the eleven-year-olds were still little boys, tiny and pudgy, like babies. But even then, hints of slim muscles rose above the baby fat in places, on their thighs and developing biceps, stretching, flexing, growing. Other boys seemed nearly like grown men, already tall and changing. It was that in-between that mesmerized Sean, the new muscular energy straining to replace childhood. All the boys yearning to become men, yet unscathed by the harsh world, beautiful and compelling.

Sean connected to the wonder and enthusiasm of youth in a way he couldn't connect with his peers, with adults. He shared the incessant physical energy, the never-ending carnal need to move. The stillness required by polite adult society was not only impossible to achieve but seemed pointless. Yet another way in which he could understand children while adults were often incomprehensible. As he watched the boys, he found himself pulling back his own foot as if to strike the ball in sync with the players. His body longed to be with the boys in every way.

More than that, he imagined having a young friend over at his place, a bowl of popcorn, milkshakes, and a scary movie. A best friend whose small body cuddled against Sean for protection, affection. They would feed each other popcorn, laugh, talk, and then sleep together.

If the child was awake or afraid in the night, Sean would soothe and comfort him. Every night might be that dreamy if he could find the right child lover to share his bed.

The boy lover would enjoy the relationship, too. That was the only way. Sex alone wasn't enough; there had to be a connection, companionship, closeness. Mutuality was key, like in any relationship. In his daydream, the boy loved Sean as much as Sean loved the boy. Sean's longing to be touched, to be physically loved, his emotional skin hunger would be satisfied. Finally, Sean would have an emotional companion, a partner, a lover, though he knew it would—could—never happen.

He watched the players on the field, how their bodies moved, their strength, their tightness, their youth. Arousal played in Sean's sweatpants.

*Shit. Not now. This can't happen.*

Fortuitously, the teenage referee blew her whistle and exited the field. Halftime. Coach Sean herded the team to the shade of a nearby tree outside the opposition's earshot. He walked briskly but relaxed, chin up, aware of his influence on the boys. They saw him as a role model, now and perhaps for the rest of their lives. They could do worse. And they had been playing extremely well, so Sean didn't need to say much. JJ ambled along behind, his eyes on the grass, hands in pockets.

As the group settled in and slurped from water bottles, Susie rushed over with a kitchen bowl of fresh orange slices to pass out. Eager hands grabbed at the cool slices of juicy, refreshing fruit. The thirsty, slurpy mouths were too busy for talk, but the silence would only last a moment. Coach Sean took advantage of the quiet nanosecond to kick off the discussion.

"Good work out there, lads. You've got their keeper on the run. He's brilliant, but you are more brilliant. Now, who wants to tell me what you're doing right?"

Josh Martin, Susie's kid, shot up his hand and, without waiting for Sean to acknowledge him, blurted out, "Coach, can I get more playtime? I should get to play more."

"Ok, Josh, let's start with you. You want more playtime. How do you earn it?" Coach Sean first squatted to address the boys at eye level, but then went ahead and sat at their level in the cool grass. Teased by the sweet, fruity fragrance filling the air, he grabbed an orange slice while waiting for a response.

The children remained silent until Josh shrugged and mumbled, "Whatever…"

"Well then, lads, who can answer that question?" Coach Sean was determined to turn Josh's inappropriate outburst into a learning moment for the boys.

"Attitude!" a chorus of sweet voices answered.

"That's right—what else? Ace, what do you think?" Coach asked.

"Don't hog the ball. Pass, but make smart passes, smart plays," Ace said. His face eagerly searched for Sean's reaction, for reassurance. Sean had called on Ace because he could rely on Ace for positivity and enthusiasm, and his answer would likely be correct.

"That's right, Ace. Attitude and teamwork, you can't beat that combo. I'm seeing a lot of that out there. Keep it up." Sean smiled at Ace and winked. Ace returned the smile. "Ok, what else? What should you do more of?"

The discussion continued like this for the entire ten-minute break. Sean questioned the boys in a juvenile version of the Socratic method. With an instinct for teaching children, he believed the best method was to pull the answers from developing brains, not feed endless loops of information. Sean caught motion in the corner of his eye, looked up at the opposing team heading back for the game start.

"Thanks for the snack, Susie. Everyone say 'Thank you' to Mrs. Martin. Now let's get back." Sean appreciated Susie standing nearby, silent and watching closely. He knew she would anticipate the boys' needs before they asked; shoelaces tied, water bottles filled, bags of ice, wrap, and bandages ready for the occasional injury. Her attentive assistance—not to mention her kindness—was invaluable to the team.

Another chorus of, "Thank you, Mrs. Martin," erupted before the boys rushed back with the enthusiasm of victory on their heels while Mrs. Martin ran about wiping sticky chins and picking orange peels off the grass.

The starters took their positions and waited for the referee's whistle.

Coach Sean forced his thoughts back to the game, back to player performance as the second half began. The referee provided a much-needed distraction by calling a foul against Josh, who had inappropriately tackled an opposing player. Luckily for the team, the referee did not give Josh a yellow, or worse, a red card. Sean would pull Josh out at the next opportunity. That boy could use some guidance. Or maybe he just needed a friend. Sean could do that for Josh.

Feeling eyes on his back, Sean turned to see JJ staring. Caught without time to look away, JJ smirked at Sean.

"Ye need something?" JJ asked. Everything JJ said came out snarky, confrontational. Sean couldn't tell if the tone was intentional or just how JJ spoke. Once again, Sean gave JJ the benefit of the doubt by not assuming the worst.

"Ya, we need to take Josh out, next break. Get someone ready to sub in."

JJ walked to the bench and tapped a couple players on the shoulder. Sean watched JJ instructing the boys to warm up, then turned his attention back to the game. Sean's coaching style was to watch silently, not to shout instructions from the sidelines. Soccer's a fast-moving game where the players need to think for themselves on the field. They cannot and should not be micro-managed, at least that was Sean's coaching philosophy. Not all coaches agreed.

The ball crossed the outer line, and the ref whistled it out. The Strikers had the throw-in.

"Ref, sub," Sean shouted.

The referee looked at Sean, nodded, and motioned for the substitution. Sean called Josh off the field and over to the side where they could chat about gameplay. Josh came over and looked up at Sean with a red, puffy face. Sean squatted to look Josh squarely in his wide, wet eyes. Josh, heaving with each heavy breath, looked away. Josh's dad Joe Martin was watching, and Joe pressured Josh relentlessly and without kindness. Here was an opportunity to show kindness to a kid who needed it.

*Change of plans.* Sean devoted a moment to Josh, ignoring the gameplay, and placed a gentle hand on Josh's shoulder until Josh lifted his head to make eye contact. "You are ok," Sean said gently, but with confidence. Children would believe they were ok if an adult told them so; asking an open question might get another answer, or worse, a tantrum.

Josh nodded with lips pressed closed.

"But it looks like ye need a breather, lad," Sean said. "Go on over to JJ, and he'll look at your ankle. Still a bother, is it?" They both knew the sprained ankle had healed weeks ago, but acknowledging the feigned excuse let Josh save face. Sean knew Josh needed a break, a friend. Josh responded well to JJ who could be trusted to lift the boy's spirits. Tender loving care and a bag of ice might work wonders for the kid's attitude.

Sean gave Josh a pat on his bottom as he made his way over to JJ. Putting thoughts of Josh aside, Sean turned his attention back to the game. This year's team was strong. His thoughts turned to the state championship.

*Ya, these lads might bring home the trophy yet.*

*****

After another victorious game, another line of hand slaps, another run across the field, another meeting with Coach, soccer for the day was complete. Ace dutifully slipped on his slides, stuffed his muddy cleats into his soccer backpack, and looked up. There he was across the field. His dad had seen him play, which was the best thing ever. He grabbed the backpack strap and swung it over his shoulder and stood to run all in the same motion. In his hurry, he tripped over his own feet, but caught himself and, laughing, ran to his father. The other players—not as excited to see their ubiquitous, helicopering parental units—ambled nonchalantly toward their rides home.

"Great game, Ace." Steve patted Ace on the shoulder, a rare show of affection, and Ace beamed in response, then dropped the soccer ball from under his arm and juggled it from one toe to the other, a skill he'd spent hours practicing.

"Did you see that play, Dad? When I passed to Robbie up the field? What a shot. I thought it would go over the net, but it was right at the top, over the keeper's fingers." Ace jumped up with his hands in the air to mimic the goalkeeper missing the ball.

"Awesome. I love watching you play. You are so good. I'm proud of you," Steve said with a grin and a tousle of Ace's hair.

"Did you see Robbie's nutmeg? He's gonna teach me that." Ace danced about the ball as though kicking the ball between a defender's legs and picking it up on the backside: a nutmeg. "Robbie knows some cool stuff he can teach me. He's a cool dude."

Steve laughed at the goofy soccer language—nutmeg—and wondered if Ace grasped the subtle implications. But Ace only absorbed his dad's smile because that's all he needed. Father and son laughed together as they shared the highlights of a close and difficult game on the walk back to the parking lot. Ace dribbled the ball with his feet the entire way. Steve silently admired his son's foot skills, but didn't give additional compliments. Although Ace made the dribble look easy, Steve knew it took extreme foot control.

When they got to the car, Ace reached over to grab the flyer stuck under the windshield wiper on the passenger side, and read it.

Across the top of the plain, white paper was the word—BEWARE— in letters cut from magazines and newspapers. This simple message was assembled underneath:

THE FC STRIKERS HARBOR PEDOPHILES. GEOGHAN IS A RAPIST. YOUR CHILDREN ARE NOT SAFE.

That was it. No other information was provided. It looked like something kids had slapped together as a joke with the words unprofessionally reproduced, sloppy.

Ace dropped his backpack and with expert speed, he folded the paper and shot the nearly perfect airplane over the car roof to hit his dad's face. He snickered and asked, "Dad, what's this mean?"

Steve grumbled something as he bent to pick up the paper airplane. After unfolding the flyer, Steve stiffened and froze, his eyes affixed to the paper in his hand. Ace watched him silently, watched his face turn white, watched his eyes glaze over, for what seemed forever. And as though he felt the nausea bubbling in his dad's gut, Ace put his hand on his own belly. Ace wanted to vomit but with effort controlled it. His thick tongue hindered the words, the words that came next.

"Dad," Ace called out, to no response. "Dad! What is that?" louder this time.

Steve's head jerked up toward Ace, eyes narrowed intensely. "What?" he snapped.

Ace could barely speak, but he had to know. "What is that, Dad?"

"Nothing," Steve smashed the paper into a ball and slammed it onto the grass, yet still didn't unlock the car. He reached for the car door but stopped and stood frozen with his hand resting on the handle. Ace seemed to disappear. Everything disappeared as if Steve were floating above, watching himself from the air. He observed himself remotely, frozen and staring at the ground, but this time, he wasn't staring at the paper. He stared at the grass: no, not the grass, the green. It was so green. Multiple singular blades reached for the sun in an overlapping pattern that wasn't uniformly crisscrossed. Each blade existed as a singular being with a diamond-shaped tip. Safety might be found in the green. It might be there, but confusingly it wasn't entirely safe either. Startled, Steve took a sharp breath, returned to his body, and then reminded himself to breathe deep and slow, the way his wife Heather had taught him.

Ace felt the nausea pass at the same time Steve did. Ace fixed his eyes on his father, studying every expression for clues as the two climbed silently into the car. Just a moment ago, they had connected. They were happy, but the connection broke and Ace didn't understand why. All he could understand were confusing emotional waves of negativity, maybe anger, hurt, depression. Their special moment inexplicitly morphed into disconnection, silence. His eleven years of life did not give Ace sufficient time to understand what was happening to his dad, and not knowing was the scariest part.

Steve usually gave Ace pointers on the way home, a critical but loving assessment of the day's play. Most kids didn't like that. The club admonished parents to limit feedback to telling the kid how they enjoyed watching their kid play, and they hoped the kid had fun. They say you should never give your kid pointers or criticize their play after a game. Steve, though, took everything seriously and Ace loved his dad's critical but well-meaning advice because critical attention beat no attention every time.

But on this drive home, Steve had nothing to say. It didn't happen often, but sometimes Steve would check out mentally, unraveling the tangled threads of some mysterious conundrum dominated his mind.

"Dad, what did you think of how I played?" Ace asked tentatively, gently probing.

"Uh, you were great."

"Do you have any pointers? Maybe something I could improve?"

Steve said nothing for a minute and then "Sometimes you poke at the ball, Coach explained that problem to you. I saw you poke again. Makes you look like a flamingo. It's better to lean into the play, into the ball, than to stick your leg out, poke at it. Remember Coach saying that?"

"Ya, I know. I did that. I'll work on it. Anything else?"

"No, really, you played great. I'm proud of you." Steve stared straight out the windshield with unblinking eyes. He held his lips closed tightly and said nothing more. Ace stopped probing.

The silent ride home seemed longer than it was. Steve drove on autopilot; the way was so routine he could've driven it asleep. Although it wasn't like he was asleep, it was more like a trance. Another being inhabited his body and manipulated the vehicle through the familiar roads. He didn't turn on the radio and didn't talk until they arrived, and Ace jumped out of the car.

"Have fun with Coach and Mr. Santos and everyone, Dad. I'll see you later," Ace said hopefully, waiting for a response.

Steve looked at Atticus as his eyes came back into focus and he said clearly, "I love you, Son," before he drove off to the sports bar to meet Sean and Gus.

Atticus watched his dad drive away, wondering what that flyer meant.

# Eleven

# AT THE SPORTS BAR
# 1998

Parched and jonesing for a drink, Steve entered the sports bar. He decided to take the edge off with a shot right out of the gate, relax, and enjoy his new soccer buddies. His body would neutralize the alcohol before the game was over and it was time to drive home, or so he convinced himself. He shook out a shiver of stress from his shoulders and left it at the door.

Steve had already forgotten about the flyer. Some people buried their life negativity deeply within themselves rather than facing the problems, but not Steve. Not that he consciously determined not to think about it. Rather, the entire event had mentally evaporated as though it had never happened. His mind automatically rejected the memory without allowing him to make a conscious decision about whether to remember.

Steve had heard about this bar but had never checked it out. Everyone called it a sports bar, but it was more like a pub because the dark mahogany décor and low light seemed rather old-fashioned to him, definitely European. Like many of the patrons, the bartender was a stout man with strong, tattooed arms and a gray goatee. He stood behind the massive wooden bar, multiple bottles of whiskey on glass shelves behind him. There were some basics, like vodka and tequila, but nearly all the bottles were whiskey. On closer inspection, Steve saw some bottles were old and empty, mementos of better times, perhaps. The place had lots of beer-on-tap options, judging by the multiple keg handles. The pub wasn't crowded, but still loud.

As Gus had promised, Liverpool battled Manchester United on large-screen TV monitors strategically located to maximize viewing. American sports bars are usually only for basketball and football, with an occasional baseball, hockey, or wrestling match thrown in, but typically not soccer. Yet, this place showed soccer, and the patrons actively enjoyed the matches. *This is absolutely a pub and not a sports bar*, Steve decided conclusively. With the location properly categorized and one more life conundrum resolved, Steve relaxed.

"Steve, over here," Gus waved from a table situated with an unobstructed view of the game, which had already begun. Sean was also there with Joe Martin, Josh's dad, who Steve remembered seeing at the soccer game earlier. It surprised Steve to see JJ there because the man didn't look 21, or much like a full grown man for that matter. On further reflection, Steve concluded JJ must be older than he looked and was probably even a few years over 21.

*Europeans start drinking at an earlier age, particularly in Ireland,* thought Steve. He mentally invoked the trope of a drunk Irishman. *Damn, that's racist. Stop that.* He shook his head as if to root out the pernicious racist tropes planted throughout his life.

Steve pulled up a chair. The men scooted around the crowded table to make room for one more. If anyone else showed up, they would need to get another table.

"That's right, scoot round here. We ain't expecting no one else. Here, squeeze in," Joe Martin said. His slurred voice projected over the ambient noise. Steve was getting familiar with that voice soaring over the sidelines at the games. Joe cheered loudest for the hard hits, as though they were watching hockey or rugby. He was known to spout inappropriate profanities when a call went against the FC Strikers. As team legend had it, Joe was the only club parent ever red-carded out of a game for mouthing off to the referee. Joe had obviously started drinking much earlier. He must have started drinking during the kids' game, which wasn't allowed but happened sometimes. Steve had not given Joe much thought after seeing him at the first game with his wife, Team Mom, what's-her-name.

*Why do I always forget her name?*

Given his size, Joe obviously worked out religiously, and Steve remembered he was a firefighter, or maybe police, something like that. The man's fair skin held a ruddy hue, with exceptionally red cheeks. *Wow, those cheeks… he must be loaded.* Steve's conclusion was confirmed by the tangy whiff of bourbon emanating from Joe.

Steve ordered a round of tequila shots for the table. They already had a pitcher of beer with an extra mug. Steve made a mental note to pay for the next pitcher. He liked to make sure he paid his way, paid more than his way, so he wouldn't feel like he owed friends for anything, even a beer. Despite his frugality, Steve was generous with friends, and always generous with alcohol. Frugality has no place with family and friends and drinking.

"Cheers! Here's to another brilliant victory for the Strikers." Sean held up his frothy mug and waited for the chorus of responding cheers before slurping at it. Steve held up his mug in salute before enjoying a long sip with his eyes closed. Beer foam soothed his throat with a chain reaction that soothed everything else, causing anxiety to dissipate. He took a deep breath before another long sip that drained his mug.

"The boys were brilliant today, fantastically brilliant. I couldn't be more chuffed," Sean continued. "And Ace, *that* boy has talent, he does. Brilliant!" Sean beamed at Steve.

"Atticus played well today, I'm proud to say," Steve responded awkwardly. He didn't take compliments easily, but his ears warmed and twitched, the only sign he was pleased, or as Sean would say, *chuffed.*

"Good boy, he is. I envy you having a brilliant son like that," Sean said.

*Wow, what a weird thing to say*, Steve thought. But he responded with grace, "I'm very lucky."

"Hey Gus, I heard that Trevor Smansky from Arsenal wants to move to Strikers. You remember him? He's the keeper on their top U-14 team?" Sean asked. "You hear anything about that?"

"No. How'd you hear?" Gus replied with a raise of his bushy eyebrows. "You know the Association doesn't let us recruit from other teams. Parents or players have to approach us themselves. We can't approach them." Gus had a note of sarcasm in his voice, implying they didn't always follow the Association rules. "Also, I don't think that kid is very talented. If he is who I think he is."

"Bloke came up to me after the game, asked how much it cost to get his kid on the Strikers team."

"Well, that depends on what talent he brings. Have him call me and I'll watch the kid play."

"I know that kid," Joe Martin added. "His dad was complaining the kid doesn't get enough playtime, the club not doing enough for his scholarship opportunities."

"Well, shit. He's already thirteen, so it's a little late," Gus said. "Besides, parents always complain about playtime."

"Already gave him your number, Gus, so you may get a call. Don't think the kid has much talent, but his da's loaded, so can contribute nicely to the Strikers. Besides, everyone knows we churn out talent at Strikers like a machine. Innate talent is a myth," Sean laughed.

"Is right. Get em young enough and we can *make* talent." Gus laughed and Joe joined him, but Steve did not.

Steve's lawyer brain realized immediately what this was, but he was still shocked. He saw Gus sneak a sideways look at him and then quickly look away again. *Wow, even at the youth level, unbelievable*, he thought. Everyone knew international soccer was corrupt, but Steve hadn't realized that corruption happened in the United States and with the children. *Parents buying spots on the team, unbelievable.*

"Well, guess it's lucky for me Ace actually has talent," Steve retorted. He joined the collusive chuckle. Gus exhaled, and his body relaxed as though he had been holding his breath, then he caught Steve's eye and winked. Steve accepted the affirmation; he was now one of the guys.

The men's attention turned to the closest big screen television when a shout went up in the bar. Something interesting was happening in the game, but Steve wasn't thinking about that. His legal mind had engaged and was puzzling over the information he had received. He couldn't think of any reason getting a spot on a kid's soccer team for a donation was illegal. Technically, there wasn't any fraud. He had never seen financial statements from the Strikers and doubted any other parents had seen financials either. The situation oozed sleaze, but not necessarily crime.

Steve looked at Gus with fresh eyes. *I wonder what his background is. Maybe it's not family money after all.* He looked at the gold watch, the designer sports gear, the stylish tennis shoes, and thought about the BMW. He wondered how much Gus paid himself for being the President of the Strikers, a not-for-profit sports team, affiliated with the umbrella Association, but with apparently no financial oversight.

*Atticus is happy.* That was it. The legal mind needed to venture no further. Happiness shut down all the legal questions. However, Steve determined the club would not make the list of the family's year-end charitable contributions. Steve made sure that the charities he supported had financial accountability. The Strikers reminded him why that was important.

Also, Steve felt comfortable with Gus and Sean, but not Joe, who he found tolerable in small doses. Nevertheless, they were enjoying a pleasant afternoon together, watching the soccer match.

*Atticus is happy. It's all good.*

But it wasn't all good because corruption followed Steve like an enthusiastic puppy, first his client, pressuring him to forge documents, and now his new friends. His refusal to accept dishonesty roiled his gut and burned his heart, as though the stress left at the front door had found its way back to him. Despite all his smarts, Steve couldn't find a path to making his family happy without engaging in immoral behavior.

"Fucking dirty players!" A Liverpool-bedecked patron jumped to his feet to share his thoughts.

"Red card!" Another Liverpool-shirted patron added to the growing fray.

"Shut your trap! It's a good goal!" This time a Manchester bedecked player jumped up for the counter yell.

Manchester United had scored a goal after—what the Liverpool fans believed was—a red-card-worthy foul against a Liverpool player. Steve watched the big screen where the game referees strode to the centerline for the post-goal kickoff and ignored the Liverpool player writhing in the grass. Everybody had something to say about that, and several patrons jumped to their feet while saying it.

"Dirty players," Sean grumbled. "We don't allow our lads to play dirty."

"That's right," Gus agreed. "We go by the book."

The collective shouts punctuated with profanity mellowed into a grumbling roar and eventually returned to the usual ambient raucousness. Steve focused his attention on the hotly contested game until Joe Martin's thundering voice pulled him back to the men at the table.

"… I think it was the damn Arsenal trying to dis the Strikers, trying to recruit our talent by spreading bullshit rumors." Joe's mug splashed down on the table, but Joe didn't notice his spilled beer. Steve noticed.

"We were talking about that damn flyer," Gus explained. "Did you see that? The one that was stuck on everyone's cars. Every single car out there, I think…" Gus shrugged and Joe interrupted.

"It's slander, it is. You should sue them assholes, Sean. Maybe we should report it to the Association. The damn good-for-nothing AAYA should put a stop to it. Damn Arsenal is cheating. Trying to wreck the best club around because their kids suck on the field."

"Nah, just jealousy, that's all. I'm over it already," Sean said. He averted his eyes and his voice weakened. Steve wasn't convinced.

"What flyer?" Steve tried to remember. He toyed with a vague remembrance of something, but his mind got fuzzy.

*Where the hell is the tequila? I need another shot.*

"Well, that's good, maybe everyone didn't get it." Always the optimist, Gus was trying to make the best of the shitty development. "Let's just forget about it."

"Assholes said Sean is a faggot, a queer, rapes boys," Joe piped up too loudly. His tone conveyed a belief that homosexuality was ethically equivalent to sexual assault.

Startled by Joe's words, Steve stared at the floor and his eyes glazed over. For a second, he forgot what had just been said, and forgot where he was. When he remembered, he looked over at Sean, who was peering silently into his beer, no doubt embarrassed by Joe's outburst.

*Doesn't seem like Sean's gay. He's not married… but so what?* Steve's mind rejected the implications of sexual assault against children. Rather, he thought they were only talking about Coach Sean being gay. He reached for his beer and shifted uncomfortably in his chair because that didn't seem right; something more was going on.

"Let's not make a big deal about it. This will blow over. You're right, Joe. It's a bunch of kids who are jealous because Strikers kicked Arsenal's ass at finals last year. You know how the kids are. This'll blow over." Sean's tone was remarkably even, straightforward.

*Nah, I don't think Sean's gay. Seems like a straight-up dude to me,* Steve thought. *But who cares? What's the big deal?*

"I agree," Gus said. "No need to get the Association involved. It's a stupid prank, probably kids. Let this blow over." Gus appeared overly eager for an easy way out. But maybe the simple solution was the best. Gus made eye contact with Steve, then glanced away.

Tequila shots arrived, providing a welcome break from an uncomfortable conversation. Steve noticed with the tequila's arrival JJ broke his brooding trance and turned back to the table for a shot. JJ didn't even bother to feign politeness and obviously didn't belong, maybe a generational difference. He was younger than the other guys. He didn't have kids, so how could he relate to parents, to the whole competitive youth sports experience?

It could also be that the other guys were jocks, and JJ didn't dress or act like a jock. He looked more goth than jock. He wore torn jeans and an old Dead Kennedys t-shirt, also torn. And even though old enough to drink alcohol, JJ clung to teenage angst and attitude. It seemed to Steve that JJ would rather be somewhere else but was under the sharp supervision of his uncle Sean. JJ swallowed his tequila without saying a word. Then he gave Steve a knowing, condescending smirk before turning his attention back to the soccer game. Steve felt flustered and exposed, like JJ was seeing him naked. Whether JJ was jock or punk, gay or straight, Irish or alien, Steve decided he didn't like the kid and ignored him for the rest of the afternoon.

*Twelve*

# It Begins

# Mid-2022

## Trial

Ace stopped on the cracked concrete steps to watch a young girl juggling a soccer ball on her tiny feet on the small patch of parched grass behind the courthouse. The girl wasn't older than ten, but she bounced the bright pink ball on her well-worn cleats as though she had been practicing for many more than her meager years. Another young girl, older but with the same bouncy blond, pink-ribboned ponytail, a sister, or cousin perhaps, rushed the little one and stole the ball. A chase ensued. The children squealed and laughed as they ran. They played with aggressive athleticism, undiminished by their girly-pink soccer ball and frayed ribbons. Their sweet laughter reminded Ace of his own soccer days, ended long ago.

Having children someday sat at the top of Ace's bucket list. He decided that if he ever had children, especially girls, they would play ice hockey. The sport had embraced women and girls, so why not? Better that than a misogynistic sport mired in corruption. The US Women's Team gave fans the best soccer America offered. And what did the women athletes have to show for it? Crap, crappy fields, crappy pay, crappy everything—and no executive respect for their achievement. And the US Men's Team? Pure soccer lameness. Fuck that. Ace was over soccer, so his kids, if ever there were any, would be ice hockey players.

*I can keep telling myself that's the reason, anyway*, Ace thought.

The younger girl tried to tackle the bigger girl but fell on the grass. She lay on her back moaning loudly—too loudly—and holding her ankle as though she needed a trip to the emergency room. Ace laughed.

*Oh yeah, she's a soccer player all right. What would happen to soccer if "embellishment" were a penalty like it is in hockey? It'd be a different game.* Sure enough, once the small girl's "injury" went unnoticed, she popped up like nothing happened and continued play.

Ace breathed in the joy flowing from the children, sucking it in like the fragrance of rare flora hidden in forgotten meadows of an anguished world, because that's exactly what it was. He closed his eyes while his hand wandered to rest on his stomach, and he submerged himself in their glee. As the sun warmed his face, images of his dad floated forward. Ace remembered his dad watching him play soccer, how his dad's sun-roughened face would soften, blue eyes bright with pride. Ace was also proud of his dad, the man who, deprived of happy moments in childhood, had nonetheless grown into a loving, supportive father.

A familiar voice broke his train of thought.

"Ace, wait up."

Robbie rounded the corner of the old building, hastened his step, and caught up with Ace. Robbie's quickened pace emphasized the awkward fit of his newish wedding suit on his bulky frame, but Robbie not only looked presentable, he looked great. He was also wearing that smile, exactly as he had as a child, easy and genuine, accentuated by dimples clearly visible on his freshly shaven face. Even facing this challenge, Robbie could—would—stay positive. It was maybe the most admirable Santos family trait.

"Dude, looking sharp."

"Sharper, if I lost a hundred pounds, quicker too." Robbie struck a mock strongman pose, making Ace snicker, even though Robbie's attempt to lighten the mood with self-deprecating humor was misplaced. The minimal effort of walking from his car had caused a sheen to break on Robbie's round face. Regardless of the size of any lawsuit award he ultimately received, he would forever wear his armored suit of fat, built from compulsively eating junk food. It was just one of many struggles Robbie had endured that brought them to this fight.

Robbie followed Ace's gaze to the rowdy, giggling girls. "Having fun, are they?" he asked.

Coming from anyone else, the question would have been rhetorical, but Robbie was one of the few people who knew Ace's secret. Ace was an empath—a true empath—not just some guy who was sensitive to others' feelings. It was more than that. Ace often internalized the feelings of other human beings as though the feelings were his own.

As a child, Ace couldn't distinguish his emotions from the emotions of others. If someone nearby was sad, Ace was also inexplicably sad, but not his own sadness. It was theirs. To bear the emotions of others is not only confusing, but burdensome. Over the years, Ace learned to recognize and set aside others' emotions, but being a human emotion sponge was never easy.

Sometimes when his guard was down, often right before falling asleep, an overpowering black wave carrying suffering, pain, hunger, or fear would slam into his psyche. Lacking a better description, Ace thought of that place where emotion bubbled as the universal psychosphere. It battered the rare empaths of the world at unexpected intervals. Because wrestling a killer wave into submission is impossible, Ace learned to surf. As empaths go, Ace was unique because he protected his sanity by radical acceptance and active management of his response to the wave. He studied the wave and then surfed it. Yo also helped him keep it together. Ace could have made accommodations to bring an emotional support animal to the courthouse, but he was concerned about how the jury might react. There was also a risk that Yo's extreme adorableness would steal everyone's attention.

Maintaining his sanity was easier when the universal psychosphere gifted Ace the pleasure of vicarious delight, like children playing. Ace's only job there was to accept the gift.

Robbie understood as much as anyone could, having grown up with Ace. They were family.

"Ya, they're really sweet," Ace said.

"You miss it."

"So do you."

The two men stood together, absorbing an unexpected, yet welcomed, moment of sunshine and joy. But a rush of excitement burst through their fleeting reprieve and broke the moment. Ace looked up to see a TV news team heading toward them. The duo had met at the early to avoid the angry crowd, but they had been spotted. He elbow-jabbed Robbie.

"Let's go. Now." Without waiting, Ace turned and dashed upstairs to the old-fashioned brass and glass doors; Robbie followed.

"Morning, Ace." The uniformed, middle-aged security guard held open the door and ushered Ace and Robbie through.

"Morning, George," Ace replied. They emptied their pockets into the scuffed beige plastic bowl on the conveyor belt, and when signaled, walked through the metal detector. They all knew the drill.

"See, you got some paparazzi again. Admin warned us there'd be a crowd today."

"Sorry for the hassle; I owe you a beer when this is over."

"Anytime, Ace, anytime." George turned his attention to the reporters, whom he would scrutinize with intentional sluggishness to allow Ace's escape. Ace and George had developed this understood ritual over the last couple of years. The ploy succeeded when the elevator doors closed on Robbie and Ace before the reporters arrived. Had he been alone, Ace would have ducked into the stairwell—it was only one floor up, after all—but Robbie wouldn't have welcomed the stairs.

The bailiff had unlocked the courtroom early, so people were already milling about inside. Seating was filling up. Ace pushed open the knee-high, saloon-style swinging doors that separated the seating area from counsel tables, the well, the bench, and the jury box, keeping the place where all the action goes down discretely apart from the watchers. The court clerk and reporter nodded in greeting as he took his place at counsel table. Most days they'd chat, maybe share a few jokes, but today the courtroom staff was quiet. A whispering hum erupted from the already seated watchers.

Reporters made up the single largest group in the gallery, but other watchers filled the hard wooden pews as well. The largest courtroom available had been reserved to accommodate all interested parties. Families, friends, silent survivors assessing their own legal options, and an occasional random lawyer ducking in to see what the fuss was about, also took seats in the quickly filling gallery. Ace was pretty sure the bulk of watchers would disappear over the coming days when boredom inevitably hit.

Scattered papers—left over from the preceding days of jury selection and motions—filled the spaces between the laptops on the tables facing the judge's bench, one table for the plaintiff's lawyers, and one for the defense lawyers. Multiple stacks of file boxes were within arm's reach, behind each table. Another stack of cardboard file boxes sat between the table for the plaintiff and the table for the defendants. In the well—that space between counsel tables and the judge's bench—sat a battered wooden desk with a single computer monitor for the judge's clerk. The room's fake walnut paneling failed to soften the harsh fluorescent lights, and there were no windows to blow out the already stale air.

Anxiety, like hunger, pinched at Ace's abdomen. His heart beat faster. With one focused breath, he mentally stepped away from the anxiety, letting it glide past him. *That anxiety might be from the press,* he thought, *or it could be mine. Study the wave…* Reporters never stop to breathe, much less think. The local community, his clients, and everyone across the country—it seemed—clamored for an encouraging word about this case, even though it was hardly the first case of its kind. The AAYA's fanatical denials of any problem were unique and divisive. News media thrived on divisiveness, driving it to an ever-uglier place. The more obvious the lie, the more the organization clung to it, doubling down at every opportunity. Even though the obvious lie caused reputational damage, they believed that insignificant compared to the reputational damage of admission, apology, and reformation. So far, the Association had gotten away with that. Robbie's case was the only one against the AAYA that had gone to trial. Every other case had been hidden in settlement or had been thrown out on technicalities.

Robbie's homosexuality brought a unique angle that also captured media attention, not only was he openly gay and married, still a bit of a novelty, but also Latinx, or black, or maybe a person of color. Attempts at correct labeling befuddled the press who finally settled on "person of color." Still, the AAYA had not been shy about victim-blaming and shaming. Media lapped that up from all kinds of political angles. Ace kept thinking they would let it go, but they always doubled down on blaming the black guy. Sometimes it felt like you were living in the twenty-first century, then you encountered this crap and wondered when and where the hell you really were.

The slowed news cycle played a key role in excessive media interest. After the craziness of the hundred-year pandemic, fueled by election-year propaganda and massive racial equity protests, the press scrounged for information worthy of the new standard for interesting. Americans became comfortable with the slow summer spread of the virus in 2021 and ignored the experts' warnings of another fall resurgence. The repetitive warnings no longer generated any interest, so the media searched for alternatives. As Ace had warned Robbie, infotainment media pushed the boundaries of American cognitive dissonance by defending the Association's denials of accusations made by a gay man of color, a favorite target for derision. Legitimate news reporting still grappled with appropriate responses to the entertainment dynamic and took the path most traveled by covering the same marginally significant story. The perfect storm of these events resulted in a circus and Ace was the ringmaster.

Ace's broad shoulders slumped under the weight of his responsibility: responsibility for Robbie, for the community, for the truth. So many exploited men deserved justice, not just Robbie, but thousands of others, maybe hundreds of thousands, or millions. More particularly, Ace sought justice for a single absent soul. As much as Ace craved justice, he could not allow himself to believe in it. Yet finding justice was the impossible task set before him.

Lupe had already taken a seat at the plaintiffs' counsel table, but not in the spot reserved for lead trial counsel. At the insistence of both Robbie and Lupe, Ace was the lead counsel and his partner was the second chair. The deep red of her buttoned-down pantsuit complimented her clear tawny skin and bright brown eyes. She wore her shiny dark hair swept into a tidy bun, barely visible behind her delicate, golden hoop earrings. Lupe favored a prim look and refused to wear the trendier messy bun. She was ready for blood. Nothing got past Lupe.

"Sit here, Robbie," Lupe said. She pointed to the seat on her right. Ace sat in the lead-counsel spot on the end closest to the defense counsel table.

"Team huddle," Ace said. The three scooted their chairs and leaned in for whispers behind the plastic pandemic shield. Confused about the ever-changing pandemic protocols, the Court staff had not removed the plastic germ shields from around the counsel tables, judge's bench, and various other spots where people were known to breathe. "Did the press get to you, Lupe?"

"No comment," Lupe winked at Robbie, who smiled in response.

"Ok, so far, so good," Ace said. He turned to Robbie. "Questions?"

"Is it too late to take the settlement money?" Robbie tapped his fingers sporadically on the table, clicking his fingernails against the laminate.

"Yes, but we can reopen that discussion anytime," Lupe said. She reached over, placing her hand gently over Robbie's. "You're strong, just let us know if you get overwhelmed and need a break."

"I'm kidding," Robbie said. "You know I don't want the money. I want an apology more than anything, though I might settle if those buttheads would at least admit what happened. When it gets tough, I'll suck it up."

"I'll know if he's overwhelmed," Ace said. "He doesn't need to say anything. I'm the one you should worry about." *And I can't let the jury see my fear*, he thought.

"I know, brother, but I've got you," Robbie said. Ace saw the determination in Robbie's eyes and knew he could rely on Robbie to be strong for them both.

"I'm not even going ask," Lupe said, but Ace could tell that she wanted to know more. She reached to her ear and rolled her golden-looped earring between her fingers and turned her attention to Robbie. "Now, do you have any *relevant* questions?"

"Ya, when's lunch?" Robbie joked.

"When your mom gets here. She's bringing her delicious Brazilian home cooking," Ace said, deadpan.

Robbie chuckled. Everyone knew his mother, Gabi, didn't cook. "Ok, you got me. But just so you know, the whole gang's coming, Mom, Dad, brothers, husband, the entire Santos clan."

Ace craned his neck to the gallery but only saw Robbie's husband, Tony, who pinky-waved

"Damn, I told him not to act so gay," Robbie said.

"He's fine, Robbie." Sometimes it seemed to Ace that Robbie would prefer hiding in the closet, maybe because he stood with one foot cemented in old-fashioned values borne from his family's awkwardness around a divergent sexuality, an awkwardness not shared by Ace. "I'm more worried about a late and noisy arrival by the Santos family." Gus and Gabi were notoriously late for everything.

Robbie shook his head. "No, I think they get it. They should be here on time. Fingers crossed."

"Enough," Lupe said. Ace noticed that the harsh fluorescent light softened when it bounced off her hair. And while her words were stern, her voice was high pitched, like that of a child, but at the same time clear and confident. The wrong person might be fooled by her endless paradoxes, but Ace found them endearing.

"Back to work, team. Roberto, you remember what we said about courtroom protocols?" Lupe asked.

"Kind of."

"Okay, a quick review: don't call the judge 'you.' It's a weird lawyer thing. The judge is either 'the Court' or 'Your Honor.' And don't say 'Her Honor' because that sounds stupid, my personal pet peeve."

"Got it, the Court and Your Honor." Robbie faked a British accent with an affected air and smirked at Ace. The men laughed.

"Come on guys, be serious," Lupe said. "If you don't know what to say, keep your mouth shut." She frowned and pulled a neatly hand-printed sheet of yellow, lined legal paper from her leather portfolio. "Okay, I've made a list of some review points for the opening statement. Quietly now…" The three heads huddled again for the last-minute review before the trial's official opening.

*Thirteen*

# DATE NIGHT
# 1998

Steve reached across the white linen tablecloth for Heather's hand. She smiled at him and extended her hand to receive his. He gave her three gentle squeezes: *I-love-you*. She squeezed back four; *I-love-you-too*. Warmth flowed through their connected hands, into the hearts of both. But it was only a moment. Steve abruptly withdrew his hand when the intimacy of the touching he desired a second ago confused him. The touching felt good and then it didn't. He picked up his wineglass in an effort not to ruin the moment.

"To us," Steve said. He held his wineglass in salute.

Heather responded as expected. "To us."

They both sipped from the crystal goblets with eyes locked.

*I'm so fortunate*, he thought. He swirled the goblet and watched how little runners of redness clung to the crystal, legs. If one looked deeply enough, the rich red sparkled in the chandelier's low light. The sparkle was subtle, not blinding, but soft, shimmering refractions of burgundy and rose. But the wine's bouquet was not subtle. Steve held the glass to his face to breathe it in, big and bold, as you would expect from a quality California cabernet. Heather did the same. Steve's free hand wandered to his stomach so he could process Heather's enjoyment of the wine. Or was it his own? Either way, he filled up with comfort and satisfaction.

Steve leaned back in the rich velvet chair to enjoy the rest of his wine. Heather did the same. Steve considered how they automatically synchronized their movements and pondered the physical intimacy that implied. Steve's body yearned for a physical connection with her.

He wanted to wrap himself up with her until their bodies joined. His cheeks turned a pale pink as he thought about the joy of sex with his wife. But those thoughts were not appropriate in public. Proper decorum restricted intimacy in a public space, and that restriction made Steve feel safe touching her hand. The touching wouldn't become more intense in public, with only hands. He considered touching her again but decided it might give her the wrong idea.

"Would we like something from the dessert cart?" The server interrupted.

Once again, the couple moved in unison, as they sat straighter to mull over the delicious-looking options.

"Maybe…" Steve said.

"Let's not," Heather interrupted. "I have a better idea." Her eyes twinkled a smile at Steve. He knew that look.

*She has a plan*, he thought. *Probably desert and port, or brandy, with live music.* One of the many things they shared was a love of R&B and funk. There might even be dancing involved. With music surrounding Steve, he could cast off his self-imposed constraints and maybe even bust a move. The neighborhood was hopping on a Saturday evening. Plenty of venues would have music. They could walk about, enjoying the fresh air and bustle of activity while perusing various clubs, looking for something new and interesting to experience. They had plenty of time before they had to relieve the babysitter.

"No, thank you. I think we'll pass," Steve replied. "We'll finish up our wine, and then the check."

"As you wish." The server topped off their goblets with the remaining decanted cabernet, pouring Heather's glass first before he wheeled away the cart. The couple settled in for a final private moment together before moving on to their next event.

"What deviousness are you cooking up now?" Steve asked Heather.

"You'll see…" she replied with her signature eye twinkle.

"Well, I suppose we don't need to check around for music, since you already have this figured out." He still expected they would end the evening in the usual way.

"Something a tad bit different this time," she taunted, still leaving him in the dark.

Steve frowned. He rarely enjoyed surprises. Routine comforted him. Certainty rendered the moment stress-free, and something new brought the unacceptable possibility of something bad. He preferred the safety of the tried and true.

"It'll be ok, you'll see." Heather had sensed his hesitation and reassured him.

"Well, ok then, are you ready?" Steve snatched the bill before Heather could peek. After confirming the itemized amounts and total were mathematically correct, he calculated the precise percentage tip he thought appropriate for the service provided.

Before Heather could grab her coat, Steve picked it up and held it for her patiently while she turned her back and plunged her arms into the sleeves. He was a gentleman and would afford his wife every courtesy owed to the woman who had earned the station of being his wife.

"Should I have the car brought around?" Steve asked.

"Oh no, let's walk. It's not far."

The city was at its best. Young, well-dressed people crowded the sidewalks and enjoyed the brisk evening. Sounds of happy chattering mixed with strains of music from the sidewalk cafes. Steve took Heather's hand, and she moved closer to him, leaning into his arm. He took advantage of the closeness to put his arm around her waist. He held her close, taking in the fragrance of her shampoo. Since he didn't know where they were going, he let her lead the way, which she did by signaling the correct direction with a slight pressure of her shoulder against his.

The city's sidewalks were home to many unfortunate souls. Even on a good night, the alleys and shadows held suffering, hooded figures, partially hidden from the affluent revelers. On the path ahead, Steve and Heather were coming up on one such figure. A dirty, disheveled creature who didn't seem entirely coherent, sitting on a tattered blanket near the edge of a dark alley. Steve had trained himself to look straight ahead and keep walking in this frequently encountered situation, but this time, he looked straight at the human lump on the sidewalk and felt a twinge in his gut. A pair of sad, brown eyes peeked out at him but didn't seem focused.

*But for the grace of God, there go I...* His hand wandered to his middle as he remembered he had broken a larger bill earlier at the gas station and still had some cash in his pocket. He fished out a twenty and put it into the outstretched cup without speaking. He said nothing because he had no comforting words, and he didn't want to draw attention to his action. But—despite his intention—Heather noticed and reached up to kiss him on the cheek.

"You are a good man, Steve," she whispered in his ear affectionately. His ears twitched—the way they sometimes did when he felt pleased—but his body stiffened. He struggled and failed to find the words to convey his gratitude for her expression of appreciation, so he said nothing.

After walking a couple of blocks, she nudged his arm toward a small storefront with an A-frame chalkboard sign on the sidewalk. The sign read: Couple's massage, champagne, and chocolate-dipped strawberries with cream. They walked into the cramped waiting room to the sound of a tabletop fountain, a little too loud, and the smell of jasmine incense, a little too strong. The décor was jewel-toned—deep purple, emerald, turquoise, and magenta—and there was a potted silk rubber plant shoved into a corner. Steve thought the spa was cheese-ball, like they were trying to appeal to an upper-class clientele with a lower-class budget.

"Is this where we are going?" he asked. Even though it was obvious, he hoped it wasn't.

"Yes, we're getting a couple's massage." Heather's voice burbled with excitement as her words tumbled out. "I saw the sign on the sidewalk when we walked to the restaurant. So, I called them when I went to the lady's room and asked if they could get us in after dinner. We've never done this before, so I thought it would be a surprise."

Steve could see her excitement and wouldn't disappoint her. A tacky spa massage wasn't his idea of a good time, but he would make the best of it. The delicious meal and wine had relaxed him, so why not?

"Let's do it!" He smiled at her and tried to sound enthusiastic.

A petite woman came out to the reception area. She looked young, in her early twenties, and professionally dressed, which Steve appreciated. She pleasantly greeted the couple with few words. After Heather signed in, the woman escorted them through a maze of darkened hallways. The place was bigger than he guessed.

She showed them into one room that, to Steve's pleasant surprise, seemed more elegant. There was a different tabletop fountain in this room, tastefully arranged with river rock and a quiet gurgle. New-age music played, giving Steve the sensation of being in another dimension of hippie spiritualism. The jasmine was subdued, maybe because it wasn't incense, but jasmine scented oil heated in a small brazier. *This is different,* Steve thought, still trying to decide if he could relax, become comfortable.

Two massage tables, side by side, stood in the middle. *But not close enough that we can hold hands.* Nestled against the back wall was an overstuffed velvet chaise, big enough for two, and in front of that, a small table with refreshments. The table held two champagne flutes, a small dish of whipped cream, a plate of chocolate-dipped strawberries, and a pitcher of ice water with cucumber slices floating in it. Next to the table was a pedestal champagne bucket filled with ice and an already opened bottle.

The woman motioned them toward the plush terry robes and indicated without speaking that they were supposed to put them on. Steve gave Heather a questioning look. She appeared to understand intuitively the unspoken process at play in this predominately female domain. *Is this genetic knowledge passed down to women only?*

"We'll let you know when we're ready," Heather informed the woman, who smiled pleasantly as she left the room.

"Here, let me undress you." Heather stepped up to Steve and reached out her hands to him.

Steve flinched. "We have to take our clothes off?" He realized as he spoke that this was obvious, but it had not occurred to him until now.

"Of course, we do, Skeeter." Heather giggled, then added reassurance. "It's ok, they have robes to wear, and on the massage table, you'll be under a sheet. They'll be discreet." She reached out to him again.

"No, that's ok, I got it." Steve bristled at her use of his old nickname.

*Damn,* he scolded himself for both his unintended reaction and the missed opportunity. He could tell she was disappointed. *This is weird, but I can do this for her.*

"Ok." Heather turned her back and undressed quietly on her own. Steve did the same. They donned the terry robes and sat together on the chaise.

"Feed me, please," Heather purred sweetly and tilted her head back. Steve took a strawberry, dipped it generously with cream, and held it over her head. He held it up high enough that she had to arch her back to reach up and nibble on it. "Mmmm, that's wonderful." She nestled into the chaise and stretched out her legs.

Steve could tell Heather was in her element, but it wasn't his. They sipped from their champagne flutes and feasted on the strawberries. They enjoyed each other's company in silence.

When all the cream was gone, Heather asked, "Should we start?"

"Sure, what do we do?"

"Take off your robe and lie on your tummy on the massage table, then put the sheet over yourself."

"Shouldn't I leave on my underwear?"

"No, it's ok. They've seen everything before. Just relax."

Steve carried out her instructions quickly, but awkwardly.

There was a tap on the door, and a quiet moment passed before it cracked open.

"You ready now?"

"Yes, come on in," Heather answered.

Two women entered the room and immediately began bustling about. Steve and Heather each lay on a table with their heads turned, facing each other.

"Close your eyes and relax," Heather advised quietly.

Again, Steve did as instructed. One woman went to Steve and gently laid her hands on his back, over the sheet. Steve flinched and the woman immediately removed her hand.

"Is this ok?" she asked Steve.

"Ya, sorry, I wasn't expecting it, that's all."

"Ok to try again?"

Steve hesitated, unsure, before answering what he didn't feel. "Sure."

The woman again placed her hand on his back, over the sheet. Before pulling the sheet down from his shoulders, she told him about her intention. He stiffened at the thought, then tried to make himself relax. As long as she told him what she was going to do first, he could get through this.

The oil on her hands was warm and smooth when she positioned them directly on his skin. Tendrils of fragrance from the oil made their way to his consciousness, and he sighed. The woman became hands, just hands, slippery warm hands. She pressed her thumbs on the base of his skull, along his neck and shoulders. Under her hands, he could feel the stiffness and pressure he carried there. He had never previously considered physical tension trapped in his muscles. The release of pressure felt good, so he relaxed into it.

The music track changed to a new melody of flutes and other-worldly-sounding instruments Steve couldn't identify. Heather moaned softly from the other table, and he opened his eyes to look at her. *Definitely in her element.* She looked relaxed, asleep even. She must have sensed him looking at her because she opened her eyes and connected. A sleepy smile spread over her face and she closed her eyes again.

Steve mimicked her and closed his eyes, too. He tried to become pliant under the warm, smooth hands, but it was a struggle. As the hands moved down his spine, he again stiffened. The masseuse stopped.

"Pressure good?" she asked.

"Fine. Go ahead."

He could hear her move over to the supply counter for more oil. When she stepped closer, he noticed her rubbing her hands together to make them warm. And then the hands were on him again. This time, he unknowingly clenched his fist, then both fists. His eyes flew open, and he wasn't in the spa room; he didn't know where he was.

Pain shot from his lower back down his legs.

But the hands remained on his skin, crawling lower and lower down his back. The hands were not small and soft, but large, rough, grabbing, thrusting.

More pain registered, this time excruciating and in his ass.

Deep rhythmic grunts replaced the music, which had disappeared. The slippery oil became the sticky goo of sweat dripping, dripping over his body. The musty odor of old dirt and sweat replaced the jasmine.

*Holy shit. Where am I?* The room darkened. All light disappeared.

Steve's heart sped up, followed by a wave of nausea.

*I can't throw up. I can't throw up.*

He choked out loud, screamed, and jumped off the table. Another painful spasm hit, and his knees buckled, nearly knocking him to the ground. He stood by the massage table, drenched in sweat and ick, suffocated by dust and muck, naked, vulnerable, terrified. Spasms enveloped him.

Then, a voice…

"Steve! Steve, are you ok?" Heather was at his side. She pulled the sheet over him, to protect him, an effort to preserve his modesty, his honor.

The nightmare faded away at its own pace. His vision slowly focused on her face. Her face was kind, her voice familiar. He remembered the gentle touch of her hand in his. A semblance of safety returned to Steve, but he was still disoriented and shivered.

"No, I'm sorry. I feel sick. I need to use the bathroom. Help me?"

"Of course," Heather replied, and then said to the women, "Give us a minute, please." After they left the room, Heather helped Steve back into the terry robe and walked him over to the toilet.

"I don't need you now," he whispered as he entered and shut the door, leaving Heather alone. He sat on the floor next to the toilet for some time, staring at the dirty baseboards and linoleum peeling in the corner. Eventually, he laid his open palms on either side of the slick white toilet.

*Maybe I should make myself throw up. No, that won't help.*

He pulled the robe tightly around himself, but his arm wrapped around his middle did little to comfort him. Another wave of nausea, smaller this time, flowed through him. He slowly leaned over until he lay on the floor, curled in a fetal position. He hugged his knees and whimpered.

Eventually his heart rate slowed, and his breathing became more even. He thought nothing. He lay on the cold floor, breathing. With each passing minute, he felt slightly less nauseous. He stood and splashed cold water on his face from the sink. The shaking stopped, but not the feeling of weakness. He looked at his face in the mirror, pale, very pale.

*What the hell is going on? What just happened?* The face in the mirror explained nothing. *Work stress, that must be it.* Thoughts about his client ethics conundrum surfaced, and he shuddered remembering that phone call, the one where the client told him to fake documents. Even though that isn't *exactly* what the man said, the meaning was clear. Commit fraud or lose the client, lose the client's revenue to the law firm, lose his career. Another pang of nausea hit him, which to his mind confirmed the source of the problem; it was the client. He saw no solution, only darkness ahead, but he pushed himself to get up, to continue life.

When Steve eventually left the bathroom, Heather was waiting, concern deep in her face. No, it was more than concern. She looked scared. He didn't want her to be afraid but didn't feel strong enough to comfort her. Not only that, but he refused to burden her with his problems. Telling her would require admitting the weakness, admitting events that still hid in the darkness of lost memory. Unacceptable. He must bear the burden alone.

"I'm sorry, babe. Let's go home. I feel sick. Maybe something at the restaurant. I… I don't think I should drive."

"Of course." Heather looked at him doubtfully. Neither one of them had experienced food poisoning like this before.

He had stayed in the bathroom long enough that Heather had already dressed. He allowed her to help him get dressed, since he still felt weak. Heather arranged for payment and delivery of the car, as Steve sat hunched over in the jewel-toned lobby. When the car arrived, Heather held out her hand to him to help him stand, but he pushed it away.

On the drive home, Heather kept glancing at him with worry as she drove. She tried to say soothing things, and while her voice was soothing, he didn't hear her words. He didn't respond. He sat and stared out the window. All he could see was darkness. They drove into the darkness together, all the way home.

# Fourteen

# ANOTHER PROMISE

# 1972

## BRAY, IRELAND

The hooligans had waited for him after school, waited to beat him with their fists and makeshift shillelaghs. Sean Geoghan tried sneaking around the back of the newly built school gym, but that strategy didn't work. As he rounded the corner, he saw the group. There were four of them, all somewhat older and all bigger than Sean. They were a scraggly group of misfits, and a fair fight was not in their lexicon. They had been tormenting Sean for the last few days with increasing intensity. That intensity had peaked earlier that day when one ruffian called Sean out.

"We're gonna getcha, ye manky freak. After school. Ye better watch yourself," the ringleader had said with a snicker. He had slid up to Sean between classes to deliver the threat in a low, rumbling whisper. Sean had seen determination in the piercing, cobalt eyes that were shrouded by greased tangles of black hair.

Everyone knew the reputation of these ruffians, particularly Sean. He had an idea what the threats might be about. That's why he had snuck away after school, to avoid being seen. But it didn't work. The boys spotted him at the same time he saw them. Without waiting a beat, Sean jumped up and sprinted for the church. If he could make it there before the boys, he would be safe. He had a chance.

The church was only a kilometer from school, but Sean took the long way. He bolted straight to the closest getaway point, the rough dirt path behind the school. The bullies frequented the dirt path because it was hidden, yet close enough that they could sneak a smoke and make it back quickly. If they caught Sean, nobody would be around to help him out of the jam. But Sean didn't have alternative options for escape.

The bullies, being daft, were slow to react. Sean had a solid head start and was also the fastest kid around. He thought he could outrun them all, even on this rocky route. Low-hanging branches grabbed at him as he dashed by. He fought his way through the brambled overgrowth, but he didn't slow to accommodate the terrain. Instead, he pushed himself to a higher speed. The hooligans scared Sean, but he was also thrilled by the chase. He couldn't help feeling gratified he was faster than they were. It was a minor victory.

His fall wasn't too bad, as falls go, except that he fell face-first into a pothole recently filled with cold spring rain. After falling, he tried to stand up too quickly and lost his balance. Once again, he fell into the muddy pothole, this time catching his cheek on the pointed edge of a rock, giving him a nice red slash. He looked back to see if the bullies had given up the chase. It seemed they had, but he continued running, a little slower and lots dirtier.

The old church was in the center of town, on Main Street. From the front, it appeared as rather nondescript, with washed-out gray stone blocks more ancient than concrete. The church itself lacked any architectural appeal from the front. Strangely, it looked beautiful from the back, as though it had been built backward. The elegant stained-glass windows could not be seen from the facing street. From the back, one could also appreciate the graceful medieval arches.

Sean entered the vestibule of the old building quietly, respectfully. He wiped his hands on his pants without considering that a good scrub would have been a better choice. His Ma would've been mortified that he entered the church dirty, face scratched, sweaty, shirt torn, like a pauper. But he couldn't help it, so he didn't bother to worry about it. He headed to the sanctuary where he knew Father John would be waiting for him. He automatically crossed himself upon entering.

"Aye son, there you are. We need to polish up the supplies and clean up the classroom. It was left a mess after catechism." Father John eyeballed Sean but didn't admonish him for being a mess. Rather, he chuckled kindly. "Get yourself washed up, my boy. You look like you've been fighting."

"Yes, Father." Sean ran out of the room. He ran everywhere. It was his way.

"And *walk* boy, you're in a church," the old priest added with another chuckle.

"Yes, Father." Sean forced himself to slow down, to walk. He would have rather kept running. If he had nowhere to be, he would have run right past the church and kept running. He could run all day without getting tired. He loved running almost as much as he loved football.

Sean trotted down the brick-lined hallway to the retrofitted toilet. A flush toilet and indoor running water were the most modern features in the building, still rendering it ridiculously antiquated to Sean's mind. He washed his hands and face. He even tried to rub the dirt off his pants, but that made the mess worse.

When he returned to the sanctuary, Father John sat, quietly waiting for him in a front pew. Sean realized he should have considered what Ma would've said: "Clean up before you go to the church." Sean hoped he wasn't in trouble.

Father John wore jeans and a tweed sweater hand-knitted for him by an old lady parishioner. The sweater was well-worn with suede patches sewn over the elbows. Usually, Father John wore his collar and cassock, but it wasn't unusual for him to dress casually for mundane chores. He had shiny cheeks, like Santa Claus, but without a beard, and was mostly bald.

He patted the polished wood next to him. "Sit here, my son, and tell me what happened." The sanctuary was empty, so nothing prevented Sean from telling the old man what had happened. But Sean was hesitant. He had always trusted Father John and loved him, his entire life in fact. Still, it was hard to talk about these things with anyone, particularly an adult.

*But if I can't tell my priest, then I can't tell God. Maybe he can help me. He is very wise and nice.*

"Did those boys give you a roughing up?" Father John asked gently, breaking the silence of Sean's hesitation.

Sean looked down at his mostly clean hands. "No, Father." This time, the priest allowed the quiet to linger unbroken, but Sean felt increasingly awkward in the silence and so he blurted "... I ran too fast for them! They are slowpokes."

Father John laughed, a hearty laugh that warmed Sean, who suddenly also saw the ridiculousness of the situation. "… and then I fell down," Sean continued and then joined in the laughter. As they shared an easy laugh, Sean became more comfortable, more connected to Father John. *I think he can help me.*

"Father…" he began hesitantly. "The boys say I'm gay. That's why they chased me. They think they'll catch me and beat the gay out of me. They will never catch me."

Father John patted Sean on the knee. "That's the spirit. I know who those boys are, and I'll speak with their parents. That harassment needs to stop."

"Thank you, Father." Sean was relieved the priest was looking out for him, but also sheepish. He was nervous about what would happen if his parents were brought in. The burning question had no obvious words, no guarantee of safety. Asking was a risk. It seemed like everyone expected you to figure out these things on your own.

He had witnessed his Ma harshly admonish his older brothers if they said anything remotely related to sex, girls, or puberty. Once he saw Ma smack his oldest brother for the audaciousness of a mildly suggestive comment. Home was not a safe place to ask questions of this nature. His da' might answer, but da' was always working or at the pub. Da' paid little attention to Sean.

There was nobody at school to ask. The nuns were even harsher than Ma. School wasn't a safe place either. But Father John had known Sean and his brothers their whole life. He had always been a kind man. When da' was sick, Father John stopped by the cottage to check in on the family. Sean trusted Father John but was uncomfortable, even embarrassed. Somehow, all the children at home intuitively understood that developing sexuality was a forbidden topic for discussion without that ever being clearly expressed by an adult. Everything sexual felt dirty, off-limits, dangerous, and oh so exciting.

Sean took a breath and squeezed his eyes closed. It was better to ask without eye contact, like confession. With eyes closed, he took the plunge. "Father, how do you know if you are gay? Maybe I am gay." There it was. He'd put it out there. He held his breath, waiting to be stricken down by God himself for bringing up such a question in a church, in the sanctuary no less. If the priest didn't smack him for impertinence, he would surely go to hell. It seemed like forever before Father John responded. His eyes narrowed sharply at Sean, and he sat up straighter.

"Well, my boy, the devil tempts us all. We cannot say if the devil will torment you with homosexual thoughts or not. Sometimes he does and sometimes he does not. There's no rhyme or reason to it. If the Devil attacks you with unholy inclinations, you will find solace in Jesus. You must pray for God to guide you on the path of chastity." Father John's voice was usually jovial, but it took on an unaccustomed tone of seriousness.

Sean tried his best to understand, but something about that still made little sense. He couldn't decipher the words *inclinations* and *chastity*. But he was not smitten by a bolt of lightning, and Father John didn't smack him. The questioning felt safer and Sean opened his eyes. He continued cautiously.

"But doesn't God make somebody gay?"

"My son, nobody is born a homosexual. God has created us all in the perfection of his own image. People who choose to be gay and follow that lifestyle have lost their way. It's a temptation from the devil. Do you understand this?"

"I'm not sure."

"Well, sometimes a man has inclinations toward other men, and those inclinations may follow him for most of his life. That alone is not a sin. That is the devil tempting you. Turn to Jesus for strength if you are so cursed." The Father examined the boy before continuing. "But—and this is very important—you must never act sexually with men. If you stay chaste, God will guide you to salvation."

Sean squeezed his eyes shut again for his next potentially inappropriate question. He imagined piles of writhing, naked people in the flaming depths of hell. If he didn't get this right, that might be his future, burning in hell, writhing and naked with terrible sinners. He struggled to find the strength to ask.

"What's 'chaste'?" He could barely choke out the words. But again, God did not smite him. He wasn't yet sure about opening his eyes until he heard a soft chuckle from Father John.

"'Chaste' is when you keep your body physically apart from other people. When you find a woman and become married, your bodies will become one. You will know what to do when the time comes.

Everybody does. But you must never allow your body to be physically close to men or women who are not your wife. That's being 'chaste,' and it's called 'chastity.' As you grow older, your body will change, and you will want to touch women. That is normal. But, you must wait until God has blessed your union in marriage with a woman, your wife."

This answer was more boring and vague than Sean had hoped. He hadn't thought of himself as ever being married, but marriage seemed as inevitable as it was boring. Everyone married eventually because that's just what adults do. Sean wondered if he should tell the priest about that time he and his mate Liam had touched each other's private parts.

They had been at Liam's house playing when Liam had said he wanted to show Sean something. Sean had been hesitant to go into the family's dank, stinky basement, particularly since it was a lovely day to be running around outside. Nasty spiders were down there, along with who knows what other scary monsters. However, Liam's sinister look made Sean think it was something really cool. With that look, Liam had convinced him. They had climbed the stairs into the dark, earthen basement. Their steps beat in time to a faint dripping sound of an indeterminable origin. When they had reached the bottom, Liam pulled on a string attached to a single low-wattage bulb hanging from the ceiling. The basement was still scary, even with a bit of dull light.

Then, to Sean's shock, Liam had opened his pants and took out his willy.

"You can touch it," Liam had said. Blood rushed to Sean's face. He was blushing, yet he felt compelled. His fingers tingled with desire. The rest of him tingled from overwhelming curiosity. His loins stirred as he stepped forward toward Liam. He reached out. And then Sean did it. He touched Liam's willy.

Liam's face relaxed, and he smiled lazily at Sean. "See, I can touch yours now, too. You'll see, it feels nice."

Sean didn't expect it, but of course, this had to be mutual. Mutuality would cement the secrecy, ensuring silence for the crime. Maybe they were committing a crime. Sean didn't know. At least, he thought, this must be a terrible sin. The problem was Liam's older sister happened upon them when she had come in to retrieve a jar of apple preserves.

"Perverts!" she had yelled out at them with malice in her voice. She was as surprised as the boys at the intrusion. Rather than climb down the stairs for the apple preserves that their Ma had sent her to fetch, she slammed the door and ran off. Liam quickly put himself back together and ran after her. Sean had assumed Liam would stop her from telling Liam's Ma. Sean followed and ran up the stairs. He kept going and ran all the way home.

Liam had successfully convinced his sister not to tattle on the boys. But Liam had been unsuccessful in getting her to keep quiet about it. She had told her girlfriends and word got around. The Liam episode was the reason the bullies chased Sean. They had heard rumors about Liam's basement. That is why they accused Sean of being gay. Sean was not sure whether he should reveal the whole story, particularly now that Father John said that stuff about being physically close. Liam and Sean had touched each other's privates, which was precisely the physicality the priest talked about.

But that wasn't the worst of it. The worst of it was that Sean liked it. He really liked it. After being introduced to it in Liam's basement, sex was all he could think about. He longed to do it again. He worried that meant he was a homosexual. *If I do it again, then I won't be chaste, then I might go to hell. Or at least I would have to confess, and confessing would be worse.*

Sean nodded at Father John to show he understood about chastity, even though he only partially understood. This was as good as it would get. He was still conflicted about discussing Liam's basement. Maybe that was better for confession. Either way, he didn't want to talk about it at all. He looked at his fidgeting hands as the wheels turned in his head. The idea revealed itself to him, slowly. No, it wasn't an idea, it was a solution, a promise. He would make a deal with God.

*I didn't know it was wrong so I shouldn't have to confess, but I promise I will never do it again. I will be chaste like Father John told me. If I am chaste, I won't go to hell. I will have a wife when I grow up, and a family, and everything will be perfect.*

"All right then, let's get to work, Sean." The old man patted Sean on the knee, then stood up and waited for Sean to follow. Sean stood up and followed, three steps behind the priest.

*I don't want to go to hell; I won't touch boys anymore; I don't want to go to hell....*

# Fifteen

# SPECIAL TRAINING
# 1998

Mrs. Santos cranked the radio and belted out nonsensical lyrics like nobody was listening. They weren't. Robbie and Josh, seat-belted in the back with Ace, ignored her; nobody sat upfront with Mrs. Santos because that was uncool.

*Just like Robbie, always singing,* Ace thought. *I wish I understood the Portuguese in this song, voo-lay-voo something. I'll ask Robbie what that means later...*

Ace wondered how Mrs. Santos could manage carpool duty in the middle of the week, the middle of a workday, as he watched her from the spacious backseat of the new Santos family car, a ginormous Lincoln Navigator. *Why doesn't she have a job?* he thought. *Being a stay-at-home mom has to be boring, but she isn't bored.* Mrs. Santos intrigued Ace. She sat up high over the traffic in her fancy monster truck. Ace placed his open palm on his stomach and channeled her sense of physical size and power behind the wheel, and the wind-in-her-hair sense of freedom. She immersed herself in the new car smell, the luxuriously soft leather seats, and fancy gadgets. While Ace didn't understand the attraction to those things, he well appreciated her uninhibited joy.

And the power sunroof was awesome, and Mrs. Santos let the boys play with that until it got boring.

"Faggot! Faggot! Faggot!" Josh muttered. Josh jabbed Robbie in the ribs along with the insult. "JJ likes you. JJ is your boyfriend! Faggot! Faggot! Faggot!" A thick lock of blonde hair flopped into Josh's reddening face. Josh's teasing popped the happy bubble for Ace, but not Mrs. Santos, who remained oblivious. Agitation and jealousy roiled, filling the backseat with negative and conflicting vibrations. Ace absorbed it all but needed visual clues to decipher the source of each feeling. Which emotion belonged to Robbie and which belonged to Josh? Without adding visual and auditory observations, Ace couldn't sort through the clashing emotional waves, so he sat still and quietly observed.

"Shut up," Robbie muttered back, returning a sharp poke to Josh's midsection.

As the new kid, Ace wasn't sure how to react. He hoped everyone, both boys, would like him and he could avoid getting in the middle of a fight. Bullying, however, was bad. He had been taught he should report bullying.

*Ya right, like anyone does that,* Ace thought.

Josh's bullying surprised Ace. Josh was helpful and nice to Ace, so this behavior made little sense. They were teammates, comrades. *It's jealousy. Josh is jealous of Robbie.* Someone had told Ace that Josh was a jerk sometimes, but Ace hadn't believed it until now.

Ace considered how his father would handle the situation. But Ace held no authority because… new kid. Before intervening, Ace had to sort through the tides of emotion drowning him.

*What would Dad have done when he was a boy?* Ace couldn't envision his father ever having been a child, although Ace spent lots of time thinking about that. He wondered if his dad had always been so serious. *Maybe that's why dad became a lawyer. Well, that and he's smart.* Sometimes his dad was aloof, but he helped Ace with homework, with soccer. Ace could always count on his dad to help him with schoolwork. Ace hoped he could be as smart as his dad someday, maybe even become a lawyer.

"Stop it, you guys," Ace said. He was frustrated with Mrs. Santos who wasn't paying attention, not doing her mom duty to stop the fracas. She ignored the rough jostling and noise of boys in the back seat; maybe that comes with being a mother to four boys. His mom, Heather, wouldn't have put up with this behavior. Ace was usually on the corrected end of corrections and so had not appreciated his mom's meddling until he realized parental authority had some utility after all.

"Come on, guys," Ace pleaded. He wouldn't take sides, even though Josh was out of line. As Robbie struggled with the abuse, his breathing became labored, and his face warmed. As Ace internalized Robbie's struggle, his own breathing became labored, and his face warmed. Robbie's frustration and agitation connected to Ace, who didn't understand what was happening because Robbie didn't understand. Ace cupped his hands over his ears and squeezed his eyes shut, but the intensity only increased.

The torment finally stopped when the big Navigator pulled up to the club fields where the boys would work on their special training session. Coach Sean and his nephew JJ were both there already. It would only be the three boys, JJ, and Coach Sean. Nobody else had scored an invitation. As the boys tumbled out of the car, Mrs. Santos reminded them that Josh's mom, Susie, would pick them up at the end of training. Without listening to the reminder, the three boys dashed off. Mrs. Santos waved to Coach Sean with a warm smile, her shiny red lipstick contrasting brightly to her shiny black car, and drove away without waiting for a return wave.

"Race you!" Robbie shouted and took off toward the Irishmen like a shot. Ace was on his heels. Josh snorted as he ran. The short distance from the car gave sprinters the advantage. Josh was not a sprinter. The commotion caught Coach Sean's attention, and he looked up.

Sean watched the boys' untied cleats tear into the damp grass, and their unzipped backpacks precariously flop about as they ran toward him. On this rare afternoon, the group had the Striker fields to themselves. The club dominated the players' spare time with mandatory practices and games. Extraordinarily dedicated athletes, however, strive to squeeze in extra training. It was those athletes Sean enjoyed most, the ones focused on self-improvement, exactly the boys running toward him. Robbie, Josh, and Ace shared a deep love of the game. These three were talented, enthusiastic. Sean made it his life's mission to nurture that spark, and fan it into a flame of lifelong passion. It was a perfect day, in the perfect place, to enjoy his favorite activity.

JJ was sulking, making the day less perfect. But Sean determined not to let JJ ruin anything. Sean had promised his oldest brother, JJ's da, he would help the troubled offspring. JJ was an adult now, but still acted the part of a surly teenager. Sean and his brother had hoped America, religion, and soccer would turn JJ around, put him on a righteous path. The results so far were not promising, but Sean would keep trying.

"Ha, I beat you!" Robbie reached the coaches first.

"No fair, you got out first. You got a head start." Josh retorted with a whine.

"Settle down," Coach Sean said. Hard work was the daily agenda. Sean didn't want them worn out before training started. Stamina management was among the many skills successful athletes learned.

"Hey, JJ, look. I can do a rainbow now." Josh couldn't contain the news of his achievement any longer. He grabbed a soccer ball and dribbled it for a few steps. He flicked the ball up behind his back, then kicked it up with his heel over his head and caught it on his feet, facing forward.

"Brilliant rainbow!" Sean said. "Glad to see you've been working at it. Great job."

But Josh tilted his beaming face to JJ, not Sean. JJ turned away. The smile dropped from Josh's face.

"Hey, Josh. Teach me that. I want to learn," Ace said.

"You guys want to work on rainbows?" Sean asked. "Watch this." Sean took the soccer ball, juggled it on his laces, circled each foot around the ball—around-the-world—let it drop, one bounce before flicking it up behind his back, and over his head where it landed back on his laces. "You guys want to do that?"

The boys shouted enthusiastic affirmations.

"Ok, well, don't expect to do that without hard work and drills. Also, I have an advantage because I'm ambidextrous, meaning I'm not a lefty or a righty, I'm both. I can do both feet the same. Usually, people have one side that's easier than the other." Sean nudged the ball away and picked up a cone. "Right then, let's do that today. First, take a lap while JJ and I finish setting up."

The boys began a slow jog toward the outer perimeter of the field. "What kind of run is that? Move your bloody arses or I'll chase you." Sean crouched as though preparing to pounce and chase, but the threat was enough. The boys laughed and picked up the pace. Sean stood and watched. He assessed the boys' physicality, their spirit. He also assessed their interactions for cooperation, competitiveness, and comradery.

"JJ, grab those cones, help me set up," Sean instructed. JJ was ostensibly running the practice, but that was a joke. Sean ended up with all the work and had given up pretending it was JJ's practice. JJ was slow to move. He casually walked over to the duffle bag full of soccer gear and grabbed some cones without speaking.

*What happened to the kid that loved to play soccer with his uncle?*

Sean's brother—JJ's da'—had warned Sean that JJ behaved like an angst-ridden teenager, always in trouble, always making poor decisions. Sean and his brother had both believed JJ would behave in America, behave around his favorite uncle. His older brother's confidence affirmed Sean's ability to handle the task which bolstered Sean's self-esteem, but progress seemed unattainable. With a sigh, Sean turned to his clipboard to review upcoming drills as the boys took their lap around the field.

The run started slowly but became competitive quickly. Each boy tried to run faster than the others until the group was racing. Robbie and Ace were the fastest, but Josh lagged only slightly. Josh was bigger than the other two boys, stout and strong. He was built sturdy like his dad, Joe Martin, but had the delicate features of his mom, the team manager, Susie Martin. The entire family had a traditional blonde-haired, blue-eyed German look about them. Sean didn't expect speed from Josh but was glad to see the boy's tenacity and effort.

The three boys sprinted toward the last bend. Robbie and Ace were neck and neck, with Ace slightly in the lead. Josh was a step behind when he grabbed the back of Robbie's jersey and yanked hard. At first, Robbie pulled away, but Josh yanked harder, causing Robbie to fall backward into Josh. The boys tumbled to the ground in a tangle of limbs, cleats, and jerseys. Sean's bottom lip dropped when he saw the scrum of wrestling boys on the grass and heard the crashing grunts and shrieks.

Josh successfully used his weight and size advantage. He flipped Robbie onto his back and straddled him in an effective pin. Sean froze as he watched Josh pull back a fist to punch Robbie in the face. Before Sean could move, it happened. Josh punched Robbie with a sickening *thunk*, fist against face. Robbie cried out.

Ace screamed, "Stop it!"

Sean dashed over to the boys. "Knock it off. What are you doing?"

Ace grabbed Josh's arm in midair before Josh could hit Robbie again. With his other hand, Ace grabbed Josh's shirt and yanked him to the ground. Deftly, Ace let go at exactly the right second in the momentum of Josh's fall.

Sean wasn't as deft. Josh fell sideways onto the grass and into Sean, who had just arrived on the scene. Josh's fall caught Sean's feet. Sean tripped and fell on top of Josh.

JJ stood watching the melee before he walked over to the dogpile of bodies.

Ace offered Robbie a hand. "Robbie, are you ok?" he asked.

But Sean already knew the answer to the question. He saw Robbie was not ok. Robbie was confused and wounded. Robbie lay still in the soft grass, looking up at the sky and then at Ace.

"I'm fine. Thanks, Ace." Robbie didn't take Ace's hand and jumped to his feet under his own renewed power. Robbie spat on the ground next to the lump of Josh. "What the hell, butthead!" Robbie shouted. "Seriously, what the hell?"

"Watch your language," Sean admonished. He rolled into a sitting position on the grass. His legs would be sore tomorrow from the fall: the price of age. He pulled himself to his knees before standing. Then to Josh, Sean said, "What was that about? Why did you hit Robbie? Explain."

Josh didn't move; his eyes flicked up at JJ, who said nothing and turned away, laughing under his breath. The sick humor surprised Sean. *JJ is pleased by all this. Why?* Sean thought.

"Robbie tripped me," Josh explained.

Sean had seen what happened, so he knew Josh was lying. Still, Sean had to pick his battles. It was more important to sort this out, get the team back in sync. That was the battle to fight.

"Don't worry about it," Robbie said. "I'm fine. Let's just practice."

Josh turned his head and glared at Robbie. "Robbie's tough, I was just testing what he can take," Josh said. "Maybe got a 'lil bit out of hand."

"I'll say it did," said Sean.

Sean puzzled over the dynamics between the two boys. Maybe they were having problems at home. Josh's dad was tough on the kid. Maybe that was it? JJ's behavior, also a mystery, confounded Sean. Why does Josh keep looking at JJ? Sean would think about it later. This was the time to set the boys straight.

"We are going to talk about this right now. Sit," Sean said. Ace sat obediently, but Josh and Robbie took their time, ultimately sitting on either side of Ace. "Whatever is going on between you, this stops now," Sean spoke firmly. "We don't be needing to bring your parents in, but I'll have no choice if you keep at it. Understood?"

Ace nodded his understanding, but Josh and Robbie stared vacantly at the ground. Nobody wanted parental involvement.

"You guys need to work together as a team. There's always people you don't like or some people you like more than others," Sean said. The boys squirmed in the grass.

"Sometimes people your age struggle at home or school. When they don't know how to handle problems, they can be mean. Do either of you feel like something like that might be happening?"

Sean's gentle voice and calm demeanor exemplified sincerity. Still, nobody answered Sean's question, which was followed by several beats of silence. The boys might be more forthcoming if he could speak with them individually. Later, he would get them alone for private discussions. He pressed harder.

"Everyone has stuff to deal with. It's not ok to take it out on each other. That's not acceptable." Sean was losing the young wigglers.

"Pay attention," he snapped. Three little faces gaped at him. "That's better. Here is what I really wanted to say." Sean waited for their undivided attention before continuing. "You can always count on me. If you have nobody to talk to and you need advice, I will keep your secrets. Your parents don't need to know."

JJ rolled his eyes and walked away.

"So, here's the deal—this is just between us. My job is to keep the team together. Part of that is helping individual players who need extra attention. If you feel you have no friends, you are wrong. I am your friend. You can trust me. Do you understand?" Three heads nodded. "Ok, good. Now, Josh and Robbie apologize, shake hands. Let's get on with our day."

The boys shook hands anemically as they mumbled insincere apologies.

"Ok, good. Now let me look at that shiner." Sean took Robbie's face in his hands and gently ran a finger over the upper cheek where the punch had landed. "Doesn't look too bad, mate." Sean leaned over to kiss Robbie on the cheek, like his own mum used to do, but thought better of it and didn't.

Robbie yanked himself away. "I'm fine." Sean gave him a quick pat on the top of his head and winked.

"Ok then, who wants to learn rainbows?" Sean asked.

The boys perked up at the suggestion and went to grab their soccer balls. JJ watched intently but wouldn't take part unless cajoled.

*I'll figure out JJ later,* Sean thought. *Now I need to get these boys working together again.*

*Sixteen*

# OPENING STATEMENTS

# 2022

## TRIAL

"All rise, Court is now in session, the Honorable Judge JoAnn Witmayer Moore presiding." The bailiff stood in the well, shoulders back, head high, and faced the gallery to make his announcement.

Buzzing in the courtroom hushed as everyone stood up. The door behind the judge's bench opened and a petite elderly woman in an oversized black robe emerged. Sticking out from her robe were two thin ankles capped with practical, black, low-heeled pumps. She was bespectacled, with gray-brown hair held in a clip at the nape of her neck. Drawing Judge Moore pleased Ace's legal team because she had a reputation for being smart and fair. After graduating at the top of her class at an Ivy League law school, she worked for peanuts to pursue civil rights when she could have made mint in the private sector, and later worked her way to the bench. She was exactly what Ace thought a judge should be.

"Thank you. You may all be seated." Authority sprung from her clear ringing voice, like grandma telling you the cookie is for after dinner. With some shuffling and whispers, everyone sat. Judge Moore waited for silence before continuing. "We are on the record in the case of *Roberto Rivelino Santos versus the Athletic Association for Young Americans*. Now, is there anything counsel would like to address before opening statements?"

It was time, and Ace was prepared for battle. He sat with his back straight, suit jacket straight, tie straight, freshly shaven, teeth brushed, and hair combed, ready to go. Pressure built against his chest and abdomen, like a giant squeezing him in its arms. It often started that way. The emotional barrage would come next. He placed his hand on his starched white linen shirt over his stomach before he remembered the rock. His mother, Heather, had given it to him long ago for protection against emotional bombardment, some New Age, crystal-magic thing.

He wrapped his hand around the polished Brazilian black tourmaline rock in his suit jacket pocket. The stone was small enough to fit into his pocket surreptitiously, but large enough to make its weight known in his palm. Its coolness and heaviness were reassuring. He grounded his feet flat on the floor and let the tide of emotion from the gallery flow through him without knocking him down. *Not sure about Mom's woo-woo shit, but I like the stone's feel. No harm holding it*, he thought.

Counsel signaled the judge it was time to proceed, and she said, "Mr. Bailiff, please bring in the jury to be sworn."

The bailiff opened the jury door and instructed the gallery, "All stand."

A fresh emotional river flowed into the courtroom with the jury. Ace allowed himself to absorb the jurors' emotions as the bailiff herded them to the jury box. *Curious, nervous, guarded, uncertain, wary, alert, uncomfortable.* Just as he expected. He was thankful that he didn't sense any bitterness, malice, or anger. Ace didn't know which exact feeling came from which exact person. Sometimes he could guess by matching the expression on any specific face to a singular emotion swirling within the morass. For now, he floated on the ripples in the pool as the jury entered.

But then he counted and attempted their classification as they entered: Juror One—stoic; Two—friendly; Three—mystery; Four—sharp; Five—serious; Six—salty. He stopped counting at Juror Six and tried not to stare. Lupe had wanted to challenge Juror Six because he seemed to be angry at the world. Ace agreed Six exuded resentment but disagreed about the challenge, and now he questioned that choice. A cranky old man, Six rather reminded Ace of Joe Martin, authoritative and brash. Yet despite all that, Ace's instinct told him to keep Six. As though knowing Ace was thinking about him, Six looked up and scowled.

*Did I make a mistake with Six?*

Act turned his attention to the other jurors and connected smiling eyes to certain individuals, careful to avoid too much eye contact, too much smiling. He balanced the right amount of each, to be cordial and professional. Most jurors avoided eye contact, but a few caught his eye for a nanosecond. None smiled. That was ok because Ace knew they were acutely self-conscious while on display for the packed gallery. Throughout the trial, they would become more comfortable as they grew accustomed to the cramped, sterile environment.

"Jurors, please remain standing and raise your right hand. Madame clerk, please administer the oath," the judge instructed.

A middle-aged woman with a bleached bouffant and clunky shoes stood behind her desk to administer the oath, reciting it from memory in a steady voice.

"Do you, and each of you, understand and agree that you will well and truly try the cause now pending before this court, and a true verdict render according only to the evidence presented to you and to the instructions of the court?"

The jurors' muttered responses of "Yes," "I will," and "I do," overlapped, making any single response unidentifiable. Good enough.

"Thank you, you may be seated. Counsel for the plaintiff, Mr. Elbridge, you may address the jury with your opening statement." The judge nodded at Ace to proceed. The jurors opened the notebooks provided by the generosity of the State.

"Thank you, Your Honor." Ace snatched the stone from his pocket and held it discreetly in his hand before he stood. "May it please the Court, counsel," Ace nodded to opposing counsel sitting at the parallel table facing the judge's bench, "and the jury." The courtroom became even quieter than seemed possible. Reporters had tablets, and some notepads and pencils, poised and ready.

It had begun.

Every eye in the gallery bored into Ace's back. Trickles of curiosity dripped onto him from everywhere in the room, like soft, steady rain. He wondered if his dad had felt this same way in court, whether he had faced juries. *Dad always did the right thing, except the last time when he was too afraid. He made a mistake. I'm afraid of doing the right thing, but unlike my dad, I'm going to do it anyway because a person can make a mistake either way.*

Ace faced the jury.

"Ladies and gentlemen of the jury, I am Atticus Elbridge, one of the plaintiff's lawyers in this lawsuit. My partner, Ms. Guadalupe Garcia…" he gestured to Lupe, who nodded to the jury "… and I are working together, so you will also hear from Ms. Garcia throughout the case." He assessed the jury's reaction to Lupe, but they remained expressionless.

"Our client, the plaintiff, Mr. Roberto Santos, Robbie, is also with us today at counsel table, next to Ms. Garcia." To Ace's relief, Lupe put her hand over Robbie's hand to stop his clicking fingernails. An astute juror might notice Robbie's shaking hands, wonder if Lupe was his girlfriend, but whatever. It was still early. They would soon understand the dynamic.

With the introductions complete, Ace pulled himself up to his full six-foot height. Most jurors, regardless of their race and gender, would be unconsciously biased—favorably—toward Ace because he was a statuesque, professionally dressed, white man. The jury would assume he was competent, smart, honest, because he looked the part. Most jurors didn't realize they would unintentionally make favorable assumptions about Ace. That was his white male privilege at work. He knew it, he owned it, and he would milk every bit to help Robbie. The team had discussed the trial's racial angles at length. Every choice was another piece of their comprehensive strategy, including Ace's delivering opening statement.

Ace knew the jury would make initial assumptions about opposing counsel, Saul Vilipend, Esq., as well. Vilipend represented the defendant AAYA, the Athletic Association for Young Americans. They could afford the best legal representation available, and they would need it. Vilipend's silk suit was custom-tailored to his small, atrophied body. He rolled his gnarled fingers across the sterling filigreed grip on his wooden cane as he sat at counsel table. As a younger man, Vilipend didn't need to use a cane, but he was obviously never athletic. As a younger man, Vilipend's mustache was as thin and his curly puff of uncombed hair wasn't so white. But he had matured into an even sharper thinker, with a quicker and more deadly mind, a formidable opponent.

Vilipend sat at defense counsel table with two other attorneys, younger white men who were whispering and passing notes. One of them was also an AAYA employee, its in-house attorney. Implausibly clean-cut, either could have played the leading role as Captain America. The defense had thrown as many expensive attorneys as it could against Robbie, against Lupe, against Ace. They had an entire staff at their disposal, including more attorneys, paralegals, and clerks back at their office. Ace wasn't intimidated, not a bit, at least not by them.

"What this case is about, ladies and gentlemen, is the defendant's failure, the Athletic Association for Young Americans failure, to protect children under its supervision. You all are familiar with the AAYA, everyone knows them as—and they advertise themselves as—the premier national organization for competitive youth sports. They've spent decades developing their image of all-American wholesomeness."

*Think about that. One beat, two beats, three,* Ace thought. "But today we talk about responsibility. Responsibility for protecting vulnerable children is the issue you must ultimately decide. In 1998, they failed to protect Robbie, an eleven-year-old soccer player, from foreseeable sexual abuse. Robbie played for the California soccer club, the FC Strikers, which was affiliated with and under the AAYA corporate umbrella."

*Oh God, Robbie. Hold it together.* Ace refused to turn his head to Robbie and—despite the sting of Robbie's shame that stabbed Ace in the back—he stayed focused on the jurors.

"When you were chosen as jurors during the question-answer process—what lawyers call *voir dire*—I told you a theme would develop in this case. The theme here is that a youth organization cannot hide secrets about dangers to children. A youth organization cannot hide secrets about dangers to children…"

"And what was it that the AAYA kept hidden? AAYA knew they had a problem with rampant sex abuse in their chapter organizations across the country. The organization attracted male volunteers because of unrestricted opportunities to molest its most defenseless, innocent members."

Ace hesitated, then took a step forward. His hand hardened into a fist around the stone. He centered himself before diving deeply into the pain, but not just Robbie's pain, all of it in the world, and the worst from deep within himself. His voice rose, his tone was adamant.

"They knew children were being raped and sodomized under their supervision. They did nothing."

*That hit,* he thought, *pause, breathe, go…*

"Defense counsel will not tell you they didn't know. He can't do that because it isn't true. They knew that the man who raped Robbie had a history of lewd conduct with children. They knew."

He lowered his voice to a near whisper. "They always knew. They knew, and they did nothing except hide their dirty secrets. AAYA is responsible for the intentional, vicious predation at FC Strikers when Robbie was a little boy." Ace took a moment to look at each juror, while his eyes laser-beamed torment. He wasn't putting on a show like some lawyers might do. This was real, it was raw, and it hurt. He wanted them to see the authenticity of pain, his own pain. He did it without pretending or acting.

Ace gestured toward the plaintiff's counsel table, toward Robbie. "Robbie is asking you today to hold this institution accountable. To hold it accountable for not taking common-sense measures to protect the children it recruited, to hold it accountable for not exercising due care, for not protecting him when he was a child. Much of what you'll hear will be disturbing, but that can't be avoided."

Ace dimmed the laser beams. *These men and women don't deserve to witness the coming torment to be presented*, he thought, *but that's how our screwed-up system works*. This was the stuff of nightmares. Some of them would finish their civic service, taking those nightmares home with them, into their own sleep. Some might even experience triggered post-traumatic stress from their own life experiences. Not much of a reward for a responsible, civic-minded citizen.

"As you review the evidence presented, ask yourself if you are going to allow organizations to continue hiding the sex abuse of children in the shadows, in locked and abandoned file cabinets." Ace swung his arm around and pointed to a stack of file boxes on the floor. "Every box here is full of files that contain witness accounts of abuse, each one a boy or girl ignored. The AAYA refuses to acknowledge anything happened. They refuse to validate the traumatic life-changing events of these children with an admission, much less an apology. But once we all know what happened to them, we can take positive steps to protect the most vulnerable among us, our children. But we have to know—to know the stories hidden in those boxes—first. Well, we know now. And at the end of this trial, you will know, too."

"Now it's time for accountability. Accountability for the extreme physical and emotional pain Robbie has suffered throughout his life.

For the costs of lost opportunities and ongoing counseling. You will learn that pain from abuse isn't something that children just get over or grow out of. Children are resilient, yes, but not when it comes to abuse. The pain of abuse follows survivors for a lifetime, destroying chances for a normal life. In some cases, destroying life…"

Ace clenched his teeth and stopped talking. He took a breath and closed his eyes but couldn't lessen the tension in his jaws. Perhaps the watchers, the jury, counsel, thought the pause was dramatic, part of his performance, but it wasn't planned. Ace had more to say but he couldn't continue, all he could think was *destroying life….* His demons stirred, and he knew he had to stop right there before everything fell apart.

Ace forced his mouth into obedience. "We respectfully ask you to consider thoughtfully the evidence and hold the AAYA responsible for its reprehensible dereliction of duty. Thank you."

Ace marched back to his spot and sat tall. Lupe patted Robbie on the shoulder, but Robbie stared vacantly with wide eyes. Ace clutched at his stone in response to the pain emanating from Robbie. Or was it his own? The jury didn't feel the same intense pain Ace and Robbie did, but he was sure they sensed it, sensed it was genuine. Ace didn't have to look. He was fighting tears, and they had only just started. *How the hell am I going to get through this?*

As though sensing his distress, Lupe—with a blank expression—switched her attention to Ace. He knew she had adopted a poker face to hide her concern from the jury, but he could feel it flowing from her like waves of warmth in a snowstorm. Maybe the jury could sense it as well, but Ace couldn't read the jury. The intense emotions from Robbie, from Lupe, from everyone in the room, and from himself confused him as though he were a child again just learning how to manage feelings. Only one emotion rose above it all: Lupe's concern.

*Her suspicions about me are getting stronger. At some point, I'll have to share my story with her.* There was a time that a thought like that would have scared him, but now it offered a strange comfort. *Maybe that wouldn't be too awful. Maybe Robbie already told her…*

He turned to Robbie who made a fleeting funny face at him, eyes crossed, tongue out—the back of his head to the jury so they couldn't see—and Ace relaxed. *Robbie is always there for me.*

"Mr. Vilipend, are you prepared to proceed?" the judge asked. Her face remained expressionless, a consummate professional.

"Yes, Your Honor." Vilipend straightened his jacket as he stood up with an exaggerated effort. He leaned heavily onto his cane as he pulled himself up. Ace noticed a dime-sized, mustard-looking spot on Vilipend's bowtie and wondered if he chose it on purpose so the jury would sympathize, then felt a pang of guilt for the thought. Vilipend's legal associates stopped whispering, fingers poised over their laptop keyboards, and focused intently on Vilipend. He stepped out from behind counsel table, stopped, and faced the jury.

"May it please the Court, counsel, ladies and gentlemen of the jury." A surprisingly deep, booming voice rocked out of Vilipend's scrawny body. The prominent protrusion in the middle of his skinny neck bobbed as he cleared his throat. He adopted a stiff, wide-legged stance and began.

"Nothing is more despicable than the sexual abuse of a child, nothing. This case will be emotionally charged, and you may be naturally inclined to sympathize with the survivors. The plaintiff will tell you a troubling story and you will feel sympathetic. But your job today is to review the facts, and—emotions. Are. Not. Facts." Vilipend lowered his voice to emphasize the sense of responsibility he strived to instill in the jury. His case depended on dividing legal issues from emotional issues. That task was formidable but Vilipend earned the big bucks for a reason. He was good.

"The AAYA is an established organization. Its mission is to provide opportunities in sports for young people. Thousands of sports clubs across the country hold an affiliation with the AAYA in every sport, from archery to volleyball. Affiliate clubs, like the FC Strikers, are not controlled by AAYA. Those sports clubs operate as independent organizations that merely choose to have a relationship with AAYA. The Strikers club itself is not here today because it was financially dissolved and doesn't exist anymore, leaving only the AAYA's deep pockets. But it was the FC Strikers, the soccer club itself, that was responsible for any harm that might have been done to Mr. Santos. The FC Strikers was a separate, distinct, legal entity from the AAYA, like two different people. The AAYA isn't responsible for what the Strikers and their people did.

"And the father of Mr. Roberto Santos was one of those people. Mr. Roberto Santos wants to hold the AAYA responsible for the actions of the Strikers, *and* for the actions, or rather the *inactions* of his own father, Señor Agostinho Santos." Vilipend said the name slowly, accentuating the foreign sounds and incorrectly using a Spanish language intonation, rather than Portuguese. He let that sink in for dramatic effect, then continued. "The truth is that, over the years, multiple false allegations have been made against the AAYA. Such is the nature of any activity involving children. But the AAYA has a *perfect* record of protecting children. It has the best record and best reputation in the country. The attempt here to sully that representation is based on half-truths and outright lies which we will expose over the course of the trial."

The cold precision of his words carried authenticity but without cruelty. Ace looked over at Robbie, who was glaring at Vilipend. He would have to talk to Robbie later about that. The jury shouldn't witness anger directed at lawyers—the defendant, maybe—but not lawyers. The jurors wouldn't like anger directed at an elderly gentleman like Vilipend.

"We expect the plaintiff will not tell you the entire story. We will provide evidence to you of the facts that they leave out. You must judge the honesty of witnesses who come before you. If you believe any witness is not telling the truth, you aren't bound to believe that witness' story. It's *not* our job today to prove to you that the defendant is innocent, rather plaintiff must prove that defendant should be held responsible. Once you have heard the evidence and considered the proof, you'll agree the AAYA isn't responsible for what happened to Mr. Santos." Vilipend opened his mouth as though another string of language might escape and then snapped it shut.

*He looks like a fish*, Ace thought.

Vilipend hobbled back to counsel table, consulted his notes on a yellow pad, and bent over to hear a whisper from one of his associates. He straightened up and abruptly concluded his opening statement. "Thank you. Your Honor, that is all." Vilipend sat down.

"Very well," said Judge Moore. "Counsel, fifteen minute break?"

"Yes, Your Honor," came the simultaneous response from counsel. Ace knew better than to object to the judge taking a pee break. They could all use a break. Especially Ace who needed to get himself centered, focused, and find strength.

"Thank you for your courtesy. We will be in recess for fifteen minutes."

As the judge stood, the bailiff announced, "All rise, Court is now in recess."

After the judge and jury left, the courtroom buzzed. A couple of reporters pushed their way to the front and tried to get Ace's attention. He ignored them. His focus was on Robbie, who was distraught, though hiding it well. *Robbie should know that he can't hide his feelings from me.* Ace sighed.

*Our legal system at its finest, re-victimizing the victims,* Ace thought, as he absorbed Robbie's anguish along with his own. *God help us survive this trial.*

*Seventeen*

# THE SHOWER
# 1998

Sunday was usually a day off. Not this Sunday. After the first game of the season, the FC Strikers administrators met to review the players' performance. Tournament organizers demanded commitments, so the club had to decide where to participate and what players to bring. San Diego held the highest-level, most competitive tournament, and the club had received a coveted invitation, so now decisions and arrangements had to be made. The Strikers clubhouse had a large meeting room, ample space for the coaching managers and board members to meet in the afternoon after church services, at least for those who attended church.

The grass fields around the clubhouse glowed brightly from an unusually wet spring. Normally, the fields were full of kids and coaches, with each newly formed team getting ready for the upcoming season. But the fields were empty when Robbie and his dad, Gus, arrived early for the meetings. Enticed by the soft, fresh turf, they went kick the ball around together until the meeting started. The older Santos boys were off enjoying their remaining summer freedom, so Robbie had his dad all to himself, a special treat. Too excited to enjoy the crisp air, slightly moist with the remnants of newly mowed grass, Robbie grabbed his ball and ran off, stretching legs that had been bent still under a pew all morning. He called for his father to follow. Robbie didn't mind that his dad was getting too old and round to keep up with his youngest son.

Robbie wanted to practice headers, so Gus threw balls quickly, one after another, toward Robbie, who had to hit them back with his head. Gus intentionally mixed up every toss to make Robbie run from side to side.

"Great job, great job with the feet, keep moving, keep moving. There you go. That was a good one!" Gus was moving his mouth as quickly as Robbie was moving his body. He continued to encourage his boy. They laughed together as a stray ball would fly off at an unexpected angle, or as Gus missed catching the balls that Robbie headed back. Even though the summer afternoon was not too warm, Robbie worked up a sweat trying to impress his father.

"Teach me, teach me the *elastico, Papai.*" Robbie could barely contain his excitement.

Motivated by World Cup dreams, Robbie always had a ball at his feet. He drilled every chance he could. He loved the game and spent nearly every waking hour eating, drinking, and dreaming soccer. Pinned to his bedroom wall behind various soccer trophies and medals hung posters of his namesake, Roberto Rivelino, and The King, Pelé. The American flag was draped behind his bed next to the Brazilian flag, creating an eyesore of clashing red, white, blue, green, and yellow. The US Men's team could barely qualify for the World Cup and would probably never beat Brazil, much less make the final championship game in his lifetime, but a boy could dream. *I will surprise those Brazilians in the final when I beat them and then yell my victory in Portuguese.*

"First you watch this, Roberto. Here, pass me the ball. I show you." Gus kicked the ball to Robbie and went out for the pass. Robbie passed the ball to Gus, immediately switched to defense, then stepped up to challenge the ball. Gus faced Robbie, then lurched to one side with the ball on the outside of his foot. That was the fake. He didn't take the ball in that direction, but pulled it back with his foot and went around Robbie's defensive position from the other side.

Even knowing the move, Robbie missed the fake and didn't have the foot skills for an effective challenge yet. Gus still had skills.

"Ok, I'll teach you now. Come here." Gus said, happy his son wanted to learn this maneuver. Gus began passing the ball slowly to Robbie. The slow movement allowed Robbie to understand the maneuvers before they took it at full speed.

"Control the ball. Gentle touches back, gentle touches," Gus coached. "Is right. Is right." His father's encouragement drove Robbie to a higher effort.

Other men arrived for the meeting as Robbie and Gus played. Robbie ignored the arrivals as long as possible, knowing this time with his dad was closing. Finally, Gus said, "Well, son. I got to head in now. You can stay here and train or you can shower and get started on your summer reading assignments."

"Right, *Papai*. Like I can't wait to start some boring reading." The two laughed.

"At least I can tell your *mãe* that I tried," Gus retorted. They both knew Robbie would take advantage of the beautiful day to stay outside for more touches. Maybe more kids would show and they could start a pickup game or keep-away.

Gus headed inside the clubhouse as Robbie practiced balancing a ball on the tip of his toe and then bouncing it up and down on the laces, without letting it hit the ground.

"Hey there, you might try alternating your feet. Sometimes it's easier to walk it forward while ye juggle." Robbie recognized the Irish accent but dropped the soccer ball in surprise. *Damn. How embarrassing*, he thought. Recognizing the chance to get a bit of extra special coaching while his father was in the meeting, the suggestion enticed him.

"Hey, you not going to the meeting?" Robbie asked.

"Nah, don't need to."

"Okay. Like this?" Robbie asked. He bounced the ball from one foot to the other while stepping forward.

"Aye, there you go, mate. Look at you, you'll make the 500 Club in no time." Robbie was close but hadn't yet achieved 500 juggles before dropping the ball. He was determined to break his personal record before the season started this year.

"Do ye want to kick the ball around? I could give you some more tips."

"You bet!" Robbie was enthusiastic. He knew he was one of the best players on his team because he jumped at opportunities to work hard. Extra training, extra coaching gave him a welcome incentive to work even harder.

Robbie drilled until he mastered every challenge put before him. He spun fantasies about World Cup finals with every drill. But after a while, the drills descended into keep-away, with the two merely chasing each other about. Eventually, they had enough. The late afternoon turned to evening, and the meeting would finish soon.

"Let's hit the showers, get you cleaned up before your da' takes you home to your Mum. You're a mess."

"Aww, let's play more," Robbie whined. "They always take forever in these dumb meetings."

"Sorry, mate. It's time to clean up. Let's go." He put his hand on Robbie's shoulder to guide him to the clubhouse showers. Robbie reluctantly but obediently went along. He wasn't one to argue with adults, particularly adults in authority. Besides, he didn't want to rock the boat. Maybe he could score extra one-on-one training again.

The FC Striker's clubhouse had a large locker room with showers added to the original building. The club reserved the best lockers for coaches, but a handful of empty lockers were available for the kids to dump their school backpacks during training. Gus had his own locker that, with help from Gabi, he always kept stocked with towels. A clean towel might even find its way into Gus's locker occasionally. Robbie grabbed a musty towel from his dad's locker before undressing to get in the shower.

When the showers were busy, hot water came out immediately. However, when initially engaged, the hot water came only after running for a minute or two. Robbie waited for the warmth outside the cold spray. Along the wall in the shower room, a few showerheads sat at regular intervals above the white tile floor. The club didn't think separate private shower stalls were necessary for the boys. Or, more accurately, they didn't see any need for the added expense of separate shower stalls.

Robbie would not be showering alone, but he was fine with that. He was accustomed to showering at the clubhouse with people around. Usually, multiple people showered simultaneously. But only two people showering wasn't unusual, either. When the warm mist lifted to his face, Robbie stepped into the stream of water. Unexpectedly, he felt the coldness of skin against his bottom. Robbie had absolutely no frame of reference for the soft caress.

Robbie jumped, startled, and turned to face a big, toothy grin.

"Hey there mate, a bit jumpy aren't ye?"

"Uh, I guess," Robbie replied sheepishly. He started to say something else, but couldn't think what to say. He turned back around and stepped into the hot water. *Why did he do that? Is that normal?* Robbie wondered. Despite the warmth of the water, he shivered. The hair stood up on his forearms.

It didn't seem normal—then again, a slap in the butt on the field wasn't unusual. He had seen that at American football games on television all the time. Maybe this was something regular guys do, maybe even all the time. His older brothers often wrestled, tickled, and generally goofed off, though nothing like that.

"Turn around. Let me show ye something."

Robbie froze. He didn't want to look, but he didn't want to disobey. Steam started filling the room as the showers became hot. Robbie's face flushed with the heat. He turned only his head, looking over his shoulder. A pale hand was stroking a full erection.

"Ahh, this feels good, it does. Ye should try. Here, I will show ye." He stepped closer and took Robbie's hand. Robbie initially jerked his hand away in a half-hearted and failed effort to get free. *I don't want to do this. Why is he doing this? If I stop, will he still be my friend? Maybe he won't hang out with me anymore, maybe he won't coach me.* Without further resistance, he mechanically watched as his own hand was placed on his penis and stroked. To Robbie's mortification, he became aroused and stiffened. His body was a traitor to his will. But he still didn't know how to make this stop, to make himself stop. *Why does this feel so good? What is happening?* But the overwhelming, intolerable horror of wrongness destroyed the physical pleasure.

"Now see, there you go, nice idn't it?" The Irish brogue crooned in Robbie's ears. He closed his eyes tightly in response, willing this to be over as quickly as possible. Someone moaned. He couldn't tell where the moan originated. For Robbie, the moment was as frozen as the rest of his body was frozen, as his mind was frozen. It wouldn't stop and it lasted forever. Except it didn't. And then it was over, this time.

"Ah, now, I knew ye'd like that."

Robbie had no idea how to respond and said nothing.

"Best keep some things private, ye know."

"I won't tell anyone, I promise," Robbie said. He couldn't imagine what he would ever say or who he would say it to.

They finished showering and got dressed. Robbie dressed as quickly as he could, despite the shaking in his hands and legs. He shoved the damp towel back into his dad's locker before he stumbled out of the locker room, mumbling a quiet, "Bye."

"Well, we'll be seeing ye later. The team will have a brilliant year. I feel it," came the good-natured response.

Robbie tiptoed into the meeting room where the men were still talking, excitement in their voices for the upcoming season. He chose a quiet spot in the corner behind his dad, safe, and plopped down onto the floor. Back up against the corner, he pulled his knees up to his chest and wrapped his arms around them. He stared at the table legs and the shoes underneath. He hoped nobody was looking at him, but he didn't know because he didn't look up. Had he chosen another spot, another room maybe, he would be alone. Robbie wished he were invisible, but he didn't want to be alone either.

The adults were preoccupied with their heated discussion and took no notice of Robbie, which was a relief. Apparently, a competing soccer club had done something bad to the Strikers with some sort of paper put on people's cars.

"They're saying shit about our club! Calling Sean a faggot is bullshit," yelled one of the more boisterous coaches.

"Calm down. Nobody believes it. Obviously, we'd never allow faggots to coach the team," Gus said with a dismissive wave of his hand. "Let's move on to other business."

The questions screaming in Robbie's head drowned out the rest of the adults' meeting. *Do they know? Maybe they already know that it happened. Maybe they know because they know what happens in the shower. God, I hope they don't know.* To avoid looking suspicious, Robbie took his summer reading out of his backpack and cracked it open. Robbie forced his focus on the words, but his mind was spinning.

*Does this mean I'm gay? Oh my god, I might be a fag. Do I have to confess this to our creepy priest? No way. That is not happening. I can't tell anyone.* This last isolating thought brought a swell of loneliness and his face warmed while his body froze. He squeezed his eyes tightly, willing away tears. He remained quiet, still pretending to read, but searching his mind for music. The music was gone. There was nothing but the wanting to go home.

# *Eighteen*
# EXPERT WITNESS
# 2022
## TRIAL

*Whoomp, there it is! Whoomp, there it is!* Robbie suppressed his mirth over the new earworm spawned in response to the next witness, the expert hired by Ace to talk about child abuse stuff. Given how much the guy cost, the moment was big. Anyway, it *should* feel big—*there it is!* Ace had convinced Robbie they needed this guy for their case. The AAYA had their own expert psychologist who got paid to say Robbie was fine, really-fine. But first, it was Robbie's turn for his expert psychologist to explain why Robbie wasn't fine, really-not-fine, why abuse distorted his normal childhood development and made Robbie the fuck-up he was. *Whoomp.*

The balding, middle-aged white man wore a tan suit with wire-rimmed glasses and sat straight, like he had a broomstick up his ass. He held his head high and pinched his nose while Ace questioned him. His tone had a casualness typical of the highly successful trying to act like, *oh yeah, Stanford, blah blah, Harvard, blah blah, no big deal*, except of course it *is* a big deal. Be impressed. Be very impressed. But the jury was rapt, so maybe the guy was worth the small fortune he'd charge.

Ace had wrapped up Dr. Schmidt's extensive education and experience in the field, then followed up with his publications in such-and-such high-brow specialty periodical and *blah blah blah*. Robbie was astonished that the jury was captivated by this boredom-fest, but they were. Ace knew his stuff and clearly picked the right guy for the job. An hour into the testimony, Dr. Schmidt described the litany of materials he had reviewed in preparation. Mostly, they comprised legal briefs, medical reports, and the like. After he established the expert's extensive background, Ace would begin questions about the doctor's formalized opinion. Robbie braced himself for this next assault when the doc would rip deeper, exposing Robbie's shame to the world. *As if they haven't seen enough.*

"Doctor Schmidt, is it your experience that children often misreport sexual contact with adults or later change their story?" Ace asked.

"Objection. Compound," Vilipend interjected.

"I'll rephrase. Is it your experience that children frequently change their stories about sexual contact with adults?"

"Yes," the doctor answered. "Children can react to trauma by shutting down, by trying to forget what happened. So, when a child is questioned near the time of the event, it is fairly typical they don't get all the details correct. Sometimes, after becoming an adult, a person will remember events more clearly than they did as a child."

"They forget…" Ace stopped mid-sentence, shook his head, and began again. "How is that poss…" Again, Ace cut himself off. He looked down at his shoes and visibly exhaled while formulating his next attempt. Lifting his head to look straight at the expert, he said, "Please explain how a child would not recall specific information soon after an incident, but could recall an incident in great detail several years later."

"It's possible that someone learned information over time from other sources and incorporated that into their own memory. In that case, it's not truly their own memory. It is also possible a child would deny something happened because they are unable to admit it, so they lie. But what happens frequently is children repress or are unable to access the memory of events because their anxiety was so great and the trauma was so threatening that they just disassociate from it; they're not cognitively aware. Sometimes it's called dissociative amnesia and it can last for many years into adulthood. So, it's not that they're deliberately lying about it or saying it didn't happen. It's that psychologically traumatized children often can't access the memory because they simply can't process it. As a protective mechanism, the mind refuses the trauma."

Ace gaped at the doctor but didn't ask another question. Moments ticked by in silence, everyone in the room staring at Ace. The jury shuffled in their stiff wooden chairs and exchanged looks. The Judge raised an eyebrow and tilted her head as she watched him, but Ace simply stood silent and stared.

Robbie considered throwing a paperclip at him as the silence lengthened, but resisted the temptation of his immature impulses. Instead, he leaned into Lupe and whispered.

"What's he doing?"

"I don't know," Lupe whispered back. Robbie could barely make out her quiet words, but he could tell that she was not only confused but concerned.

Ace remained frozen as the courtroom grew even quieter.

"Mr. Elbridge, did you have more questions for this witness?" the judge asked loudly.

Ace snapped his head to the judge like he had forgotten where he was. "Yes, let me just look at my notes," he murmured. Ace grabbed a yellow pad and stared at it, flipping through the pages.

Robbie couldn't believe what he had heard. That wasn't Ace's voice. His confidence was gone. Ace's hands hung limply at his side, no hand on stomach, no stone. *It's not his emotion thing*, Robbie thought.

"I'm sorry," Ace said, his confidence returning. "I just…" He looked down at his yellow pad again, then turned his attention back to Dr. Schmidt, his voice back to normal. "So, how does a traumatized child who has repressed the memory of a sexual assault remember what happened when he becomes an adult?"

"Objection. This isn't a repressed memory case, Your Honor," Vilipend pleaded.

The usually poker-faced judge slipped a puzzled look at Ace before responding. "I'll allow it. But counsel, you'll need to get to the point."

"Yes, Your Honor," Ace said. "Dr. Schmidt, do you need me to repeat the question?"

"Yes, please," the witness responded.

"Ok, how does a traumatized child who has repressed the memory of a sexual assault remember what happened when he becomes an adult?"

"There are several ways that can happen. At the time of a traumatic event, a child's mind associates feelings, sights, sounds, smells, tastes, and touch with the trauma. Later, similar sensations may trigger the memory. Sometimes people first remember past traumatic events during therapy, but most people begin having traumatic memories outside of therapy. They may start having nightmares, or anxiety." The doctor paused, but Ace only listened silently, so he continued. "Once triggered, the person might experience a post-traumatic stress episode, like they are reliving the event. Triggered memories may have serious psychological impact, eating disorders, anxiety attacks or even self-harm or suicide attempts."

The doctor stopped, but Ace had spaced out again, staring straight at the doctor with his mouth hanging open, his arms again limp by his side.

"Did that answer your question?" the doctor asked.

"Yes, yes, I'm sorry. It did. That answered my question." Ace again flipped through his yellow legal pad before continuing. "So, I want to go back to something you said earlier. I believe you said a traumatized child may lie about abuse because they simply cannot process what happened at the time. Is that correct?"

"Yes."

"And as I understand you, that situation differs from a child who has a repressed memory, even though in both cases the child will say nothing happened when it did?"

"Yes."

"Please explain the difference between the two situations for the jury."

"The child with the repressed memory is not really lying, because the child doesn't remember the event. The child who lies remembers the event but can't understand it or isn't ready to admit what happened. In both cases, the child is traumatized."

"Based upon your review of the record in this case, including Mr. Santos's medical records, is it your opinion that Mr. Santos lied about his abuse as a child because he was traumatized after it happened?"

"Yes, the record is clear that this is not the case of a repressed memory being brought back. From the witness statements and evidence, it is my professional opinion that Mr. Santos lied as a child but when he matured and developed enough psychological strength to face that trauma, he could eventually admit it to his therapist, and thus admit it to himself and others."

Ace walked back behind counsel table and leaned over for a quickly whispered consultation with Lupe.

"That's all we have for this witness now, but we reserve the right for re-direct," Ace said to the judge before taking his seat.

"Fine. Mr. Vilipend, do you have questions?" the judge asked.

"Yes, Your Honor," Vilipend said. He pulled his cane closer, raised himself to stand, then slowly made his way over to the well in front of the witness box.

While Vilipend was questioning the doc about his background, Robbie grabbed a legal pad and wrote a note for Ace: *You OK?* Lupe glanced at the pad and, with a curious look at Ace, passed the note to him. She had to give him a gentle kick under the table to get his attention. She raised an eyebrow at Ace while he read it.

Ace picked up a mutilated red pen to write back: *YES*

*Could he be more cryptic?* Robbie thought after reading it. *I'll find out later when he's not in the middle of this witness.* Ace appeared intent on Vilipend's examination, but was staring at the lawyer, almost like he wasn't there.

"Dr. Schmidt, are you familiar with False Memory Syndrome?" Vilipend asked.

"Yes," the doctor replied.

"Good." Vilipend turned to face the jury for his next question. "Will you please explain to the jury what False Memory Syndrome is?"

Lupe looked aghast at Ace, who sat like a big silent lump, so she jumped to her feet. "Objection. False memory is not an issue in the case," Lupe said.

"Your Honor," Vilipend replied. "Counsel covered the issue of memory on direct. False memory is my response."

"Counsel, sidebar, now," the judge said.

Ace, Lupe, Vilipend, and one of the Captain America lawyers all hustled to the bench where Judge Moore peered down at them over her spectacles and covered the microphone with her hand. Though tight, her lips moved fast, but Robbie couldn't hear what she was saying. She appeared annoyed. Robbie noticed the jurors watching the display with some interest, though they wouldn't have been able to hear either. After a minute or two, the lawyers made their way back to their spots and the judge spoke.

"Ladies and gentlemen, please disregard the comments by counsel regarding this objection. I will instruct you in more detail about this later, but the lawyer's comments are not evidence for you to consider. The objection is overruled."

Robbie hoped the jury couldn't read Lupe's agitation, but he could. While she was a master at controlling her frustration, he could read it just the same. *Something's wrong*, he thought.

The judge turned to Vilipend. "Continue."

"Yes, Your Honor," Vilipend replied. "Dr. Schmidt, please explain what False Memory Syndrome is."

"Sure. First, false memory isn't really a *syndrome* per se. But false memories occur in people sometimes for several reasons."

"And isn't it true that false memories can be implanted into a person, through certain therapeutic or other techniques?"

"Yes, that can happen."

"Please explain how that might happen."

"Human memory is highly suggestible and false memories may be created through various techniques, including guided imagery, dream interpretation, hypnosis, or other means. A leading expert in the field, Dr. Loftus, conducted a famous study where a false memory of being lost in a shopping mall as a child was suggested to test subjects and it was found that twenty-five percent of those subjects developed a memory of the event even though it never occurred. The subjects thought it did."

"In the 90s, so-called recovered-memories therapy saw a rise in popularity but often resulted in extreme and obviously false memories in the subjects. This was a time when there was rampant fear of satanic rituals involving child sexual abuse. Perhaps the most famous being the McMartin preschool, where elaborate theories of abuse developed, including assertions about grave robbing and underground sex tunnels which didn't exist. Ultimately, the experts struggled to distinguish false memories from genuine memories, a challenging task given the ages of the children involved. Lots of psychiatric malpractice litigation was initiated and today, legitimate therapists are extremely careful about the possibility of suggestion."

"So, it is widely accepted among professionals that children are uniquely vulnerable to the suggestion of false memories?" Vilipend asked.

"I would say so, yes."

"How can you distinguish a false memory from something that really happened?"

"The best way is with corroborating evidence, witnesses, or other evidence."

"Doctor, you have reviewed all the medical records of Roberto Santos on this matter. Is it your opinion that Mr. Santos's memory could have been falsely suggested during therapy?"

"In my opinion, there is corroborating evidence here that shows the abuse actually happened."

"That's not what I asked. Please answer the question." Vilipend raised the volume substantially, causing anyone who'd been dozing to snap to attention. "I'll ask again. From your review of Mr. Santos's psychiatric record, is it *possible* that his so-called 'memory'—"

With dramatic effort, Vilipend fingered air-quotes around the word 'memory'

"—could have resulted from improper suggestion?"

"Well, it's always possible, but in this case, I think—"

"Thank you, Dr. Schmidt. That will be all," Vilipend snapped, cutting off the witness before he could finish the sentence.

"Thank you, counsel," the judge said. "Mr. Elbridge?"

Ace stood. "No re-redirect, Your Honor. The witness may be excused."

"All right, the witness is excused. We will take a fifteen-minute break," the judge said.

After the judge and jury left, Robbie, Lupe, and Ace put their heads together at the table in the team-huddle style frequently employed during the trial.

"I don't understand. Is Vilipend saying I made everything up?" Robbie asked.

"It's more nuanced than that," Lupe replied. "He is going to argue that you *might* have a false memory and that abuse never actually happened. It's on us to prove abuse happened. All Vilipend has to do is raise doubts. We should bring out the prisoner to testify."

Ace's face turned pale, and when he spoke, a slight tremor accented his words. "That's risky, Lupe. He's a liar and could flip. Maybe he'd say it never happened, that Robbie's lying. He could say anything. Besides, it's not been done before in any of these cases. We couldn't find any legal precedent for it. You researched everything; I called friends from the plaintiffs' bar. Nobody's done this."

"Exactly, they won't expect it. It will shut down this line of argument. They've always denied that anything happened, and they've always gotten away with it. We have a unique opportunity to prove otherwise. Our witness will prove it once and for all." Lupe turned to Robbie. "I know this will be incredibly hard for you. We didn't want to do it if we could avoid it. But I'm worried that the jury was believing Vilipend's bullshit. I think we should take the risk." Lupe was very convincing when she wanted to be, and neither Ace nor Robbie could find an argument against her idea. Compelling, but not oblivious, she turned to Robbie and asked gently, "But you have to be okay with this. Can you handle it?"

Robbie stiffened and didn't respond. He stared at his hands opening and closing into tight fists, again and again, before he turned his head toward the gallery, looking for his husband Tony, but Tony was chatting with Robbie's mom, Gabi, and didn't see. *At least Mom likes him*, Robbie thought. "Can I talk to Tony about it first?"

"Sure," Lupe and Ace answered in unison.

"You go do that. I need to talk to Ace," Lupe said. As Robbie left to grab Tony, Lupe grabbed Ace by the elbow and escorted him, not gently, outside the courtroom and into a private conference room.

Once they were inside, soundproofed from the world with the door tightly shut, Lupe let her anger show. "What the actual fuck, Ace? Why did you bring up that memory stuff? You opened the door for Vilipend to question whether the abuse really happened. They *never* admitted the abuse happened, but they didn't deny it either."

Ace averted his eyes.

"Now we have to prove Robbie was raped because Vilipend will say that his memory *could be* faulty," Lupe said.

Ace kept his eyes averted. Her frustration was penetrating, and he didn't have an excuse. There was no brilliant legal strategy at play here. He couldn't pull a rabbit out of a hat, leaving the crowd awed by his genius. The truth was, Ace had made a critical mistake in the middle of trial. When he answered, his voice was soft. "It's personal; the doctor's testimony explained something to me I never understood. I let a personal problem impede my work."

Lupe stared, incredulous. Her disappointment hit Ace like a cold, hard slap in the face. Instead of letting her emotion wash past him, he absorbed it; he took the hit. *I deserved that,* he thought.

"The memory thing?" Lupe asked.

"Yes."

Lupe nodded, and Ace could see her mentally wrestling with the little information he gave her. "What is going on with you, anyway? What are you not telling me?" she asked.

Ace sighed as he weighed whether to tell her, and if he did, what would he say?

She looked at him, giving him a chance to respond, but he remained silent, so she continued, "Look, I don't know what's going on with you, but I know you can set this aside, whatever it is." She placed her hand on his shoulder and squeezed, then repeated her encouragement. "You've got this, Ace." The confidence in her voice was infectious.

Ace found a modicum of courage, enough to look up, look Lupe in the eye. "I'm sorry, Lupe. It was a mistake. It was my own personal mistake, and I should've never let it happen. This is supposed to be about Robbie, not about me, and I got lost in my own problems. I fucked up." Ace had been holding his breath while he spoke and exhaled with a huff. "I'll talk to Robbie about it. You don't have to do that. I'll fall on my sword because it was my fault."

Lupe's face softened because she could see how hard this was for Ace. Here was the price of justice staring directly at her. "Not now, because we don't have time for that. We move on."

"Okay then, what now?"

"We'll have to bring him in. He said he'd do it. He'll admit to the rape," Lupe said.

"You know it's an enormous risk. It could blow up everything."

"Yes, I know. But the alternative is worse. The jury might believe that the rape never happened. We can't take that risk. Honestly, I think that would be the worst thing for Robbie—if the jury didn't believe him."

"You're right, of course," Ace nodded.

"Look, I'll do the witness," she said. "You take Robbie's testimony on direct, just as we planned, then we do the prisoner after Robbie. I'll make the arrangements. Okay?"

"I don't know if I can do it now. Maybe you should take over—"

"Damn it Ace, this isn't like you at all. You can do this. I've seen you unwind more complicated legal tangles lots of times. Whatever this is, know that I am here for you; Robbie is here for you. Everyone in that gallery is here for you, too. You can't back out now. How would that look to the jury? You've got this."

Ace nodded reluctantly, then pulled himself up straight. He grasped his pocketed stone, but it offered him no protection from himself.

"All right, let's go find Robbie and see what he and Tony are thinking." Lupe again took Ace's arm, gently this time, and they headed out, putting the incident behind them, for the moment anyway.

# *Nineteen*
# ADMISSION
# 1998

Sean had prepared a simple meal to share with his nephew JJ: roasted potatoes and braised brisket with carrots. Although he enjoyed cooking, gourmet was not Sean's style. He preferred basic, old-fashioned meals, eaten in moderation. While his meals weren't fancy, they were delicious, and constructed with special attention. JJ was late. He had a quick errand after practice and said he'd be home for dinner, but still hadn't arrived. Dinner would stay warm in the electric slow cooker, at least for a while. If JJ didn't come home soon, Sean would eat alone, and JJ could survive on leftovers.

Sean settled into his overstuffed brown leather recliner in front of the television; with a pull of the side handle, he raised his feet. Sean's youngest sister had visited recently from Ireland and orchestrated his interior design. Though she favored modern styles, he insisted on traditional. Good old-fashioned Irish was the most comfortable style imaginable, doilies and all. To Sean, modern furniture seemed cold and bare, though he appreciated his sister's helpful intentions. He surfed channels, looking for an interesting program, but nothing appealed. Sean stretched out his long legs over the recliner's footrest and thought about sneaking in a quick run. He got little exercise at training earlier and was itching to run.

*Besides, running makes the world better. I should've run a lap with the kiddos.* Sean's toes twitched under the hand-crocheted afghan, eager to run, but JJ's car pulled into the garage and JJ entered the adjoining kitchen door. Sean promised he'd double his efforts to ten miles later, tomorrow.

"Hey-ho, Unc', smells good."

"Dinner's ready; grab a plate." Sean rose and headed to the kitchen to join JJ at the table.

The heavy comfort food silenced the men, and Sean reminisced about their last special training session. Maybe if he had run with the boys then, Josh wouldn't have picked a fight during laps. Sean puzzled over Josh's actions. The boy had become downright belligerent and—that day—violent. After what happened, Sean couldn't deny the emergent behavior pattern. Maybe Josh had been experiencing growing pains or problems at home.

Sean had seen some tension between Josh's parents, team manager mom Susie, and firefighter dad Joe Martin, but it didn't seem cruel or violent. Many times, Sean observed Susie's extra caring touch with all the boys, including her own son, Josh. She attended to shoelaces and scraped elbows with care. The team was lucky to have her as the manager because she handled every boring administrative detail with a smile. Josh's dad, Joe, had high expectations for his son, pushing him to excel, shouting from the sidelines. Joe could be harsh—not untypical soccer dad behavior—but Sean had assumed the harshness came from a place of love. Sean had seen no behavior he would characterize as unusual or abusive.

Josh usually followed JJ around like an attention-starved puppy and JJ usually afforded him plentiful attention, affection even, but not at training that day. JJ had been aloof, uninterested in training, unin-terested in Josh. Sean accepted JJ's mercurial mood swings, but Josh may have felt rejected and had acted out for attention. Sean watched JJ going after his meal with gusto, grunting as he wolfed the food. It occurred to Sean that Josh and JJ had connected, had become friends, so maybe JJ knew something.

"Meant to ask you after training the other day, something going on with Josh Martin?" Sean asked.

"Don't know what ye mean."

"He punched Robbie at our special training session. When they were running laps?" Sean examined JJ's face for any clue pointing to comprehension. "You saw how he was."

"Suppose so, strange that," JJ mumbled through a mouthful of brisket. "Robbie's a popular kid, lots of friends, everyone likes him. Maybe that's why Josh is jealous."

Sean took another bite, chewing as he considered JJ's sneer. JJ stared straight into Sean's eyes as if intentionally confirming Sean's suspicions yet daring him to ask more. Sean swallowed, then took the dare. "I think there's something with you and Josh. What is it?"

"Nothing."

But Sean could tell from the twitch of JJ's lips and the twinkle in his eye that he was lying. Because the discussion might get ugly, Sean chose his next words carefully and delivered them in a flat voice. "Come on JJ, what's the deal?"

"Well, I think the boyo likes me is all." JJ winked.

"What?" Sean squinted at JJ, mentally sorting the puzzle pieces. JJ had befriended Josh, but why would that make Josh punch Robbie?

JJ shrugged and continued eating. He spied an errant crumb near his plate and, squeezing his thumb and forefinger together, flicked it to the floor. He didn't bother to look where it landed.

*Oblivious*, Sean thought. *He's never cleaned floors and once again, someone else will clean that mess up—me.* Sean waited for more of a response, but JJ kept eating.

"Damn it, JJ. Tell me."

"Weren't nothing. Boyo's randy, maybe a homo."

"What?"

"Maybe he likes boys."

"I know what 'homo' means, but he's just a kid." Sean's face reddened, he raised his voice and clumped his hand into a fist.

"Told you, weren't nothing."

"Damn it, JJ." Sean's fist hit the table.

"Ok, fine. I'll tell ye what went down." But JJ didn't speak immediately. He lingered over another tasty morsel before speaking further. Sean glared at him while he chewed, assessing the obvious reluctance and afraid of what might follow. "Boyo and me jerked it a while back," JJ finally said.

"You what?"

"Jerked it. Come on Unc', ye know what that be." JJ sounded exasperated but not embarrassed.

Sean gaped as he struggled to process this crushing new information. His brother had warned him that JJ had masturbated with a young boy and had begged Sean to turn JJ around and make him stop. Sean thought it was over, that JJ was interested in women. He had caught JJ with computer porn of naked—adult—women, and let himself believe that porn was the problem, that JJ would grow out of it. JJ's admission opened an abyss of dreadful possibility and destroyed the safety of Sean's denial. Now Sean had another, substantially more serious, mess to clean up.

"You know better. You have to stop. Just stop!"

"We were just horsing around, no big." JJ stood to walk away, leaving behind his dirty dishes.

"Sit!"

JJ didn't sit but stopped in his tracks to stare down Sean. "What now?"

"You know what. You can't do that to kids. For one, it's illegal. You could go to jail."

JJ shrugged. "Nah, I didn't hurt no one. Boy wanted it. Liked it."

"No. You could've hurt him, hurt him psychologically, seriously. Don't you understand?"

"Whatever."

"Did you do it to anyone else? How many times did you do that?"

"Are we done?"

Sean had avoided speaking with JJ about why he came to America. Another failure, since that dreaded discussion, was the primary purpose of his visit. It had to happen and there was no better time.

"You know why your da' sent you to America?"

"Ya."

"Tell me."

"Jeez Unc', do we have to talk about it?"

"Yes. Tell me."

"Fine, guess I'm randy. Don't matter if it be men or women, boys or girls. Same to me. I don't hurt nobody. Them kiddies, they like it."

"No! It's wrong. You don't know how much they could be hurt, maybe lifelong hurts."

"Nah, they want it too, always asking for it, ye know. Flirting, begging for it."

"They're only children. They don't know." Sean searched JJ's face for any glimmer of empathy but didn't find it.

"Come on, Unc' ye like the little ones, dontcha?"

"I don't touch them, not like that. Never."

"Liar." JJ laughed with surprising viciousness. "If they be hurt, 'tis their own fault for doing it."

"That's not true; they're only children. You are an adult now. Why don't you stop?"

"Grown women get me going, ye know, the kids aren't like that," JJ gave Sean a moment for reaction, but received none, "… but women are harder to get with. It's just playtime with the kiddos, they're easy pickings, and the boys, the boys don't say nothing to nobody. I like it that way."

*He isn't even attracted to children; he wants women but preys on children*, Sean thought. "So, you do it because you can control them? Is that it?"

"Pretty much."

JJ confirmed Sean's nightmare. JJ molested children because he could easily dominate, manipulate, and deceive them. Children, particularly insecure or needy children, wouldn't stand a chance against JJ's cunning. His victim choice was pure predation, driven by opportunity and depravity. Sexual attraction was not JJ's primary objective.

"Stop, JJ. It's unacceptable, illegal. You'll go to prison. Do you even care about that, about going to prison?"

JJ shrugged. He didn't appear concerned with the inevitable consequences and couldn't be convinced about the immorality, illegality, perversion, or depravity of his behavior. Even if Sean could convince him, JJ wouldn't care. That was the worst part. He wouldn't—or couldn't—care.

"We done now?" JJ asked.

"No. San Diego's coming up. No sex play, no masturbation, no touching boys. Promise."

"I could stay here. I don't have to go." The corners of JJ's pale, fleshy lips slowly turned upward.

"I'll think about it. But promise you'll never touch another kid, not while you're here, not while I'm responsible for you."

JJ sighed loudly.

"Promise."

"Ok, fine." JJ walked off, again ignoring his dirty dishes.

"I mean it." If JJ had heard that, he ignored it and apparently had nothing more to say.

Sean puzzled over the conundrum that was JJ while staring at the closed door and not eating. He wanted more than anything to believe that his nephew would keep the promise, but after everything, believing was more and more difficult. At some point, Sean would have to tell his older brother, JJ's dad, about the problem, too. That was not a conversation to look forward to.

Sean sat, speared a carrot and examined it as though it were extra-terrestrial. Things that grow underground should be brown, not orange. Orange belongs to fruit trees basking in sunlight. Sean contemplated the paradox of bright orange underground vegetables, then stuck the fork in his mouth and chomped both the carrot and thoughts about the carrot into oblivion. As intriguing as carrots are, he had to resolve the JJ problem. He would rather contemplate the color of carrots.

Sean stood, cleared the table, and filled the sink with scalding, soapy water. JJ should help, but asking would undoubtedly create more conflict. Sean scraped the crusty dishes into the garbage disposal side of the sink and unceremoniously dumped each dish into the soapy water on the other side, careful not to touch the scorching water. One benefit of ambidexterity was the ability to speed-wash dishes. As he worked, Sean wondered if JJ resulted from some gene mutation or alien body swap.

He seemed to have been born wired with obliviousness to the human condition, devoid of empathy. If JJ was born like that, would change be impossible? Sean considered differences between his brother, JJ's dad, and a fine man, and the pugnacious twat that was his son JJ. Maybe this kid wasn't blood; maybe his sister-in-law lied. The entire Geoghan clan was loving, empathetic, but not JJ. *Why would God give our family this person, this challenge? JJ's a dangerous asshole. Maybe he belongs in jail.*

Was it possible to love sociopathy away? If so, JJ should be normal. JJ's mother, Sean's sister-in-law, was all love and lilacs, all the time. Sean remembered the last time he saw her—back when he was playing professional ball—cheerfully waving from the sidelines, cheeks ruddy in the crisp wind. She didn't have an evil bone in her body. If love were the determining factor, JJ would be a goddamn saint.

Sean's brother was the same, all love, no evil. Love ran rampant in Geoghan children, all the children, and grandchildren, except JJ, who must be some sort of weird genetic throwback. Everyone else in the family was blond, except ginger JJ. Not that it was a stretch for an Irishman to be redheaded, but as far as anyone could remember, there had been no Geoghan redheads.

Red hair and maliciousness were not family traits, but what about sexuality? Maybe certain kinds of sex attractions run in families. Sean jumped when he stuck his hand in the sink along with a drinking glass. The water was too hot, and he wasn't paying attention. He dried his hand on the nearby dishtowel, then rubbed in some aloe vera hand lotion.

Young neighborhood boys were playing baseball in the street outside his kitchen window and he watched them closely, rubbing his hands together; the lotion soothed his burned skin. The boys were the cutest age possible, pre-teens, energetic but not yet egocentric. At that age, they didn't yet know to hide their yearning for adult approval and showed unrestrained affection. Their own developing sexuality barely peeked through, but mostly the boys were too busy being boys to dwell on that. Girls were still icky and had cooties. So cute.

Sean longed to be with them. He felt called to their playground in the street, to play, to mentor, to love, to touch. He could show them how to hold a bat and in doing that he would get to touch their smooth, unscarred skin. To teach proper athletic technique, he could stand close behind a boy, rub his bare arms, put his hands over the boy's small hands gripping the bat. But Sean understood his love for boys couldn't be physical. He couldn't do what JJ did. Sean had promised. He had promised God.

Under the sink, Sean kept a spray bottle of diluted ammonia among the cleaning supplies. He opened the cabinet, pulled it out, and turned it over in his hands until the spray nozzle pointed to his face. With his eyes squeezed shut, he held his breath and sprayed his face. He did it again. The ammonia stung his skin and burned his lungs when he finally sucked air. He slapped it around his face like aftershave, except he slapped viciously. When he opened his reddened eyes, the neighborhood boys were still there, still adorable. Sean had heard the ammonia technique might rearrange—or reassign—someone's sexual urges. But even through the resulting nausea, his attraction persisted. He hung his head, disappointed. *How can a person change their sexuality? How can that be possible? I don't know what to do.*

Sean turned his back to the window and slid down the sink cabinet until he was sitting on the floor. Again, he slapped himself, over and over, harder and harder, until his cheeks matched his bright red eyes. Pain pounded at his head—even when he stopped slapping himself—and he cried a puddle of shame and ammonia.

*Am I a monster?*

*I can never—will never—have a relationship with a child; I will never have a spouse, significant other, partner, or lover; I will never have a family.*

When he stopped shaking, Sean stood and turned his attention back to the sink, the window. The dishes were dry, but Sean stood there, staring out the window, watching sweet boys play baseball in the street. He could inspire a team of boys like that, take charge and coach them to win. But his mentoring of JJ was ineffectual, pathetic. JJ didn't take him seriously.

If JJ was faithful to his promise, if he stopped the behavior, then Sean wouldn't have to take corrective action. Problem solved. But his gut was sending him a different message. Something was still wrong. If Sean disclosed the JJ problem, there would be hell to pay, particularly with Josh's family, Susie and Joe Martin.

The sound of JJ's footsteps on the stairs interrupted Sean's thoughts.

"Hey, I'm heading out to hang with my mates. Back later," JJ said. Sean stood quietly and listened to him leave. The kitchen door slammed, and the garage door opened. Sean watched JJ sulk down the driveway, toward the playing boys, and speak, probably telling them to move out of the street. They all laughed as though JJ had shared some hysterical joke before moving away. JJ's car pulled out of the garage with a squeal as the boys waved.

The neighborhood children would be vulnerable when Sean and the team went to San Diego. If JJ stayed here alone, what would happen to the neighborhood kids? He couldn't trust JJ alone. JJ's friends were thugs, and they might do illegal drugs at the house. He doubted that a last-minute flight to Ireland could be found, at least not at an affordable price. There would be trouble leaving him home, but having JJ around the kids in San Diego was risky, too. The road trips were chaotic. Monitoring JJ's actions would be tricky. It was a no-win situation.

*Gus Santos has four boys, I'm sure he's seen everything. He'll know what to do,* Sean thought. He also remembered the Strikers' manual, a loose-leaf binder imprinted with the name of the AAYA. That manual surely had rules or advice about this type of thing. At the next opportunity, Sean resolved to tell Gus everything.

Sean sighed, rested his limp, burned hands on the sink, and stared out the window until he couldn't see.

## *Twenty*

# CONFESSION-INTERVENTION 1998

Sean paced in front of the large picture window facing the street in front of his house. A pitcher of ice water and three glasses sat ready on the coffee table. A few days after the dinner with JJ, Sean had asked his local priest, Father John, to visit. Funny how many Father Johns exist in the Catholic world, but the American priest was nothing like the Irish Father John, dead for many years. Irish Father John had already been ancient twenty-plus years ago. American Father John was an athletic and energetic middle-aged man who planned to stop by after a basketball game with disadvantaged youth. Sean couldn't imagine the Irish Father John ever playing basketball.

Just like the Irish father however, Sean could confide in the American Father John. Sean believed in the institution, his faith unwavering. He had outgrown his childhood idea that priests were manifestations of God on earth, but still found solace in their ministry. Then again, Sean never dared confide the most troubling secret he carried. Disclosing the burdensome dilemma could destroy Sean's life.

That secret wasn't about JJ, it was Sean's secret. Sean had asked the priest for help with JJ, and JJ would arrive later. But Sean had hoped for a moment alone, just a moment, because it was time. JJ's depravity illustrated the disastrous pitfalls of Sean's own struggle. His greatest fear was that he was no different from JJ, or possibly worse. Why did God make Sean this way? Why would He do that? Sean had to know; he had to accept the disclosure risk to find answers.

Society loathed pedophiles without qualification or mercy. Even the safety of children was secondary to the hatred; laws were designed to punish, not protect, not rehabilitate. If protecting children required honest understanding and treatment of pedophiles, then maybe children would never be protected. Nobody talked about chaste pedophiles; then again, perhaps the concept itself was oxymoronic. If a person was sexually attracted to children but didn't act upon that attraction, were they still a pedophile? It was all so confusing, and frightening. Sean didn't know the answers to any of these questions. All he knew was fear, the utter contempt the "pedo" label would bring, not garden-variety contempt, but a nuclear explosion of life-wrecking hatred. No friendship would withstand the shattering divulgence of his terrible secret. The secret pushed him into a lonely place where help was unavailable. Worse yet, the secret made friendship and companionship unavailable. People could not be trusted to see the goodness in Sean if the truth of his nature became exposed.

*I have to tell him because I need assurance. He might reject me, but I need help and have to take that chance.* An old Buick pulled up and parked on the street. Sean was at the front door before the priest exited his car.

"Father John. Thank you for coming. Come in," Sean said.

"Hello, Sean. No problem at all," replied Father John. He was wearing old sweatpants cut off above the knee, a plain gray tee-shirt, and high-top tennis shoes. Sweat darkened his underarms, revealing a rigorous workout.

"Kids go easy on you today, Father?" Sean asked.

"Never," the Father laughed as he entered the house and settled on the front-room couch. "How are you holding up?"

Here was Sean's golden opportunity. Sean rubbed his thighs with both hands. This was his chance, but he wasn't ready yet, so he started easy. "I don't know what to do about JJ, Father." He had already told the priest what had happened over the phone. Father John suggested he stop by to talk about the matter in person. "JJ's not home yet. He'll be here soon." Sean twisted in his chair. He was finding it difficult to sit, much less sit still.

"Well, let's talk about it before he gets in. You said JJ had a problem in Ireland, that's why he came to America?"

"Yes, this isn't the first time. My brother was ashamed; he thought JJ could get better help in America where the church is more modern. And my brother might have guessed about my own situation, but I don't think he knows." Sean's voice softened and slowed. He dug his toe into the old brown shag carpet his sister said needed replacement, as he waited for the question that he had just baited.

"I don't understand. What's your situation?"

Sean sighed with a silent prayer and dove in. "It's been this way since I was little. I promised God I would never do anything... you know... anything sexual. I swore chastity until I got married and had a family." Sean stopped. He averted his gaze away from the priest's scrutiny. He didn't know how to verbalize his quandary. Saying it out loud would make the admission true. Once it was out there, he wouldn't be able to take it back. He squirmed as he searched for words.

"Are you trying to tell me you're gay?" Father John asked kindly. "It's pretty common. I've helped lots of men find solace and forgiveness for those sexual feelings." His face softened, and he leaned forward slightly toward Sean.

"I don't know. I don't think so. Oh, God... how can I say this? I'm not attracted to grown men."

"It's ok, whatever it is, you will be forgiven. I can help you work through it."

Sean looked up, believing for a split second that he had found help before sinking again into doubt. *But will they really help me? Will anyone help me, or will they think of me as a monster?* He couldn't bring himself to tell Gus, not really, but a priest should be safe, maybe. Nobody else was safe, not even a therapist or a doctor. Even if Father John rejected or ostracized Sean, the sanctity of confession bound the priest to silence. Sean had been attending the local Catholic church for years and he trusted Father John. He sincerely believed the Father was strong, ethical.

"You will think less of me, but I can't keep this to myself anymore. I need help. Not just JJ, I need help, too."

"No, I won't think less of you. I've heard everything, so you won't surprise me. Let me help."

Sean gathered his thoughts by staring out the window and willing tears away.

"I can't help it. I'm sexually attracted to boys, to children. Not men, children." Saying it out loud was new, but the attraction wasn't new. Often Sean wondered if his sexual growth had been stunted somehow, perhaps by the incident in Liam's basement. As Sean's emergent sexuality developed, the source of his attraction never changed. Children often explore developing sexuality with their peers, and as they grow older, they remain interested in companions of comparable age. Sean did not experience that growth, rather, his sexual interest remained as it was when he was a child, with children. He'd been too afraid to ask, and even had he found the courage, there was nobody he could trust enough to ask.

The priest's face went slack; he didn't respond but leaned back, brought his hand to his chin, and looked away. Sean took a breath and lifted his eyes to the man who appeared lost. The silence niggled Sean; he couldn't remain quiet any longer. He gulped at the air before words tumbled from his mouth.

"I don't want to be like this, but this is how I am. I don't know how anyone can say God didn't make me this way. It sure feels like that is how I was made, and I don't know why. Do you still love me? Does God still love me? How can anyone love me?"

"Yes, you are loved. God loves his children and knows they make mistakes…" The priest's words trailed into an awkward silence before he continued with a stammer. "But tell me, have you done anything about it? I mean… anything sexual… with kids?"

With disappointment, Sean realized the priest was more concerned about potential child victims than about Sean's plight. He knew Father John was not required by law to report possible child harm if the information was disclosed during a penitential communication, but Sean wasn't sure this discussion legally qualified as a confession. Sean posed no threat to children and never would.

"Father, is this confidential? Like confession, even if we aren't at church?"

"Yes, Sean. I'm bound to keep our discussion confidential. You are safe to tell me whatever you wish, but I'm concerned about the welfare of children." The priest's voice remained soft, but his words became stiff.

"I understand, but you need to understand that I've harmed no children. I am not a rapist." Sean remembered sitting in his church in Ireland, his childhood promise to God, the promise of chastity. With diligence, he had kept that promise. "But, I love boys. I want to be sexual with them, but I'm not because I know it's harmful, and I love them. I don't want to harm anyone, particularly the boys." Sean's words tumbled from his lips.

"Yes, it's harmful to kids and to you because it's a sin. If you've acted sexually outside of marriage with a woman, confess your behavior and seek forgiveness."

*He doesn't believe me. He thinks I've molested boys*, thought Sean. "I haven't done it. I want to sometimes, but I haven't." Sean pled for understanding. He tried to make the priest believe him.

The priest cocked an eyebrow as he looked at Sean. "But your job is working with boys. How can you do that?" he asked.

"How do regular men work with women? Are all men rapists? What, are they supposed to never be around women because they have sexual attraction? But for me, I'm not allowed to be around children?" Sean was adamant. "I am not a rapist!" He knew he would get this response from the priest. Everyone thinks about the children. *I get that; I love them so much. But nobody ever talks about a person who has sexual attraction to children. Nobody wants to help me. Everyone would be horrified if they knew. I would be ostracized.*

"I understand," said Father John.

*No, you don't.*

"So that's why my brother sent my nephew to America," said Sean. It was time to get to the point. "My brother sort of knows about me. He knows I don't hurt anyone, and he thought maybe I could teach JJ," Sean said.

"Sort of knows…?"

Sean shrugged.

"But it hasn't worked out," Father John said.

"Exactly, JJ is different. He doesn't care about the kids. He worries me. I can't reach him."

"Some men need intensive help. The church has programs for some of its priests that can't seem to stop. You know, the bad ones. They are removed and treated. Maybe JJ is like that."

"I hoped you could help, that maybe the church could help. I hoped there's a simple answer to help me, to help JJ," Sean said. The other Father John, the one in Ireland, had guided Sean through childhood. He was invariably there with kindness, but even he didn't have a solution. The American Father John was also always there with kindness, but he didn't seem to have a solution either. If a solution existed, it wasn't obvious, and it wasn't simple. Chastity alone wasn't good enough anymore.

The door flew open. JJ and two of his friends burst in, laughing loudly.

Sean stood up. "JJ! What the—" Sean stopped himself from using profanity in the presence of a priest.

"Hey, Sean, hey, Father." JJ giggled. "Me and my mates wanted to grab a bite. We're hungry."

*Damn, he's stoned again*, thought Sean. He could tell the priest saw it, too.

"You were supposed to come alone. This is when we're meeting with Father John." Sean spoke a little too loudly in his frustration.

"Sorry, Father." JJ giggled again. His friends giggled with him like this was the funniest thing ever. Sean blushed at the grown men acting like teenagers. His nephew was an embarrassment, an embodiment of his own failings.

"JJ, your friends have to leave." Sean walked over and ushered the man-boys out the door.

"Sorry, lads," JJ said. "I'll catch up with ye later." His friends stumbled out the door, still laughing, still loud. When they were gone, JJ's tone changed immediately. "Ye didn't need to go doing that now, did ye? Can't we do this later?"

"Come on in and take a seat," Father John said. His voice was quiet but firm.

Sean thought the Father was relieved for the interruption because it detracted from Sean's shocking disclosure, and Sean shared that relief.

"Yes, Father. What's this about?" JJ sat on the furthest end of the couch, as far away from Sean as he could get. Sean also took his seat, and the room was quiet.

Father John spoke first. "Your Uncle Sean tells me you had inappropriate contact with a young boy. He told me what happened." The priest commanded the room, speaking authoritatively. Sean could see he had no intention of letting JJ slip away from the confrontation.

JJ turned and glared at Sean, and raising his voice, said, "What the fuck? What the fuck did you tell him?"

"I told him the truth, of course." Sean had never lied to a priest. Even though JJ's question was rhetorical, the implications surprised Sean.

"Did ye tell him, Unc'? Did ye tell him that yer a kiddie-diddler, too?"

Nobody wanted to say it out loud, and the resulting silence was ominous. Father John again spoke first.

"Look, I already know. Sean already knows. Let's talk about you and what you should do. I take it you understand your actions were a sin?"

"According to you," JJ replied.

The priest pressed on, undeterred by irreverence. "You understand the boy might be harmed by what you did?"

"Nah, I didn't hurt nobody. Just havin' a little fun is all. Just horsing around. It's not a big deal. Anyway, the kid liked it, so I don't see what the problem is," JJ shrugged.

Sean sucked his lower lip so hard his shoulders spasmed. The lack of concern was inconceivable. How could anybody not prioritize protecting children, even if there was an infinitesimal chance of harm? Sean's eyes widened, and he realized, *JJ understands, he doesn't care.* Sean turned to the priest, hoping the church would have a solution this time. Surely, he had seen this before.

"Have you been to confession recently?" Father John asked JJ. "It would do you some good to cleanse yourself from the burden of your sins."

*Of course, faith is the solution*, Sean thought. Father John would encourage JJ to find salvation in Jesus. Sean's faith had provided him with the strength to remain chaste. Perhaps this would work for JJ, too.

"I don't believe in that shit anymore," JJ stared the priest down as he dropped the unthinkable bombshell. "Ye can't save me from nothing. I'll do what I like." JJ oozed hostility. "I'm done with this chat. Ye both can go to hell." He stood and stormed out, leaving the two remaining men stunned.

"I'm sorry, Father…" Sean began but couldn't finish his sentence. The priest walked over to Sean and put a comforting hand on his shoulder.

"Let's pray for him together," Father John replied. The men bowed their heads together while the priest called on the higher power for help.

*Please Lord, help my nephew find his way back to Jesus. Please help me keep the boys safe in San Diego.*

*Twenty-one*
# ROBBIE TESTIFIES
## 2022
### TRIAL

*I've dreaded and wanted this moment forever. This part will end soon, today, but it will still last forever. This will never be over, but I must take this step now. I can do this. I can do this.* Robbie clumped his beefy hands into fists to minimize the shaking.

"This is it, the big one. This is for the championship. You ready?" Ace turned his head to whisper at Robbie and Lupe.

"Damn straight." Robbie and his legal team stood for Judge Moore.

The murmuring dimmed as the judge took her place and settled into her chair.

"You may be seated. We are back on the record in *Santos versus the Athletic Association for Young Americans.*" The gallery was still fidgeting and whispering. Judge Moore glared at the squirming crowd with eyes that demanded attention. The crowd obeyed and stilled. Once she established her command, the judge turned her focus to Ace expectantly. "Mr. Elbridge, you may proceed."

"Thank you, Your Honor." Ace stood and straightened his suit jacket. "Plaintiffs call Mr. Roberto Santos." Robbie didn't need to turn around to know multiple eyeballs were staring at his back. He looked straight ahead, not making eye contact with anyone, but painfully aware of the mumbled whispers that followed him.

*Let them think what they want.*

Robbie shifted his focus to the small box next to the judge and walked over to it. He wondered how long he'd be confined to the witness stand. "It may feel like it takes forever," Robbie remembered Ace telling him when they had prepared for this critical moment. "But you will get through it. Whatever happens, I believe in you." Robbie took Ace at his word and the affirmation imparted strength.

The court clerk administered the oath to Robbie and asked him to state his full name for the record.

"Roberto Rivelino Santos." He sat down.

"Good morning, Mr. Santos," Ace began.

"Good morning, Ace, uh, I mean Mr. Elbridge." Ace and Robbie's eyes connected in a flash of understanding, but without smiling.

"Mr. Santos, do you understand what it means to testify under penalty of perjury, to tell your story to this jury of citizens here today?" Ace asked.

The citizens in the jury box scrutinized Robbie. He could feel their eyes on him and knew they were judging him, judging his integrity, honesty, character. But he didn't care because he intended to tell the truth in the best way he could, regardless. The truth was worse than any lie. *Lying would be easy. If I lied, we wouldn't even be here. This trial wouldn't be happening. But they might not stop the abuse if I don't speak out. I must explain, so they understand. They must believe me. Maybe these people, this jury, can make it stop.*

Robbie looked straight at Ace. "Yes, sir. I do."

"Thank you, Mr. Santos. You are the named plaintiff in this case against the Athletic Association for Young Americans, are you not?"

"Yes, sir. I am."

"What is your occupation?"

"Teacher. I teach fifth grade for the public school district."

"What is your connection to the AAYA?"

Robbie glanced briefly at the jury box before looking at Ace to answer the question. "I played soccer as a kid, me and my three brothers. I'm the youngest. We played with a club called FC Strikers. The FC is a European thing that means football club. Anyway, the Strikers were a member club of AAYA. It was a local sports team underneath the AAYA."

*Maybe I should explain more? Maybe I should stop talking?* Robbie remembered Ace telling him, *When in doubt, say less, stop talking, I'll do the work.* Robbie stopped talking. Ace knew what he was doing.

"Please explain for the jury in more detail the relationship between the team you played soccer on, FC Strikers, and the Athletic Association for Young Americans."

"The AAYA is the umbrella organization. They set the rules that the clubs and the teams have to follow. They handle all the clubs and teams in their association, for policies, rules, and stuff like that."

"And for how long did you play soccer with this AAYA soccer club?"

"From when I was seven until fourteen." He watched his folded fingers wiggle in his lap, then added softly, "I love soccer, but I quit playing competitively when I was fourteen."

"Mr. Santos, as the plaintiff in this case, why did you not sue the FC Strikers, the actual soccer club that you played for, in addition to the AAYA?"

"The Strikers don't exist anymore. The club fell apart for financial reasons. They had some financial problems."

"Is it your understanding that the AAYA took responsibility for the FC Strikers?"

"Objection," Vilipend blurted. "Calls for a legal conclusion."

"I asked about his own understanding, Your Honor," Ace said.

"Overruled." Turning to Robbie, she added, "you may answer the question to the extent of your own understanding."

"Well, I understand AAYA made all the rules. The coaching staff made sure teams followed the AAYA rules. We always did what they said."

"Mr. Santos, you have made profoundly serious allegations against the defendant. Please explain to the jury the basis for your claims."

"Objection. Calls for a legal conclusion." Vilipend's voice exploded before Robbie could open his mouth.

*Butthead!* thought Robbie. *He's trying to make Ace mess up, make me nervous. Well, it won't work.* Vilipend's squinting eyes landed hard on Robbie's. *Back at you, Butthead.* Robbie had faced the opposition lawyer, Vilipend, on a handful of occasions over the last few years, at depositions and hearings. Despite the tough questions, the snarky questions, Vilipend failed to crack Robbie, at least during the confrontation. Vilipend had pulled out every nasty trick possible, looking for any advantage.

Robbie had recalled the looks of contempt Vilipend had given him during the depositions when the Captain America-looking lawyers grilled him about his most embarrassing and painful moments as a child. The look on Vilipend's face telegraphed blame like he thought Robbie was responsible for the abuse, particularly after the defense lawyers learned Robbie was gay. Before that moment, it felt like Vilipend blamed Robbie for being black. Though nothing blatantly racist was said, Robbie was all too familiar with the elitist snarls and sideways looks. Vilipend had no qualms about exploiting Robbie's race, Robbie's gender, Robbie's sexuality, everything about Robbie, to find any viable defensive edge.

Even though Ace had said Vilipend was widely respected, Robbie perceived a smarmy man wearing an expensive suit. The man's voice was deep, which didn't fit his slight, thin bearing. His use of voice to command the room was remarkably effective. Inexplicably, he exuded an aura of royalty despite his decrepit appearance.

"Overruled. Please answer," Judge Moore instructed, interrupting Robbie's thoughts. Looking past her poker face, Robbie saw a flash of exasperation.

"I'm sorry, what was the question again?"

The judge nodded at the court reporter, who fumbled through the tape on her machine. Reading from the tape, she repeated the question verbatim: "Mr. Santos, you have made profoundly serious allegations against the defendant. Please explain to the jury the basis for your claims."

The judge turned to Robbie and asked, "Can you answer that based on your own understanding?"

Robbie took a slow breath. *I can do this; I can tell them what happened. Ace will get me through it.* He replied softly, "Yes, Ma'am, I can do that..." *... and away we go...*

The direct testimony went exactly as Ace and Lupe said it would, smoothly. Robbie told the story about what happened in the shower, what happened in San Diego, and what happened on a couple of other occasions. Although he had told these stories multiple, multiple times, to many, many different people, he still felt awkward, embarrassed. He just hoped the jury didn't read his embarrassment as dishonesty.

Robbie stared each jury member in the eyes, daring them to do the right thing, challenging them to judge him poorly, but looked away when he realized staring aggressively was inappropriate. Not yet. Robbie switched his focus to his hands, folded and fidgeting in his lap. He needed a rest, but Judge Moore wouldn't give him time. Ace had warned him he'd have to power through. No breaks while a question was pending, and none before cross-examination started.

"Your Honor, that's all I have for this witness. We reserve the right to recall for rebuttal," Ace said. His clear voice resonated throughout the courtroom. Robbie never doubted that Ace would pull through, and he had. Robbie was proud of him.

*We should all be so strong. After everything he's been through, he can still do this for me, for his father...* Robbie thought.

"Mr. Santos, please remain in the witness box. Mr. Vilipend, your witness," said Judge Moore. Ace returned to counsel table and sat down.

"Thank you, Your Honor. If I may request the Court's permission to remain seated during the questioning."

*Oh please, she already said it was ok. Butthead.*

"Of course, proceed," the judge said.

Vilipend's baritone boomed out of his decrepit frame. "Good morning, Mr. Santos."

Because it wasn't a question and Robbie had no desire to be polite, he looked at Vilipend without responding. Vilipend apparently didn't expect a response because he didn't skip a beat before launching into the questioning.

"Mr. Santos, I'd like to follow up on something you said earlier. You indicated that the FC Strikers club failed for financial reasons..."

"Objection," Ace interjected swiftly. "Lack of personal knowledge, foundation."

"Your Honor, this topic applies to the defense. If I may lay the foundation for the witness' knowledge on this matter, it will tie into the responsibility of the FC Strikers compared to the responsibility of defendant AAYA for the events that occurred." Mr. Vilipend replied before Judge Moore could rule.

"As I recall, the witness referenced this on direct examination. The objection is overruled. You may ask the question," The judge ruled.

Robbie glared at Vilipend and sat up straighter, ready for whatever might come next.

"Mr. Santos, we previously heard the testimony of your father, Mr. Agostinho Santos, regarding the financial situation of the Strikers. And you previously testified that the Strikers failed for financial reasons. How are you aware of the financial issues?"

"Only based on what I've been told," Robbie said.

"Isn't it true that your father caused the Strikers' failure by taking exorbitant amounts of money out?"

"Objection, hearsay," Ace said.

"Sustained."

One defense lawyer leaned in and whispered something to Vilipend, who listened briefly before speaking. "Very well, we'll move on to another topic."

*Got you there, Butthead*, Robbie thought. A micro-win was still a welcome win. Robbie steeled himself for the next onslaught. Usually, a defense lawyer will tiptoe around an abuse survivor, but not always. Ace had warned him that Vilipend might bet on juror homophobia and racism. It was risky, but Robbie was a gay man of color, fair game. Vilipend wouldn't dare aggressive questioning against a sexual assault survivor who was also a heterosexual white man.

Vilipend consulted his neatly typed notes. "Mr. Santos, isn't true that at the time your lawsuit was filed, you issued press releases about it?"

"Well, my lawyers did that."

"I'm not asking about the advice given by your lawyers. But it's true, isn't it? You approved making press releases?"

"Yes."

"And you've been interviewed, been on television, haven't you?"

"Yes."

"That's quite a lot of attention, Mr. Santos. Do you intend to sell your story for a book or television show?"

"After everything I've been through, probably not."

"But you've received offers to sell your story, haven't you? Very lucrative offers, in fact?"

"Objection, compound," Ace interjected.

"I'll clarify, Your Honor," Vilipend replied. Judge Moore nodded at him to proceed. "You've received offers to sell your story, haven't you, Mr. Santos?"

"No. I've been approached about that, but I wouldn't say that I've received offers, only discussions."

"Aww. Discussions…" Vilipend turned to the jury and raised an eyebrow. "Discussions that could give you more attention and more money, right?" He faced the jury to continue examination with his back to Robbie.

"Objection, argumentative." Ace said.

"I'll allow it. Overruled," the judge said. As always, she ruled without hesitation and without doubt. She turned her gaze from Vilipend back to Robbie, obviously engaged with Robbie's testimony.

"I don't know," Robbie answered. "I haven't agreed to anything." His voice wavered, but he kept his chin up. *Oh my God. Would you want to be violated, raped so you could expose your shame to everyone? Is that really what people think?*

"But you could sell your story if you wanted? This lawsuit, this trial might be quite lucrative for you."

"Objection, Your Honor, this is badgering," Ace said. He stood as he pled his objection.

"Sustained. That's enough, counsel. Move on," Judge Moore ruled.

"Yes, Your Honor," Vilipend said.

*He's sneering again, what a snarky sneering slimy snaky shark.* Robbie shivered instinctively, but a hint of a smile turned his lips in response to his silly mental alliteration.

"Mr. Santos, when you were a child, your parents asked you about the alleged assault didn't they?"

"Yes, they asked."

"And you told them nothing happened to you, didn't you?"

Robbie trembled, but Ace and Lupe had prepared him for this question. He would answer honestly. "Yes, when I was a child, I lied to my parents about it." He stopped, even though he wanted to say more because Ace had told him to say as little as possible under Vilipend's questioning. Every question could be a trap.

"So are we to take the word of a confessed liar, that you were lying then or can we infer you are lying now?"

"Don't answer that." The Judge interjected before Robbie could speak. "Mr. Vilipend, you will withdraw that question as argumentative, and I will have no more of that in my courtroom. Move on."

"Yes, Your Honor," Vilipend conceded. "We will change topics. Mr. Santos, are you married?"

"Yes."

"And your wife is here today in the courtroom?"

*Fuck you. Fuck you. Fuck you.* "My husband is here."

"Oh, your husband…" Vilipend turned again, addressing his comments to the jury. Again with a raised eyebrow, Vilipend asked, "So you are in a… same sex marriage?"

Juror Six snapped his head up at the question and glared at Robbie.

"Yes." Robbie refused to look at Juror Six or at Tony. Rather, he narrowed his eyes on Vilipend.

"Were you always homosexual?"

"Yes, because that is how God made me."

An audible snort came from the jury box, Juror Six no doubt, though Robbie refused to look at the jury for confirmation.

"Your Honor, move to strike everything after 'yes' as non-responsive," Vilipend sneered.

"Denied. Move on, counsel." Judge Moore clipped her words and wrinkled her forehead. Robbie could see that she was weighing how far to let Vilipend go with this questioning, but Robbie knew where this was going and he was ready. He sat up a little straighter and met Vilipend's eyes.

"So the incident in the shower, you were homosexual when that happened?"

"I was eleven."

"Did you know you were a homosexual when that happened?"

"I think so, maybe, but I was only eleven years old."

"And you agreed to shower, get naked, with a grown man. Isn't that correct?"

"I was eleven. He said I should shower after the workout."

"But you weren't forced? It was your decision?"

"Yes."

"And it was your decision to participate in masturbation, wasn't it?"

"I was only eleven. I didn't know." Robbie's head dropped, and he stared at his feet, wondering why this had to be so hard, so weird. In his peripheral vision, he noticed Juror Six was shifting uncomfortably in his wooden chair.

"Please answer the questions. I'll ask again. Did you ever say, 'No'? 'No, I won't do that'?"

"No, I never said that." Robbie forced his head up, forced himself to look at Vilipend, unaware he was biting his lower lip as he did so.

Vilipend locked eyes with Robbie, then turned again to his typed notes.

*Ha! You looked away first; I win.* Another micro-win, another iota of strength, and he was still there, still standing, still fighting. The nightmares would doubtless come again tonight, and come again for weeks, but Robbie was still there, still fighting. *I can do this.* Robbie snuck a furtive glance at his husband, who was watching intently. Tony winked and Robbie suppressed a smile, opting instead to breathe deeply, slowly. *Thank God for Tony, but focus, focus.*

Vilipend and his legal associates had their heads together, whispering, shuffling papers. Vilipend nodded his head at his colleagues before he looked up at Judge Moore. "That is all we have for this witness on cross-examination, Your Honor. But we've listed Mr. Santos as a hostile witness for the defense, so we reserve the right to recall him."

"Very well," the judge said. "Mr. Santos, you may step down, but you are not free to leave. They may require your further testimony."

"Thank you, Judge," Robbie said. As he tried to stand, his knee buckled, his legs shuddered. After raising himself an inch, he sat again, closed his eyes, and took a breath. *I can do this.* He opened his eyes, smacked his hands on the armrests, and pushed himself up forcefully. Willing himself strength, he focused on each tortuous step back to counsel table. All his efforts concentrated on keeping his back straight, his eyes dry, and forcing one foot in front of the other, as every person in the courtroom stared. One step, another step…

Once Robbie settled back with his legal team, Lupe surreptitiously patted his hand and Ace looked at him with a slight nod.

"Mr. Elbridge and Mr. Vilipend, I understand there are special considerations related to the next witness, is that correct?" the judge asked.

Ace stood. "Yes, Your Honor."

Turning to the jury, the judge said, "We have some preliminary matters to discuss with counsel before we can proceed. I will dismiss you for a short time while we work these issues out." She turned to whisper something to her clerk as the lawyers stood and the jurors exited.

"The bailiff will prepare the courtroom for an incarcerated witness," the judge said. "And we'll be in recess until then." She nodded at the bailiff, who acknowledged the instruction with a return nod.

Robbie had agreed to face his rapist, and after some discussion, Tony supported that decision. Now Robbie doubted his strength to face what would come next. Though Robbie's exhaustion had robbed him of his usual coping mechanism—humor—he still had Tony. *Thank God for Tony.*

*Twenty-two*

# REPORTED

# 1998

Gus frowned at the stack of papers on the desk in front of him; his tummy rumbled with hunger. Gabi wasn't the best cook, but she would feed the boys something, probably delicious takeout from a favorite restaurant. Gus sighed and looked out the dusty window at the darkening soccer fields, empty late in the evening. He'd rather be home eating with the family, but the wretched, never-ending paperwork desperately needed his attention. He'd already missed a few bogus paperwork deadlines.

Unaccustomed to office work, he thumbed the stack of papers grudgingly and stretched his back. *Even when I hire people, I still have paperwork. It never goes away.* The Strikers had converted a small farmhouse bedroom into an office. It wasn't comfortable and was rarely cleaned, but Gus spent little time there. Gus preferred being outside, where he could move his body in the sun and feel the softness of cool grass under his feet. Being outside was even better with companionship, with kids, colleagues, everyone having fun. His office was lonely, stuffed with gray filing cabinets and a small steel desk. The visitor's chair was empty.

Gus thought he was alone at the clubhouse and jumped slightly when someone knocked on the closed door to his office.

"Ya, come in," Gus called out. He welcomed a distraction from the tedium.

Coach Sean entered the office awkwardly and plopped down in the only visitor chair stationed in front of Gus's desk like he had a thousand times before. But something was different this time. Sean's face was pale, his expression stern. He smelled like sweat, nervous sweat, not sweat like you get from a good workout, but the kind you get from stress, sharp and sweet. "Hey, saw the light on and thought I'd stop in. I need to talk. Do you have a few minutes?"

"Sure. Can I grab you a beer? Everything ok?" Gus asked. He reached under his desk for the mini-fridge that he kept under there. He didn't deal with late-night paperwork often, but when he did, it helped to have refreshments.

"Yeah, that'll help. Everything isn't ok."

Gus popped open a couple of beer bottles and handed one to Sean. "So, what's the word?"

Sean took a quick swig of beer, then set the bottle on the edge of Gus's desk. "It's not good." He faltered and kicked at the floor with the toe of his running shoe. "Damn it, Gus. It's not good." His voice rose and quivered. He swallowed hard and looked Gus hard in the eye.

"Ok, hit me. Whatever it is, we'll figure it out." Gus had never seen Sean like this. He was typically easy-going. Even when he was pushing the boys, his tone was never harsh. Sean's intensity surprised Gus. But it wasn't quite anger, not quite. Gus couldn't read Sean but registered serious trouble. Sean's usually perfect hair was tousled, strands out of place, and the rims of his eyes were red. Damn if Sean didn't look like he was going to cry.

Then he began. "It's JJ…" He stopped there for a second, then began again. "It's JJ, he molested one of the lads."

"What the hell!" Gus exploded, his eyes wide. "What the hell happened? How do you know?"

Sean's words jumbled hurriedly as though speed-talking might lessen the blow. "JJ told me himself. Well, I asked him about it because something was wrong. I could tell something was off. He told me he touched Josh Martin; that they jerked each other off. He showed Josh how to do it."

"Ok, slow, slower. When did this happen?"

"I'm not entirely sure, sometime over the summer, I think. After JJ came over from Ireland."

"Does Josh's family know?" Gus asked.

"I don't think so. Joe would have said something. I can't imagine Joe keeping quiet about something like this."

Gus considered Sean's point a good one. Josh's dad, Joe Martin, was a blusterous man, homophobic. He sometimes seemed violent when a referee made a bad call, or an opposing player was vicious, then cheered the Strikers' players for the same vicious play. Joe would bring down the house if he knew.

"Should we talk to Joe, tell him what happened to Josh?" Gus asked

"Shit, I wouldn't want to be the one to tell him. He'd kick my ass."

Gus nodded. Violence was definitely a possibility. But maybe it wasn't that bad. They'd figure it out either way by investigating.

"Was it only Josh? Do you know? Were there other kids?"

"I don't know. I don't think so. JJ only told me about Josh." Sean grabbed his beer and drank quickly before continuing. "Damn it, Gus. I'm so sorry. I should have known better and shouldn't have brought him here. He needs more supervision than that."

"So, what do we do now? Maybe we should tell Joe," Gus replied.

"Ya, that's probably the right thing to do, but I don't know how he'd react. Things could get ugly. I don't know. I don't know what to do."

Gus considered what might happen if Joe found out. He would be angry for sure. He might cause enormous problems. Joe wouldn't let something like that slide. He was unreasonable, even though it was just kids goofing around, as kids do. True, JJ was not a kid anymore, but he acted immaturely. JJ was barely an adult, barely drinking age. There was a ten-year difference between JJ and Josh. It didn't seem like much. Josh wasn't hurt. *It was only masturbation. Boys do that.*

"Is Josh ok?" Gus asked.

Sean shrugged. "He seems fine. He's a tough lad."

Gus agreed. Josh was a strapping boy, strong. *Anyway, children heal easily.* He couldn't imagine anyone taking advantage of Josh against his will, particularly scrawny JJ. "Kids are resilient, Josh will get over it. Do you know how often this happened?"

"No. JJ didn't say, but hopefully only the one time. We keep close tabs on the lads. JJ is almost always with me," Sean replied.

"We shouldn't say anything yet, at least until we know more. It sounds like it only happened once and not to any other kids," Gus said. "But JJ can't do that again. You must be clear. He absolutely can't touch kids again."

"Abso-fucking-lutely. Soon as I can, I'm hauling his ass to church for confession. I already talked to our priest about what to do. The church has experience with this stuff, you know, what you're supposed to do. He said we need to pray and get JJ to church more."

"Good idea," Gus said. Gus had faith in the church, a value shared with Sean. Both men believed in God's power to forgive and the priests' ability to guide them through tough times. The church was their safety net. Taking JJ to church was the best course.

"But you know, the priest didn't say what to do outside of praying and church. It seems like we should do something else. Are we supposed to report this to somebody else?" Sean asked.

Gus considered the question. It was a good one, and he didn't know the answer. "Maybe…" Gus swiveled in his chair and began rifling through a neglected stack of papers on the filing cabinet behind him. "I've got the Association manual here somewhere. Here it is." Gus held up a thin, wire-bound notebook with a translucent plastic cover over the page bearing the Athletic Association for Young Americans logo. He started flipping through the pages, mumbling. "Injuries… no, that talks about sprained ankles and stuff, get a doctor. Behavioral problems… no, that talks about the asshole kids, kick them off the team. Blah blah blah…" Gus continued to flip through the manual, looking for any useful advice as Sean watched. After a few minutes, Gus shook his head and set down the notebook. "I see nothing saying we have to report to anyone, not the Association, not the police, not anyone." He handed the notebook to Sean.

Sean searched the manual with more attention than Gus had given it. The office was silent as Sean carefully reviewed the table of contents and the index. He even read some entries out loud. Nothing was on point. Nothing even came close to providing needed guidance to the men.

"You'd think they'd address sexual conduct. Did they ever say anything to you? You know, like in case it happened, what to do?" Sean asked.

Gus scratched behind his ear as he considered the multiple Association meetings over the years. Every time the Association rolled out a new policy, they'd hold boring meetings, or phone calls, or seminars, or something. Not that Gus paid close attention, but he would've remembered discussions about sex abuse. The Association never mentioned sex, he was certain.

"No, nothing," Gus said.

"Maybe we should talk to Steve Elbridge? He's a lawyer, so he'll know what to do."

"Hmm," Gus pondered whether they could trust Steve with this information. He decided they could. Steve had shown himself to be dependable and would have the club's best interests at heart. Steve hadn't seemed phased by the banter about club contributions that time at the pub. Still, any discussion involving sex abuse would be ridiculously uncomfortable. Gus dreaded the thought of opening that can of worms. "Josh didn't get hurt, so there aren't questions here. I trust Steve, but we can't take the chance this gets out. We've had problems enough with rumors." Both men thought about the flyer.

"I don't know; it seems like we should tell somebody about this."

*Shit. He's right*, Gus thought. "Ok, let's call Steve." Gus picked up the phone and dialed. No answer. Gus hung up. "Maybe I should leave a message?"

"Ya, do that."

Gus called again. Still no answer. After the beep, Gus left a message: "Hey Steve, Gus. We've got a situation here and need to talk to you urgently. It involves possible sexual abuse… I shouldn't say more until we talk. Please call me right away."

"I feel like we should do more." Sean pressed. "We should send a report to the Association."

*Shit. Right again.* "Ok, I'll email the national administrator." Gus pulled out his keyboard and played hunt-and-peck for an inordinate amount of time while Sean waited.

"Mark it as urgent so they get back to us immediately," Sean said.

"Good idea. Ok, done and sent. Let's wait until they get back to us about it before talking to Joe or Susie. The Association can guide us through the next steps."

"Good idea, but should we report something to the police? Isn't this a crime?"

"Probably, but I don't know. It's just boys playing around. The police… that seems so serious. Maybe JJ would go to jail."

"Maybe, I don't know, probably... maybe that's where he should be," Sean said and hung his head in disappointment.

"Let's wait to hear from Steve and the Association. They will tell us what needs to be done."

Sean nodded. "I'm so sorry. It's my fault. I should've..."

"Nah, boys will be boys," Gus cut him off. He intended to reassure Sean, but Sean's head jerked up and if Gus didn't know better, Sean was glaring at him. *Did I say something wrong?* Gus wondered.

"No, seriously, it's not your fault. You couldn't have known," Gus continued.

"No, damn it. It is my fault. I did know. I should have known." Sean barely choked out the words. "He did it to another boy, in Ireland, the masturbation thing, but that boy was older than Josh. JJ got caught. That's why my brother sent him away, so his family wouldn't be shamed. He thought maybe an American church could help JJ, away from home. But my brother doesn't know about me, about how I am, well I don't think so anyway..." Sean looked into Gus's eyes, then looked away quickly, grabbed the beer bottle, and emptied it with one last long pull.

*What does his brother not know about how Sean is? What's he talking about? No, it can't be that.*

Gus reached for a couple more bottles. This was a two-beer discussion.

"Do you remember the volunteer form we sent to the Association about JJ?" Sean asked. He scratched at the bottle's label, curling off one long continuous peel.

Gus shook his head.

"You didn't read it, I guess. They asked about any prior abuse history with kids. What they asked was about convictions."

"And?" Gus asked.

"Well, JJ was never convicted, but I put some information on the form anyway. Did you keep a copy?"

Gus shrugged. Maybe he kept a copy somewhere, but he didn't even know where to begin looking.

"I explained JJ had a problematic history, but we were working on it, going to church. I asked the Association to contact me, or you, if that was a problem."

"And, let me guess, you heard nothing?" Gus asked. "I know I never did."

"Right. Exactly. But I wrote it on the form, so if it was a problem, they should have told me. I really didn't think JJ was a threat, but I disclosed it anyway."

"Well, shit. They already knew about JJ." Gus processed this unexpected information. "Probably nobody read the form, they just stuck it in a file. Nobody paid attention." He said nothing more for a while. He tensed his forehead and sipped carefully at his beer. This was a bigger threat. Worse than boys horsing around, maybe JJ was a pervert. Maybe JJ would do something worse someday. Maybe he would molest Roberto.

*No, Roberto would tell me because he is a good boy. I would know if he were hurt, and my son is no fag. No, not Roberto.* With his eybrows squeezed tight, Gus tried to clear away frightening thoughts about his son; he refused to allow his thoughts to take that path.

Gus considered other consequences if it happened again. This kid had done it before so that makes it worse, it's a history. If word got out, somebody might investigate. The police might get involved. That might bring down the club. He had worked so hard to build the club's reputation and now that could be ruined—*would be* ruined. The shame of it would be unbearable. The family might have to move to a new neighborhood, maybe a new state entirely.

Nobody would send their kid to a club where they could get molested. The charitable contributions would stop. The sponsorships would stop. Gus and Gabi might have to repay the bank loan because of the guaranty paper they signed. Gabi wouldn't understand. They didn't have money without the Strikers, they might lose everything. More shame compounded on shame.

The club was everything. Without the club, Gus didn't have the income to support his family. Soccer was what he did, what he knew. His English was ok, but he still spoke with an accent. That accent added flair to his mystique as a soccer professional, but in other settings, the accent might be an impairment. He couldn't think of alternative options. The club had been so successful that losing it to a couple of masturbating kids would be outrageous. Donations would stop. But worse, somebody might scrutinize past financial practices.

*Somebody might look at the club's files, at all this paperwork. They might figure out what happened to all the money. It's my club, my money. I did nothing wrong, but they might accuse me, anyway.*

"JJ has to leave the club," Gus said.

"I'll send him back to my brother, back to Ireland. I'll tell my brother it didn't work out."

"That is a good idea. We can't be letting this thing happen again."

"Ok, but what about the San Diego tournament? This is last minute, but he shouldn't go," Sean said.

Gus nodded. Even though JJ was already registered and held multiple assigned tasks, if the team needed the help, somebody would step up. They could get by without JJ.

"The thing is, if he doesn't go, I can't go either."

"What? Why not?"

"He needs to be supervised because I don't trust him. I can't leave him alone at my house. I'm sorry, Gus, but I'll have to bow out. It's more important to keep JJ away from the children."

Gus tightened his brow over this new problem. Getting a replacement would be difficult this close to the tournament. Losing Coach Sean at the last minute would discombobulate the kids. They would have to lie to the kids, lie to the parents, and invent some plausible excuse for Sean's absence. At this late date, any reason would arouse suspicions. It might affect how the kids played. Why jeopardize the Strikers' chance to bring home more trophies?

"We need you. The boys need you. You can't back out now."

"But JJ…"

"I think it will be ok," Gus said. He couldn't keep the doubt out of his voice. *Nobody was hurt; it was just masturbation. Boys do that all the time.* "Let's watch him, though. Never leave him alone with the kids. That should be fine."

"I disagree. JJ shouldn't be around kids he can abuse. I should back out. I'm so sorry."

"No. You are the best coach in the state. We need you—the kids need you—at this tournament. You made a commitment to the children that you must keep. We can figure everything out later."

Sean nodded and one blond lock of hair landed over his eye. Rather than fix it, he took another swig of beer and stared at the floor.

"Ok, Gus. You're the boss, so it's your call. I'll do it. I guess I'll just have to watch JJ closely; we both will." Sean rubbed his hands on his thighs as though wiping off collected moisture.

Gus looked at Sean closely. It was clear that Sean was distraught. The Strikers had to work hard to bring in a European coach. Gus thought a Brazilian coach would have been a fantastic boon for the FC Strikers, but club parents were more excited about bringing someone from Europe. Gus figured that was the secret code, the dog whistle, for rich, white parents who wanted someone white, but he went along with it. Sean had done a fantastic job for the club and a fantastic job with the kids. The boys all adored him. Sean had a natural ability with children.

But it was more than that. Sean had become his friend. They were together frequently, socializing and working. Their mutual love of soccer connected them. Their Catholic faith and immigration status connected them. Their mutual devotion to the boys connected them. Gus did not want to punish his friend. *He is taking this too hard. It sucks, sure, but it's not that bad. It isn't his fault.*

"No worries, man. You handle JJ and don't kill yourself over this. Like I said, we'll work through it. We keep a lid on this thing and that's the end of it. Let's not talk about this again, at least until we hear from Steve and the Association," Gus said.

"Thanks, man. I'm so sorry for all this. Thanks for listening." Sean finished his beer and tossed the bottle in the full garbage bin next to the desk. He stood to leave. "See you around."

"Yeah, see you around," Gus said.

After Sean left, Gus stared at the ubiquitous papers strewn across his desk. He shifted in his chair uncomfortably and reached out to grab a random page. The paper shook in his hand unseen as Sean's words replayed in his head. *Fuck this paperwork. I'm going home*, he thought. He clicked off the light, then shut and locked the door before walking out to the car and heading home.

*Twenty-three*

# THE PRISONER (PART 1)

## 2022
### TRIAL

Sean pulled the hood of his old gray sweatshirt up and kept his head low. It wasn't sweatshirt weather, too warm, but Sean thought hats might be forbidden inside the courtroom. Hoodies might be acceptable—doubtful, but possible. Not being devious by nature, he had no better ideas for eluding detection. His oldest brother had begged him to attend JJ's testimony. As much as he hated returning to California to revisit his ultimate failure, family came first. He promised his brother he'd show and report back. Time permitting, Sean might schedule a jail visit with JJ.

The gallery was crowded, but Sean spotted an empty spot conveniently located in the back. He slid his butt along the hard wooden pew which shone from the polishing of countless prior butt slides. Even better, he sat right behind a tall guy who blocked the view if anyone looked in Sean's direction. Sean immediately recognized Ace and Robbie, and after looking around, spotted Gus, Gabi, and Heather. He also recognized Team Mom Susie, who had not aged well. She appeared deathly thin and her once bouncy, shiny hair looked brittle and dull. Her son, Josh, sat next to her in his military fatigues and—unlike his mother—looked fit, obviously the result of an intensive physical fitness regimen. Sean slumped deeper and tightened the hood's lasso string.

Peering out under his hood, Sean switched his attention to Gus, who had not aged a day. Gus and Gabi, inseparable as always, hunched together, holding hands. Sean's mouth tightened as he remembered their friendship. Unexpected regret struck Sean, who had never mourned that loss. He had not considered the pain of seeing lost friends. Suddenly, Ace's head snapped around and looked right at him. Sean barely had time to duck.

*I don't think he saw me*, Sean thought. He peeked out enough to see Ace's eyes searching about the gallery. *No, he didn't see me. Thank you, Lord.* Sean instinctively bent, pointed, bent, and pointed his index finger, a minuscule gesture no less whole-hearted but less conspicuous than a full-scale Sign of the Cross. He rubbed his moistened palms on his pants.

Sean hadn't seen the old Strikers gang since he had moved to Boston for the seminary. Priesthood hadn't worked out for Sean. His church provided minimal psychological support to priests who had acted on their pedophilic attractions, and none for those who abstained. The irony—or perhaps the hypocrisy—of that never sat well with Sean who ultimately felt compelled to leave but not completely turn his back on the church.

Determined to find explanations, Sean had turned his attention to studying psychology and the counseling arts. Despite years of study, he found scientific research about people sexually attracted to children scarce and conflicting. The researchers all agreed on one point; no "cure" exists for pedophilia and the limited treatment options are largely ineffective—assuming the goal is to eliminate the attraction. But why have that goal? Why should there be a "cure" for those who abstain? People have all sorts of unusual fantasies and sexual attractions that are never actualized and don't require a "cure." Regardless, Sean resolved he should stop working with children and, as much as he missed them, he did exactly that.

Research on pedophilia historically focused on offenders, and the incarcerated, but Sean was no criminal, and maybe JJ wouldn't have been a criminal in a better world. JJ had pled guilty to burglary and because the crime involved a firearm, and wasn't his first offense, his sentence was long. The District Attorney had dropped the sexual assault charges for a guilty plea, but Sean had little doubt that JJ had raped the middle-aged woman who lived in the house JJ tried to rob. Professionals would study psychopathic JJ during his incarceration for his narcissistic proclivity for sexual assault, but was he studied as a rapist or a pedophile? Sean knew JJ was not a pedophile because JJ was not specifically attracted to children. Therefore, by definition, JJ was no pedophile. Rather, JJ was an opportunistic predator and children were easy prey. How could JJ ever have understood his own problems, his violent sexuality? What chance did JJ ever have to stop himself from offending? Would it have been possible to teach JJ how to control his urges, how not to offend?

And professionals had offered Sean plenty of contempt but no help as he struggled to understand his own sexuality. Even the professionals couldn't understand the difference between someone like Sean and someone like JJ. Sean never found sufficient safety in seeking help, only hatred, bizarre, crazy, and irrational hatred.

*What can men do against such reckless hate?*

The ammonia tactic—sexual aversion therapy, he had learned— was nothing more than bullshit at best, pointless cruelty at worst. The best Sean could do was remain vigilant in protecting children and keep his chastity promise to God by staying connected to the church. But he didn't have to remain silent—maybe anonymous sometimes—but not silent, because silence is the friend of abuse. He had discovered multitudes in the muted community of non-offending, minor-attracted persons. Together, they would research, study, and educate how to protect children using a scientifically accurate understanding of human sexuality. His path wasn't easy, but at least he had discovered a support network.

From Sean's extensive studies about childhood sexual abuse survivors, he made suppositions about Robbie, Josh, and the others. He knew Robbie must have undergone tremendous psychological work to accumulate strength enough to accuse JJ. The survivors that Sean spotted in the courtroom—including Josh—and others following the television press coverage would all be in different places of recovery, unlikely as advanced as Robbie, who was advantaged with a loving, supportive family. Unabused family members of the survivors would endure their own difficult and guilt-laden path.

Sean turned his attention forward when the bailiff announced Judge Moore's entrance and the gallery stood.

"You may be seated," the judge said. She squinted at her computer monitor, adjusted her glasses, and seemed to be scrolling while the room silenced. Eventually she peered over her glasses to look at Ace. "I understand that there is a preliminary matter to be addressed before we call the next witness. Mr. Elbridge?"

Sean again slumped, adjusted his hood, and settled in to watch the proceedings. He determined to remain a neutral observer with no expectations.

Ace remained standing while he addressed the Court. "Yes, Your Honor. With permission of the Court, Ms. Garcia has prepared to argue."

"Certainly. Ms. Garcia?" The judge nodded at the woman sitting next to Ace. Sean didn't recognize her, but apparently, she was one of Robbie's lawyers and worked with Ace.

The woman lawyer stood and adjusted her suit jacket. "Your Honor, the plaintiff would like to call Mr. JJ Geoghan to the stand, but the Defense has objected and has moved to request the Court to disallow the testimony, a Motion *in limine*," Ms. Garcia said.

"Very well." The judge turned her attention to Vilipend with a curious look. "Mr. Vilipend, this is your motion; go ahead with your argument."

Saul Vilipend straightened his shoulders and addressed Judge Moore. "Thank you, Your Honor. We object to the testimony of this witness as being unduly prejudicial. We expect the witness to testify about his role in the sexual abuse that occurred at FC Strikers. Plaintiff doesn't need this evidence. We're concerned that details related to the alleged abuse are graphic, unnecessarily disturbing to the jury."

"Ms. Garcia, what is your response to the argument?" the judge asked.

"Your Honor, I could make an offer of proof to the Court. However, the witness is available in the courthouse now. Since the witness is incarcerated, we had to make special arrangements to have him present here today. For that reason, I request the Court allow us to take *voir dire*, preliminary testimony for the Court to review *in camera*, outside the presence of the jury. With that background, the Court should have sufficient information for ruling on the Motion *in limine*."

*Well-spoken, smart woman… best I can tell from looking at her back*, Sean thought.

Judge Moore turned her attention back to Vilipend. "Is there any objection to this proposal, Mr. Vilipend?"

"No, Your Honor."

"Has the witness been advised by his counsel about this testimony?" the Judge asked while peering over her glasses at Ms. Garcia.

"Yes, Your Honor. We have confirmed that with the public defender representing him," Ms. Garcia responded. "His counsel was unavailable for court today, but gave us permission to go ahead in her absence."

"Very well. The court will review the proffered testimony of the witness. Do either of the parties wish to have the courtroom closed to the public for the hearing on the defense motion?"

Sean watched Ace lean into Robbie and whisper. Robbie's face tightened and Sean thought he saw a twitch in Robbie's shoulder, but Robbie nodded to Ace. Ace's shoulder also twitched, and he nodded to Ms. Garcia. Like a weird game of telephone, the message was passed along.

"Your Honor, this is Mr. Vilipend's motion, but the plaintiff has no objection to an open courtroom. We've instructed the jury not to watch the news, so if the press reports on any testimony given in Court, the jury shouldn't be impacted," said Ms. Garcia.

"Mr. Vilipend, my inclination is to keep these proceedings open to the public, but I will entertain any argument you have on that point. Courts have interpreted the first amendment on multiple occasions to require press access. However, that right may be outweighed by countervailing considerations. Do you wish to close the courtroom?"

"Your Honor, the Defense has no objection to an open courtroom," Vilipend replied.

One lawyer at defense table shook his head angrily at Vilipend, but Vilipend gestured him away, mouthing something indecipherable.

The gallery erupted into an excited buzz. The perpetrator's testimony would make sensational news. It's what everyone wanted to hear, the depraved pervert spilling out his lurid story. Artists in the gallery pulled out fresh sketch pads, pastels, and charcoal. Judge Moore had disallowed cameras, including cell phones, so the reporters had to make do with hand-drawn renderings. The evening news would include drawings of JJ.

*Great, just great,* Sean thought. *This will get to Ireland and my brother—the entire family—will see JJ on the news. My da' will see his derelict grandson trotted out for international derision.*

"Settle down," the judge snapped. The murmuring stopped, but not the shuffling, as the gallery obeyed. Reporters finished gathering their supplies and stopped fussing under the judge's glare.

"Ms. Garcia, you may proceed."

*They're having the woman lawyer question a rapist, interesting,* Sean thought. *JJ won't like her.*

"Thank you, Your Honor. Please have the witness brought out," Ms. Garcia said.

Judge Moore nodded to the bailiff. He stepped out and returned immediately with an armed police officer and JJ wearing an orange jumpsuit, ankle cuffs, and handcuffs. JJ had not aged well in prison; his skin had leathered like a man many years senior, which made his neck tattoos blurry. Or maybe that was just how prison tattoos looked. JJ's red curly hair had darkened and lay flat in greasy twists on his head. If it was possible, he seemed skinnier than he had looked twenty years ago. Sean shivered as though JJ brought a waft of frosty air with him. He noticed Ace and Robbie shiver in unison. *Weird.* JJ stepped into the witness box and sat down.

"Mr. Geoghan, please remain standing. Madame clerk, please administer the oath."

The clerk stood and walked toward the box, but not too close. "Raise your right hand."

JJ stood, held up his handcuffed wrists, and smirked at the judge.

"Please remove the handcuffs," the judge said. The police officer shrugged and complied without comment.

Sean noted the sneer on JJ's face. *Disgusting. He's loving this attention and the vacation from lockup.* JJ rubbed his red-striped wrists when the cuffs were gone.

After the clerk finished administering the oath, the judge asked, "Mr. Geoghan, do you know why you are here today?"

"I reckon it's got to do with them kiddies what got me in trouble a while back."

"You have the right to a lawyer, do you understand?"

"Ya, I don't want one. I told Robbie's lawyer I'd talk. I'ma do it."

"Well, okay," the judge said. She turned to Ms. Garcia. "You may proceed."

"Thanks, Your Honor," Ms. Garcia said, and began her examination. "Do you remember when you were an assistant coach with the FC Strikers?"

"Yes."

"And do you remember attending a soccer tournament with the team in San Diego in 1998?"

JJ sat up straight in the witness chair and stared straight at Robbie, the grin never leaving his face. He licked his lips before responding. "Oh ya, I remember well…"

Despite himself, Sean covered his ears and hung his head to his chest, perplexed by his irredeemable nephew, who refused to find salvation. Not for the first time, Sean despaired over his helplessness to rescue JJ. Then he remembered where he was. He looked up at Robbie, who was frenetically tapping the tabletop with his fingernails. *Robbie can sit through this, so can I.*

Sean uncovered his ears and clasped his hands together, keeping his head bent. *Lord, hear my prayer…*

# Twenty-four

# SAN DIEGO
# 1998

The road trip had been long and boring. Ace's excitement had worn off long before Mr. Santos pulled the big Navigator into the wide roundabout fronting the hotel. Ace peeked through the window from the backseat at the double-story, beige brick building where he would spend the next couple of days. It looked like many other hotels they passed along the way. Hopefully, this one had a pool. He brightened at the thought of swimming.

"You boys can get out, stretch your legs while I make sure everyone is checked in," Mr. Santos said. Robbie and Ace were already piling out of the car as he spoke. Mr. and Mrs. Santos exited with less speed and more stiffness.

"Look, Ace, they have cookies," Robbie said, pointing. "Last one there's a rotten egg." And with that Robbie was off the mark.

Through the glass entry doors, Ace saw a buffet laid out with coffee, bottles of water, and sure enough, cookies. The lobby was furnished with well-worn but comfortable-looking armchairs, tastefully arranged. In front of the buffet was an A-frame chalkboard with a picture of a soccer ball that announced in brightly colored chalk: "Welcome Strikers!" Energized by the prospect of unrestricted sugar, the boys bolted into the lobby to feast on treats laid out for their benefit.

Hanging out with Robbie had been better than riding with his boring parents and dumb sister, Lisa. He was mostly glad it worked out that way. Sure, having his mom and dad at the tournament to watch him play would've been great, but this was his first road trip ever without his family. Ace welcomed both the freedom and responsibility of his independence. Heading out for an entire weekend with his team was a big adventure.

The Martins—Susie, Joe, and Josh—had already arrived. Susie was busy at the front desk, coordinating all the player rooms and putting the key cards into envelopes for distribution to assigned parent chaperones. Even frazzled by the long car ride and rambunctious boys, Susie was beautiful in a casual sundress and sandals. She was in her element, the director of a complicated production.

"Hey, Gus," Joe said. "You need help unloading your rig?"

"Sure," Gus replied.

"Susie's got the team room already, so we can bring the stuff there."

The Navigator was stuffed with water bottles, snacks, ice chests, soccer balls, team flags, the works—enough for the entire team for the entire weekend.

"Such a good husband to give me such a big car. I love you," Gabi said, beaming with infectious enthusiasm. Unlike Susie, Gabi was immaculately coiffed and wrinkle-free. She had even applied fresh red lipstick upon pulling up to the hotel. Gabi suddenly gave Gus a big hug for no obvious reason. She could be unpredictably affectionate like that.

More players arrived as the men hauled ice chests and gear. Soon, boys—and the noises excited boys make—filled the lobby. Their first game started later that afternoon, so the kids had to be gathered, fed, dressed, and shuttled to the fields. They didn't have time to swim before the game, but maybe later.

"All right everybody, attention. Let's get the meeting started," Susie said. She fluttered about, doing her best to herd everyone to the meeting room. She added volume to her voice as an additional incentive to the chattering group. "It's the room down the hall." Ace was looking up at her, wondering at her fussing, her energy, her unending kindness. She noticed him watching her and smiled.

"Ace, honey, be a love, and help me get everyone moving," she said.

"Sure, Mrs. Martin," Ace replied. He started tugging at the boys, gently nudging them forward. "Come on, guys, I think they've got the snacks in there." Robbie bounced along after Ace, shirt spattered with cookie crumbs, laughing, joking, but also helping Ace with the herd. Eventually, the crowd meandered down the hallway to the hotel meeting room.

The hotel provided a handful of folding tables and multiple chairs for the group. Coach Sean was chatting with someone's mom about something or other. She seemed to be asking him a question. He gestured over at Mrs. Martin, who was busy fussing with the boxes of pretzels, goldfish crackers, and granola bars.

"Ok, everyone, a few quick announcements before we head out to the fields," Coach Sean spoke up, and the chattering subsided. "Susie Martin has already passed out the chaperone's shift schedules, room assignments, ride assignments to and from the fields. If you don't have it, there are extras over there." Sean pointed to the edge of a table with multiple sheets of paper neatly stacked.

"Four kids to a room and chaperones hold the room keys. Chaperones are responsible for all kids until they get turned over to the drivers. The drivers are responsible for getting the kids to the fields and back to the hotel, at which time, responsibility is returned to chaperones on that shift." Sean turned to Mrs. Martin. "Did I miss anything, Susie?"

"Yes, of course you did," Mrs. Martin laughed. "Parents, please remember that the chaperones have full charge of your children. If you need to pull your kid, you *must* check-in and check-out with the assigned chaperone." Susie held up a clipboard to illustrate the process. "Parents not on chaperone duty are kid-free, so enjoy yourself, but not too much." Snickering broke out among parents. "If you all have questions, you can ask me." Mrs. Martin waved at the group of parents from her snack-protection post. Without constant supervision, the snacks would disappear too quickly.

"Susie has done a wonderful job of organizing everything, so let's give her a big Strikers' Thank You!" Coach Sean said. Polite applause followed, and Mrs. Martin beamed. Ace closed his eyes and immersed himself in the effusive cheer resonating throughout the room. The Strikers started the weekend with an undefeated record. The boys rode the high of victory, confident in its infinity.

Even though Ace's teammates were excited about the upcoming game and the special privilege of being part of a premier club, and the parents were mostly happily chattering among themselves, something was off. Ace put his hand on his stomach when he felt an unexpected tightness there. He searched the room and found JJ quietly lurking in the back corner, watching the boys with a sneer. An icy pick of coldness pierced Ace's bones and spread throughout his body completely and instantly, like electricity. He shivered. Something wasn't right, but he couldn't figure out what.

*****

It wasn't yet dark when the team caravan crawled its way back to the roundabout at the hotel. As each car pulled up, handfuls of dejected boys crept out, dragging their backpacks. Joe Martin and Gabi Santos, the next shift of chaperones, counted each boy and made check marks on their clip-boarded sheets until they confirmed all the boys had arrived safely back at the hotel. Susie had assigned Joe and Gabi the night shift, which ended at eleven, late enough to ensure that lights stayed out after lights-out, and the boys were truly asleep.

"Can we go swimming, Dad? Please…" Josh Martin was begging his dad with a good whine.

"You played like shit. Maybe you should practice foot skills." Mr. Martin towered over Josh and glowered at him. Josh shrunk back, but before he could respond, Mrs. Santos interrupted. As always, she astutely read the situation and knew it needed immediate correction.

"Yes, yes, Susie has it right here on the schedule. We all go swimming! Come on boys, go get your swim trunks." She handed Joe a few envelopes with room keys and headed down the hall, unlocking the boys' rooms as she went.

Mr. Martin stared down at Josh, who was looking at the cleats he wasn't supposed to be wearing in the hotel.

"Git," Mr. Martin said sharply. Without waiting, he turned and stormed down the hall to help Mrs. Santos unlock the doors. Ace followed Mr. Martin because Ace needed to get his trunks and had the same assigned room as Josh. A refreshing swim might wash away the greasy grime of an ugly loss after the Strikers had gotten their asses royally kicked.

"Hey Joe, some of us are heading over to the hotel bar to grab a drink," one dad spoke up as he walked past. "You coming?" Ace wasn't sure whose dad that was. Keeping all the parents straight was difficult. This guy—athletic gear, Striker's baseball cap turned backwards, the works—was a generic soccer dad to Ace, just another somebody's dad.

"Can't now," Mr. Martin replied. "Stuck with the night shift for chaperone duty."

"Ahh man, I feel your pain," the soccer dad snickered as he walked away.

"Ya, whatever," Mr. Martin grumbled to himself.

A handful of boys pushed past in their swim trunks, running at full speed for the pool.

"Walk, goddammit," Mr. Martin shouted out from the doorway of Ace's room. "You're in a damn hotel." Hands on his hips, Mr. Martin looked like he might chase after the boys, but they slowed to a trot, so he didn't.

While Mr. Martin was distracted, Ace deftly ducked past him and into the room, determined to change as quickly as possible. Josh was there, sitting on one of the two queen-sized beds. The room was already a disarray of uniforms and miscellaneous garbage strewn about. Ace crinkled his nose at the stink of sweaty socks.

"Hey Josh, you swimming?" Ace asked.

"I don't know, I guess." Josh didn't move from the bed and didn't look at Ace.

"You ok?"

"Leave me alone," Josh snapped.

Ace had no words to comfort Josh over his father's nastiness. So, he shrugged, pulled off his uniform, and after rifling through his duffle bag, found his swimming suit and put it on. His entire uniform hastily dumped on the floor joined the sweat-drenched piles of discarded clothes from the other boys.

"Ok, see you there," Ace said and ran out the door. Josh seemed to take the loss pretty hard, and his dad was mean, but Ace figured he'd get over it and join the team at the pool soon.

Ace stopped running when he saw Mr. Martin in the hall and remembered the reprimand against running. Thankfully, Mr. Martin ignored Ace and entered the room with Josh, shutting the door behind them. Ace absorbed the anxiety flowing from the closed door and considered doing something, but what? Mr. Martin's yelling reverberated through the thin hotel walls, but Ace heard no sound from Josh. Befuddled by the lack of options, Ace walked alone to the pool.

He hoped Josh's dad wouldn't be too mean. Ace now understood why Josh was a bully sometimes. Josh got bullied at home. *I'm lucky my dad isn't like that.*

The hotel pool wasn't big enough for all the boys, much less anyone else. The team dominated the too-small pool to the exclusion of other guests. Moisture hung thickly in the room and gave it a subtle, dank, and slightly moldy smell, overpowering the hint of chlorine. Damp towels littered the tile floor. Mrs. Santos was there, ostensibly to watch the boys, but she was busy chatting with another soccer mom while the kids ran wild. Mr. Martin and Josh—apparently finished with their discussion—joined the party. *It's good everyone knows how to swim.* Ace not only was an accomplished swimmer but was well versed in basic water safety. That might come in handy, given the raucous horseplay.

A cannonball competition was underway for the biggest splash, but Ace didn't join the contest. He entered carefully from the shallow end steps, wading out to waist-deep water, and then went under. He swam slowly underwater, watching wide-eyed and avoiding the bodies bombing into the pool from every direction. The water embraced him, muffled the chaotic sound for him, and cleansed him.

Ace surfaced for breath and looked around. Nobody was telling the children to stop running or be quieter. Surely, the hotel people didn't like this behavior. Ace didn't want to be the spoilsport that ruined everyone's fun, so he decided he would watch in case anyone got into trouble and needed help. Maybe when he grew up, he could be a lifeguard and live on the beach, maybe even in San Diego. He had caught glimpses of Southern California's long sandy beaches on the drive down. Every glimpse triggered a yearning for the ocean. Maybe someday… San Diego.

Ace took another deep breath and once again submerged himself in the enveloping calm underwater. He swam around like a shark, watching legs kicking and water churning. But he was a nice shark, not a mean shark. He circled the perimeter on the lookout for distressed swimmers, but he would not attack. He was a hero shark. If someone needed help, Hero Shark would be there, silent and swift. Until that time, Hero Shark would continue its methodical circling.

The roiling water muted the bright colors of the boys' swim trunks as Ace carefully made his way around each twisting, splashing torso. The legs mostly looked identical, identifiable sometimes by the variation of flesh tones. A body bomb landed in front of him, but he deftly avoided it by changing direction. Then ahead of him was a pair of legs that didn't belong to a boy. They were adult legs, skinny, white, and somewhat hairy, red hair. That must be JJ.

Surfacing again, Ace spotted JJ and Josh splashing each other. They sliced the water hard with their palm's edge, over and over, each time sending a directed spray to the face. Their laughter masked the violence of each blow on the water's surface. Ace frowned. He took a quick look around to confirm nobody else needed the services of Hero Shark and dove again. With lidless shark eyes, he saw JJ grab Josh's wrist under the water and yank him roughly. There was a large bulge in JJ's shorts and he pulled Josh right up next to it. He made Josh touch his private parts. JJ grabbed Josh's waist and ground his hips into the captive child, all the while with Josh holding JJ's privates. The electric ice pick feeling from earlier, in the hotel conference room, hit Ace again, hard. His hand shot to his stomach. He felt nauseous. He needed air.

Ace shot up out of the water. *Did anyone else see that?* Nobody seemed to notice or care. The designated chaperones, Mrs. Santos and Mr. Martin—who was more relaxed now—were chatting poolside. Reclined on lounge chairs, they halfway paid attention to the swimmers. Ace assumed all the other parents had gone drinking with generic soccer dad and crew.

Ace didn't want to be Hero Shark anymore. He swam back to the shallow end, got out, and grabbed a freshly folded hotel towel from the stack a thoughtful somebody—probably Susie Martin—had brought out. He wrapped himself in the soft towel and stood dripping, allowing himself to absorb its comfort as it absorbed the chlorinated water from his skin. Looking back to the pool, he saw Josh had escaped JJ's clutches, and the two were swimming around, laughing, and splashing each other. *Should I tell anyone what I saw?*

Ace walked over to the chaise lounges where Mr. Martin and Mrs. Santos were happily conversing. Gabi's sunny nature had won over Joe, who was no longer cranky. *Mrs. Santos is nice. I could tell her what I saw*, Ace thought. It was a thing that should be told, but Ace was so overcome by its weirdness, he couldn't find the right words. As he stood dripping in front of the adults in the lounge chairs, Ace wondered if Josh would get in trouble. Ace had seen enough of Mr. Martin's meanness to be concerned. He quietly watched them chat and pondered possible word choices, but none seemed correct. Maybe what he saw was nothing. Maybe the adults would get mad at him for being weird about a weird thing.

A cannonball splash sprayed Ace and the lounging, chatting adults. The volume of the swimmers' shouts spiked, and additional splashes followed. Joe Martin looked up.

"Hey, keep it down or we'll get thrown out," he said. Then noticing Ace, he asked, "Do you need something, son?" Mr. Martin wasn't being mean, but anger lurked behind his words. Ace had observed that a shadow of anger followed Mr. Martin everywhere. Even something small might make him angry. Something weird probably would too. He might turn that anger on Josh. Maybe he would direct his anger at Ace. Suddenly Ace realized speaking up was a risk that could backfire on him instead of Josh or JJ. Maybe Mr. Martin would yell. Ace shivered and hugged the protective towel tighter.

"May I go back to the room? Can you let me in?" Ace asked timidly to either or both adults. Now that he was a coward, he couldn't look them in the eyes.

Gabi looked at her watch. "*Meu Deus!* We are late. We must head back now. It's time to get ready for bed." She stood and shouted, "All right, boys—bedtime."

Nothing. The kids kept splashing and playing, pretending they didn't hear. The noise became louder because they refused to acknowledge playtime's end. Mr. Martin stood up, stuck two fingers in his mouth, and whistled loudly. The room was suddenly quiet.

"Get out now," he shouted. Nobody wanted to cross Mr. Martin. They had all seen how he treated Josh. The boys quietly grumbled and reluctantly made their way over to grab a towel. Mr. Martin lined them up and began a march down the hall. Teeth would get brushed, pajamas put on, lights turned off and with no complaints, at least not to Joe Martin.

*****

As tired as he was, Ace couldn't fall asleep. Even with all lights out, the hotel room glowed. Light from the neon signs in the parking lot and street sneaked past the curtains, giving the room a strange pinkish, pulsating glow. The room wasn't quiet either; its thin walls did little to mute the endless sound of endless traffic outside the window. At one point, Josh unintentionally gave Ace a swift, but weak kick. Ace decided he might sleep better on the floor.

Ace gathered his pillow, grabbed a spare blanket from the closet, and made a nest, sandwiched in the narrow path between a queen-sized bed and the wall. Before snuggling down to sleep, he went searching for a spare bottle of water. Not finding that, he filled a plastic cup at the bathroom sink after pulling off the plastic sleeve. San Diego tap water tasted nasty, so he made a mental note to have a water bottle with good water nearby before bed the next night.

He heard tapping on the door. The knock was soft enough not to wake anyone sleeping, but loud enough to get the attention of anyone already awake. Ace wasn't tall enough to look through the peephole. He laid his hand open-faced on the door so he could channel a feeling, any feeling, from the other side. All he felt was the warm, smooth wood. All he heard was silence.

"Who is it?" Ace whispered.

"It's me, Robbie. Let me in, I'm locked out."

Ace hadn't noticed that Robbie had left. Wandering the hotel after lights-out without a chaperone was against the rules. The boys had left the chain lock on the door unfastened to allow chaperones unrestricted entry. Ace cracked open the door and peered out at a disheveled, pajama-clad Robbie in the hallway.

"Hurry, let me in," Robbie said. His hushed tone magnified the desperation in his voice.

"Ok, ok," Ace replied. He opened the door wider to allow Robbie to enter. "What are you doing out?"

Robbie pushed past him, straight into the bathroom. Ace's stomach flipped over, and his skin froze where Robbie touched him. Maybe Robbie was sick. Maybe he was going to throw up.

"Are you ok?" Ace asked.

Robbie wrapped his arms around his middle as though trying to protect himself against the pelting ice of a winter storm, and he flopped down onto the floor next to the toilet. He stared at the toilet and said nothing, but he didn't shut the bathroom door either. Instinctively, Ace wrapped his arms around himself, mimicking Robbie.

Robbie rocked forward and back with his chin on his chest, and he wanted to cry but couldn't cry through the pain.

*I feel pain like razors tearing me apart from the inside, but it's Robbie's,* Ace thought. *Robbie is hurting. Am I imagining this?* Ace's found the answer to his question when he saw the large bruise on the inside of Robbie's thigh.

Ace sank to the bathroom floor next to Robbie to share because maybe sharing would make it stop.

Yet there was something else, too. Something worse. This new feeling wasn't pain, wasn't obvious, wasn't sharp, and didn't cut. It crept up to the boys, first puddling around their bare feet. The feeling, like wet muck thick with the stink of sewage, seeped into their skin through their pajamas. It oozed over their shoulders and up their necks until it covered their heads like a moldy shroud.

Neither boy had ever experienced and had never channeled shame so deep. Like quicksand, the shame sucked them deeper into its swampy depths. Sludge filled the open and bleeding lacerations inside them, making way for infection to take hold.

*Something bad happened to Robbie.*

"What happened?" Ace asked. He gasped trying to lose the swamp feeling.

Robbie stared straight at the toilet and was silent, but he didn't tell Ace to leave.

"Should I wake up your mom or Mrs. Martin?"

"No, please, please don't. Don't say anything. Not to anyone."

"I don't know what happened, so I can't say anything, but you aren't okay. I think you need help."

"No."

"Okay." Ace sat quietly with Robbie, sharing his pain, just being there with him because that was all he could do. Mostly he said nothing because he didn't know what to say. The Hero Shark couldn't slay the bad monster Robbie was battling because that monster was invisible. Ace had no words for what was happening to Robbie, what he felt happening to Robbie. Just being there didn't seem enough, but there was nothing else.

"Where did you go?" Ace asked.

"With JJ. I don't want to talk about it."

"Okay," Ace said, for lack of anything else to say. The memory of JJ and Josh in the swimming pool came back to him. The cold shivery feeling that memory carried was like Robbie's swampy feeling, but not exactly the same. Still, Ace couldn't connect the events. *If I wasn't afraid to tell what I saw, maybe Robbie wouldn't have gotten hurt.* A twinge of guilt made itself known through the suffocating shame.

Eventually, Robbie pried himself off the floor.

"I need to go to bed. I'll be fine in the morning," Robbie said.

Ace grabbed another blanket from the closet, another pillow, and made another nest on the floor for Robbie, who curled up into it and became still. Ace nestled into his own spot and fell into a disturbed sleep. He dreamed he was Hero Shark, swimming around the pool, but the water wasn't clear and chlorinated. Dank swamp sludge filled the pool.

Slinking through the sludge, Hero Shark sensed an evil presence. Another shark was there, a bad shark. The bad shark attacked young swimmers, tearing at the flesh of their limbs. Ace was afraid of the bad shark, afraid to help the boys. He tried to help anyway, despite his fear, but he couldn't move. He couldn't breathe and drowned in the billows of blood flowing out from the torn bodies of children.

*****

"Stop it, Ace. Lemme sleep." Robbie rolled his back to Ace, pulling the hotel blanket over his head as Ace shook his arm.

"Get up. We've got a game this morning. Remember?" Ace peeled back the blanket to expose Robbie's closed eyes. "Come on, Robbie." Josh and the other boy sharing the room had already dressed and were lounging in the dual queen beds watching cartoons. They paid no attention to Ace and Robbie on the floor.

"Go away." Robbie's hand shot out to grab the blanket but came up with someone's damp sock instead. The smell just about made him gag, and the sock wasn't his, so he tossed it aside.

"If you're hurt, I can get your mom or someone. Are you sick?"

Robbie shivered under the thin blanket, unsure how to respond. He reached for a memory through the mire of pain, but it was gone. There was only soreness. He couldn't admit to Ace he had been hurt. If he told someone, there would be more questions. Questions he couldn't answer, not even to himself. If he didn't admit to being hurt, he had to get up and play. Robbie groaned.

"I'm fine."

"No, you're not. I can tell."

"No, you can't."

"Yes, I can."

"Whatever. Leave me alone."

"Dude, seriously…"

Four loud raps on the door rang out and Mrs. Martin, freshly showered, brushed, and blow-dried, clipboard in hand, marched into the room.

"Let's go. Breakfast, *now*." Unfazed by mounds of empty wrappers and discarded clothes littering the room, she shooed the other two boys out before looking over at Ace and Robbie. "Come on, guys. Robbie, why aren't you dressed? Are you okay, honey?" She switched to her worried-mom tone and bent in for a closer look, which meant Robbie had to choose; be sick or be okay.

"Ya, just sleepy." Robbie squirmed himself to a sit, expending unusual effort, and winced. He saw Ace wince but ignored that and looked instead to Susie's loving-mommy-eyes.

"Come on, honey. Let's get going now. Ace, be a love and help Robbie get dressed."

Ace nodded, but his face was tensed.

"Okay, I'll leave so you can get dressed, but I'll be right outside the door. You have five minutes." Mrs. Martin stood and backed away through the door, not completely closing it behind her. Robbie could see her back through the crack she left open.

"Dude, what happened last night? I know something happened," Ace whispered after she was gone.

Robbie squeezed his eyes shut. Something did happen. JJ was… and then it was gone again. Robbie swept the last wisps of unidentified memory from his mind. Not now. He had to focus on the team, the game, the tournament. There was so much going on. He sat starting, still sorting through multiple sensations, multiple events.

"It would be okay to tell Mrs. Martin. She's really nice. She could help."

"Tell what? What are you talking about?"

"You're hurt. I can tell."

"No, I'm not."

Ace sighed.

Robbie and Ace stared at each other. *How does Ace know? He always knows*, Robbie thought. He trusted Ace, but the words weren't there. His memory of the night before fuzzed into his dreams. Maybe it was just dreams and not the other thing. What would he even say? He didn't know the words for what that was, not even in Portuguese.

Ace took a deep breath and gushed the lyrics of a popular song about an all-star athlete, completely off key, and the sour notes hit Robbie in the head like a sledgehammer.

"Oh my God, Ace stop—you can't sing."

"Dude, get up." Ace toed Robbie through the blankets.

*He's trying to make me feel better*, Robbie thought. And it worked; the earworm had invaded Robbie's head. Once the music arrived, everything got better. Ace knew that would happen, even though he couldn't sing.

"I'll get up. Sorry." Robbie moved slowly but stood.

"Hurry up or I'll sing again." Ace handed Robbie his jersey and stuffed a couple of extra water bottles into Robbie's backpack as Robbie dressed. The boys barely made it out the door before their five minutes were up.

# Twenty-five

# The Prisoner (Part 2)

## 2022

### Trial

Sean didn't have a tissue, so he pulled on his sleeve and held it to his eyes to absorb the unexpected moisture. He hadn't heard the shocking details before. Those had been disturbing enough, but hearing them from his nephew's own mouth was horrific. More horrific was watching JJ speak, his tone, his body language. JJ's blatant enjoyment of retelling the San Diego debacle extinguished any flicker of hope Sean still held for his nephew. He dreaded having to tell his brother.

*I'll bet JJ masturbates in jail to that memory*, Sean thought. His gut flipped and a cough-like blubber escaped his lips. Violence against children made him sick. Sean pushed thoughts of rape away and forced his focus back on the lawyers. He couldn't look at JJ.

"That's all I have, Your Honor. That's the testimony plaintiff wants to present to the jury." Ms. Garcia stood until Judge Moore responded dismissively.

"Thank you, Ms. Garcia. Mr. Vilipend, do you have questions for this witness?" The judge asked.

"Yes, Your Honor, a few follow-up questions," Vilipend said.

"Very well, proceed."

"Mr. Geoghan, isn't it true that you came to America because your uncle, Sean Geoghan, who was also the team coach, was also known to be a pedophile?" Sean shoved his dampened sweatshirt sleeve into his mouth and bit down hard. He could never change that narrative, never shed that detested label.

"Ya, it were something like that," said JJ. He grinned at Robbie with a broad, self-satisfied sneer.

"Your uncle knew you had sexually assaulted children in Ireland before you came to live with him, didn't he?" Vilipend twirled the end of his thin mustache. His voice took a menacing, conspiratorial tone.

"Well, sure he did. My da' said as much." JJ turned his gaze back to Vilipend but kept smiling as though at a party. JJ was having a disgustingly grand time.

"Who else with the Strikers knew you and your uncle were pedophiles?"

*Damn it. JJ isn't a pedophile, he's a rapist. I'm the bloody pedophile,* Sean thought. *I'm the one attracted to children, but I'm not a predator. I'm not a rapist and I've never hurt anyone.*

"Objection." Ms. Garcia jumped out of her chair. "Coach Sean Geoghan was investigated but he never sexually assaulted children. JJ Geoghan acted alone. The defendant is held to know everything that Coach Geoghan knew because that knowledge is imputed to the defendant, but that's the only relevance, Your Honor." She remained standing, straight and firm, impressing Sean—and everyone else in the room—with her resolve.

"If I may respond, Your Honor?" Vilipend asked. The judge nodded at him to proceed. "Coach Geoghan and his nephew had a pedophilic conspiracy they hid from my clients. If this witness testifies, that information must also go to the jury." Vilipend sneered as though he had scored some major points.

*He's crazy. Pedophilic conspiracy? That isn't even a thing,* Sean thought, lifting his head. *Why does anybody think that's really a thing?*

"You think it benefits the Defense to prove there was a ring of pedophiles conspiring to assault the children on their soccer team?" The judge peered over her spectacles at Vilipend. If her sharp words didn't telegraph her position on the matter, her eyes did. The reporter-artists caught her expression and scribbled away on their pads. "I thought not. Continue, Mr. Vilipend."

"Surely Her Honor meant to say that—"

"Are you correcting me? Is that a shot at me counsel?"

Vilipend opened and closed his mouth like a fish, but he had no response. The courtroom became pin-drop quiet as Judge Moore glared at Vilipend.

"I've heard enough," the judge said suddenly. Her lips tightened, and she turned her bespeckled eyes to Ms. Garcia. "The defendant's motion *in limine* is granted. The Court finds that the proffered testimony of Mr. Geoghan would be highly prejudicial and confusing to the jury. Therefore, I will not allow this witness to testify."

*That has to be a good thing*, Sean thought. He watched Robbie, whose face turned dark. Robbie's hands were opening and closing in fists as he glared at JJ.

"Mr. Geoghan, you are dismissed. Bailiff, please escort the witness out. We are in recess." With that, the judge banged her gavel, stood abruptly, and left the courtroom. The door slammed behind her. The gallery loosened up with a collective sigh, but JJ held everyone's attention.

Sean puzzled through what had just happened. Apparently, JJ had finished testifying and wouldn't be required to return. Sean watched JJ rise and stretch his uncuffed hands over his head while surveilling the gallery. *What now?*

Following the judge's instruction, the bailiff and the police officer approached the witness box. JJ, still with the shit-eating grin on his face, lowered his arms and held his wrists out in front for the handcuffs. He sauntered out of the witness box, ignoring the cop's efforts to move him along. He walked straight toward Robbie, back the way he came. His ice-blue eyes gleamed as they focused on Robbie.

From his years of counseling trauma patients, Sean recognized Robbie's tensed muscles as a fight-or-flight response. Ms. Garcia put her hand over Robbie's trembling fist and whispered something to him. If she was trying to calm him, her effort failed. Every muscle in Robbie's body looked ready to explode. Robbie's lower lip quivered as he glared at JJ.

As Ms. Garcia spoke to Robbie, JJ sauntered past the table. Unexpectedly, JJ slapped his bound hands on the flimsy plexiglass virus barrier and flung it aside. JJ leaned into Robbie, stuck out his tongue, and flicked it wildly in Robbie's face, grunting profanely.

Robbie jumped out of his chair. He swung his fist back and smashed it into JJ's face. He brought his other fist around and hit JJ in the face again. JJ crumpled to the ground. He tried to use his hands to break his fall, but the handcuffs prevented that. Instead, JJ fell awkwardly on his side at Robbie's feet.

The bailiff and the cop each grabbed Robbie's arms and pulled him back. As he leaned back into the officers, Robbie kicked JJ in the gut. JJ grunted loudly. Then, as the officers backed Robbie away, JJ inexplicably started laughing.

"I should kill you, kiddie-fucker!" Robbie shouted.

Ace leaped out of his chair and held his palm up toward the officers. "I got this. I can take him out of here. Please let me take him out to cool down," Ace pleaded with the cop and bailiff.

"Good idea, Counselor," the police officer replied, stepping back for Ace to take over. Police weren't often sympathetic to child molesters and seemed inclined to let Robbie's assault slide as an infraction not worth their time.

"Robbie, *Robbie!*" Ace snapped.

Robbie turned his head to Ace. His eyes blazed.

No sound came from the gallery, not so much as a pencil scratch, though news ratings would skyrocket that night. Sean shrank into the bench, wishing to melt into the polished wood. In front of the courtroom and no longer the center of attention, JJ sat up on the floor. Blood leaked out of his face, down his nose, and onto his orange jumpsuit, where ruby brown blotches blossomed. His nose was bent and undoubtedly broken. His face was turning purple where Robbie had hit him. As the officers lifted JJ by the armpits to haul him off, dark red blood soaked into the beige carpet. JJ didn't stop laughing.

Ace gripped Robbie's forearm to guide him through the gallery to an isolated conference room. As they walked through the gallery to leave, Sean could hear Robbie tell Ace, "Whatever happens, that was so worth it."

Josh Martin was in the gallery and stood at attention in his camouflage fatigues, as they passed. Sean saw Josh and Robbie lock eyes. They shared a smile. Sean remembered the time twenty years earlier when Josh had punched Robbie. Apparently, adulthood had brought them a deeper understanding of their common plight.

"Good for you, man. I wish it were me!" Josh stood and called out to Robbie, raising a fist in solidarity. The reporters all started sketching Josh, and would no doubt soon flood him with questions.

As Ace was propelling him through the crowd, Robbie looked up and saw Sean.

"Hey, Sean, what are you doing here?" Robbie said.

Ace followed Robbie's gaze, and so did Josh. Multiple heads turned toward Sean as everyone wondered what violent action would erupt from Robbie next.

"Sean?" Robbie spoke again, louder. Buzzing voices erupted in the courtroom.

*Oh, Lord, they saw me*, Sean thought. *I have to get out of here.* Sean stood, pushed his way to the aisle, and ran out the door to avoid any further confrontation or violence. If the reporters figured him out, they would pester him unmercifully. He would have liked to connect again with his lost friend Gus, but that couldn't happen, would never happen, even somewhere different. Friendship was dangerous territory for Sean because intimacy leads to discovery, and discovery leads to contempt. Sean had learned that painful lesson from his destroyed friendship with Gus.

Sean knew it was best to leave, so he did. Having been long abandoned by friends, Sean had to find his own path. The Santos family would never forgive him—should never forgive him. Sean couldn't forgive himself for not protecting Robbie. Being a pedophile required no forgiveness; it was something he didn't want and couldn't change. While he had no say in the development of his sexuality, he had complete control over his actions. He had never touched—and never would touch—a child sexually.

Sean knew he shouldn't have returned, and he never would again. He ran back to his life without looking back. Reliving the pain of a lost friendship reminded him of his important work ahead. Maybe he could make a difference for others like himself if he kept working and ignored the near impossibility of his goal.

*****

Robbie trembled with anger, but Ace held him steady through the door and out to the hall, where Ace caught a last glimpse of Sean dashing away. The psychosphere dumped a sludge of putrid swamp water over Ace, who as an adult now fully understood this emotion as shame. But he also knew that it wasn't Robbie's shame. It was from somewhere else, perhaps a random feeling floating about, that he happened upon. Unlikely. Once Ace and Robbie slumped onto a hallway bench, Ace's hand went straight to his middle rather than to his rock. He had not forgotten the pocketed stone, but he wanted this one, this emotion; he wanted to know where it came from. Ace's hand trembled, he closed his eyes, and with focus, he deduced the feelings were Sean's.

*But definitely shame. Why shame? Why self-loathing?*

Ace shook his head, and it still made little sense. He expected Sean would exude guilt—and there was some of that—for not protecting the children from JJ. But the shame felt substantially stronger. Ace had always looked to Sean as a mentor and the best soccer coach in California, so why was he consumed with self-loathing? *Why?*

Ace gazed down the empty hall that Sean had just left and wondered if they would ever meet again.

*Twenty-six*

# BLOOD

# 1998

Heather held down the fort by her lonesome since Steve was still working in Chicago for an important client. Lisa, the ever-social child, was at a friend's house in the neighborhood, "hanging out," whatever that meant. Atticus was upstairs in his room, maybe still asleep in the late morning. He had come back from the San Diego tournament late the night before, exhausted.

Gabi and Gus had briefly filled Heather in on the tournament losses—a Strikers club disaster—when they dropped off Ace. They hadn't stayed to chat because they needed to get home, to get Robbie— sound asleep in the back seat—home. Heather had learned enough to let Ace sleep in. Losing is bad enough, but losing when you are playing poorly is the worst. The team was better than the performance they had delivered. Atticus had no obligations that day, no school, no soccer. She figured Ace would've finished his homework, and even if he hadn't—so what—the kid was getting awesome grades. A growing child needs sleep.

Since she had adequate staff coverage at the bakery, Heather also had no work obligations for the day. If the bakery needed her, she was only a phone call away. Her most urgent chore was defeating the laundry monster, that ruthlessly regenerative beast. Well, most urgent after getting some coffee. After pouring herself another cup, she began the trek around the perimeter to round up all the wayward towels, socks, t-shirts, underwear, and everything else strewn about the place. She could scrub the floors while the machines were running.

Ace's soccer backpack and duffle bag were in a pile near the front door, and she gathered those too. She had to make choices about the mountains of dirty cloth surrounding her in the tiny laundry room. Sorting laundry in her unique way, she would wash the smellies first. By tackling the nastiest tasks first and leaving the less disgusting work last, she ended chores with positive momentum.

Heather began by throwing her gym clothes in the wash because the person doing the work deserves fresh gym clothes. Lisa's gymnastics gear and Steve's running socks, shirts, and shorts went next. Finally, the washer still had enough space for Ace's soccer uniform. She zipped open his Strikers' backpack and pulled out the damp uniform, along with some random other items that didn't look familiar. Then again, she didn't take inventory of everyone's clothes in the house.

*Not. My. Job.*

She stuck her hand deep into the backpack and fished around the shin guards and cleats to find one last item of cloth that belonged in the washer, underwear. She almost shoved the tighty-whities into the wash without looking, but she didn't; she looked. And there was blood. She stopped and examined the streaks of blood on the underwear.

*What the hell? Oh shit, Ace must have been hurt.* She thought about this for a minute since he had seemed fine last night, tired but fine. The Santoses said nothing about him getting hurt. *Do little boys get hemorrhoids?* That seemed ridiculous. She dropped the red splotched undies on the washer and went to refill her coffee. As she stirred in half-and-half, she tried to fathom what might have happened. Ace was a skilled athlete, but he wasn't rough and tumble and reckless like other boys that age. She looked at her watch and decided Ace had slept enough for the morning. It was time for him to get up.

She climbed the stairs and was relieved to hear Ace already awake, brushing his teeth, such a good boy. He rinsed his mouth, spat into the sink, and grabbed a nearby hand towel that hadn't been clean for some time. Heather made a note to grab the hand towel on her way back to the laundry room.

"Hey, Buddy, how you feeling this morning?" she asked.

"I'm fine, Mom. We lost. We lost every game. That kinda sucked, but except for that it was good." He looked up at her and her heart melted. He was trying to be optimistic, to see the good in a sucky situation, such an endearing quality.

"Did you get hurt?"

"No, but I didn't play great. I mean, I was okay, but I wished it was better."

"Oh honey, I'm sure you played fine, that's not what I mean. I'm doing the laundry and there is blood on your clothes. How did that happen?"

"What blood? I don't know what you mean."

"I'm sure it's blood," Heather hesitated. "Lemme show you, come here."

The two went downstairs to the laundry room where Heather showed Ace the blood-stained underwear.

"That's not mine, Mom."

"It was in your backpack." Heather pointed to the backpack on the floor.

"That's not my backpack."

"Oh." They both stared at the mysterious backpack. Atticus picked it up for a closer look.

"Look, it's Robbie's. That's his jersey number right here. I must have grabbed his by mistake last night. He probably has mine."

"Did Robbie get hurt?" Heather asked.

Ace's eyes widened at the question. He looked stunned and didn't answer. Heather's mom alarm started beeping, lights flashing, and without being told she knew something was wrong. She knew it by the look on Ace's face, by his silence. Time to break out the mom voice: "What happened to Robbie, Atticus?"

"I… I don't know," Ace stammered. "Really, Mom, I don't know, but I think he might've been hurt, maybe." Ace mumbled these last words while looking at his tennis shoes and then volunteered a bit more. "He made me promise not to tell."

Heather squatted to look Ace in the eye. "I understand your promise to Robbie is important, but it's more important that adults know if a child has been hurt. We can only protect our children if we know, if we know what happened."

Ace remained silent and his little body stiffened perceptibly.

"What's my job?" Heather asked.

"To protect me and Lisa." Ace had answered this question multiple times.

"Gus and Gabi have the same job for Robbie. We need information to protect our children. Please help us out here, please tell me what happened."

Ace nodded his understanding. "Mom… I think Robbie isn't okay. I don't know because he didn't tell me, but he was acting kinda weird. Something mighta happened…" Her son let the worry for his friend pour out. He relayed the story of Josh and JJ in the swimming pool. He also told her about Robbie being with JJ after lights-out, and what they discussed—and didn't discuss—on the bathroom floor.

With each additional detail, Heather's hands clenched into fists, and her beeping mom alarms exploded into full-blown sirens. She focused on balancing careful listening with breathing—mindful breathing to silence the blaring sirens—but it took effort.

Heather weighed her words before responding. "Ok, Buddy. I'll call Gabi and find out if the Santoses have your backpack and I'll have to tell her. I know you don't want me to tell, but it's very important. It's part of my job as a mom. You did the right thing."

"Mom, I'm sorry I didn't tell what I saw in the pool. Maybe Robbie wouldn't have been hurt if I told. Maybe it's my fault."

"No. Maybe nothing happened. We don't know." Heather tried to sound convincing. "Anyway, if something bad happened, it most definitely was *not* your fault. Do you understand?"

Ace nodded but seemed unconvinced.

"I'll find out if he's ok, all right? And I'll tell you what I find out." She bent down to give him a hug for reassurance. "I'm sure he's fine," she added disingenuously.

"Thanks, Mom." Ace turned and walked away slowly.

*I can't hide anything from this child. He knows I'm worried.*

Heather fumbled through the scattered papers on the kitchen desk, looking for the team contacts sheet. When she found it, she sat down and dialed the Santoses' number. She allowed eight rings because somewhere she'd heard eight was the right number, not too long to be annoying but long enough for a person to get to the phone. No answer. She hung up the phone and drummed her fingers on the contact sheet.

*What the hell could the blood be? Why on his underwear?* She could accept any plausible explanation except the most dreaded, the most obvious. She considered calling Susie Martin to find out what happened in San Diego, to ask if anything had happened to Robbie, but instead phoned the Santoses again. Still no answer.

*Damn.*

She held the phone in her hand and started tapping it on the sheet. The tapping didn't help her think it through. Not entirely convinced she was doing the right thing, she found the Martins' phone number and dialed.

Susie answered. "Hello?"

"Susie, it's Heather, Ace's mom…"

"Hey Heather, we missed you at the tournament, but you picked a good one to skip. The boys were crushed."

"Well, actually, that's why I'm calling. Did, uh, did something bad happen at the tournament? Did any kids get hurt?"

"Oh no, honey. Tyler twisted his ankle, but he'll be okay. The kids are disappointed about losing, but I'm sure we'll do better at the championship games."

"No, I mean… Well, this is kind of weird, but the backpacks got switched and Ace has the wrong backpack. I'm doing laundry and I found underwear. There is blood in it, a fair amount of blood. Ace thinks maybe something happened to Robbie…"

"Oh no, honey, Robbie's fine. He was maybe quieter than usual, but he didn't play his best. So he may have been upset."

"But blood in the underwear…?" The line was silent for a moment. Susie was also stumped.

"Maybe he has some kind of condition or something. Did you talk to Gabi Santos?"

"Well, that's the thing, why I called you. I tried, but couldn't get Gabi on the phone. Ace thinks maybe something bad happened to Robbie, but he doesn't know what. This whole thing is weird."

"Are you sure it's Robbie's underwear?"

"Well, no. It was in his backpack, so I assumed."

"Every tournament the kids come home with different stuff. It could belong to any of them. The rooms are chaotic. Impossible to keep track."

"This is awkward, but there's something else you should know about your son, Josh. If it were me, I'd want to know."

Heather conveyed both the story about Josh Martin and JJ in the swimming pool and how Robbie had snuck out after lights-out.

"So, you see why I'm worried here. With the underwear, and all that… Well, I don't see how we can ignore what might have happened." Heather's mouth twitched with her jumbled words. *Breathe.*

Susie was silent on the other end of the line. After a few seconds, she mumbled, "Is Ace sure? He's such a good kid. I don't see him making it up, but maybe he thought he saw something he didn't really see."

"It's possible with all the horseplay in the pool, but I believe him. What should I do?"

"No worries, honey, I'm on it. I'll get it figured out."

Heather hung up the phone hesitantly. Susie sounded so confident, a true Soccer-World pro, and had been through lots of tournaments. Surely, she had seen all kinds of strange things like this. *But bloody underwear? Maybe I'm overreacting.* Heather drummed her fingers on the contacts sheet again as she thought about trying Gabi Santos one more time. *No, I'll let Susie work it out. Susie's a pro, I can trust her.*

Heather went back to the laundry room to focus on something productive.

*****

When Susie hung up the phone she dinged her not-yet-dry pinky fingernail against the receiver.

"Damn it," she said aloud to no one and reached for the nail polish to repair the damage.

"Josh!" She called for her son while opening the bottle and he was there before she accomplished that task. He had been there the whole time, listening, wide-eyed and silent. His white face was frozen in an expression she'd never seen on him before.

Her own eyes widened in a mirror of Josh as she searched his face for absent answers. Josh had apparently heard, but he didn't move, didn't respond, a statue staring her down.

"Sweetie, did you hear me talking to Mrs. Elbridge, Ace's mom?" Silence.

"She thinks maybe something happened at the tournament. Maybe something bad to one of the boys…maybe Robbie."

Silence again, but his marble face cracked before it hardened once more, and that caused a tingle behind her ears, momma Spidey-senses.

"Sit here." She patted the closest breakfast bar stool and Josh complied, still quiet. "Sometimes moms know things about their kids. I know that something's up. I see it in your face, so let's talk." She clanked the unopened nail polish jar onto the breakfast bar.

The bottle's clunk on the granite countertop startled Josh to the moment. He listened carefully, trying his best to make sense of her words. Something about bloody underwear, Robbie, men who touch boys in unnatural, wrong ways. The thunks in his chest thunked harder, faster. His tongue swelled, filling his mouth so full he couldn't speak and then he couldn't breathe. Insisting on air, his lungs forced a gasp from his lips and Susie stopped talking.

She reached for his hand, and when her fingers touched his, he jerked. Trapped, he had to think up something fast, an escape.

*She thinks it's Robbie, but it's me*, he thought. *I have to lie.*

"Momma, Robbie did something bad, but he told me not to tell. He said if I tell, he'll hit me again." Josh's eyes shifted from her to the floor and back again. He was the one that had hit Robbie at their special training session a while back, but he had lied about that and she had believed him then. Maybe stringing lies together stabilized, strengthened the story.

*This might work.*

"That's not going to happen again," Susie said in her reassuring mom voice. "I need you to tell me what happened in San Diego, please."

Josh kicked at the legs of the stool with his eyes glued to the floor. His mind spun with various plausible stories. Knowing the most convincing falsehoods are based on truth, the story he'd tell would be true. The lie would be that it happened to Robbie and not to him.

"Robbie let him touch him in bad ways, where people aren't supposed to touch other people." Josh held his breath hoping this story would pass muster.

"Who touched him, Josh?"

Josh twitched. He had not expected this question, which was obviously inevitable. He should have thought of that before and now he was trapped again. If he told the truth, his mom would confront JJ, who might confess what happened, that it was Josh, not Robbie, who was molested. Then everyone would know what Josh did with JJ. He couldn't bear that thought, but before he could puzzle his way through the problems, his mom offered the solution by asking, "Was it Coach Sean?"

"I don't know. I think so. It must have been Coach Sean. I think…" He stopped, but his mom patted his hand.

"It's ok, honey. Don't you worry about it. I'll take care of everything."

"Thanks, Momma." Josh jumped off the stool, but before he could take flight she continued.

"If anything happens, if you ever need to talk to me, I'm here for you. Has anything like that ever happened to you?"

"Not me. Thanks, Momma." He dashed away but turned his head before the final exit to add: "Love you."

He was gone before she could say "Love you too, Joshua."

## *Twenty-seven*

# RUMORS
# 1998

*L*aundry, check. *Floors cleaned, check. Shopping, check. Dinner, check.* Heather raised her hands high over her head, *stretch. Maybe some yoga now*, she thought. Then, *no, the damn bills. I'll pay the bills, then take a break and do some yoga.* Once again, there was one more thing. Heather turned on the family computer on the kitchen desk, a small counter hardly worthy of the moniker *desk*. As she waited for the computer to boot up, she sorted mail, separating the crap mail and the real mail languishing among the disorganized mess.

"You've got mail," the computer informed her in a friendly male voice.

*No shit*, she thought. She wondered, though, who would send her email. She received emails sometimes, but most of it was crap. Spam, they called it. Electronic junk mail was as ubiquitous as snail-mail paper crap. Heather gave her arms and neck a good stretch before she would read her email. *Yoga after this, just one more thing.*

Heather scrolled to the oldest unread email on her list, from outragedparent@usaprovider.com. Her eyes widened as she absorbed the message.

"STRIKERS PARENTS—DURING THE TOURNAMENT, ONE PLAYER WAS SEXUALLY MOLESTED BY THE COACHING STAFF. THE CLUB REFUSED TO TAKE ANY ACTION. BOYCOTT THIS CLUB NOW! PROTECT YOUR CHILDREN! SIGNED, AN OUTRAGED PARENT."

*What the hell? Oh my God, this must be what happened to Robbie, but why is it anonymous? Who sent this?*

She read the message again but couldn't tell who Outraged Parent might be. *What a chickenshit thing to do, hiding behind a fake email address.* A barrage of responses to the original email stuffed her inbox. Judging by the number of names listed in the "To:" line, Outraged Parent had emailed the entire club distribution list. It wouldn't have been hard to get, since the club sent multiple email updates showing everyone's email addresses. However, that meant every response and the responses to responses all repeated the list until the emails became ridiculously unwieldy.

*Tea.* Heather stood, filled a mug with water and a mint tea bag, then stuck it in the microwave. As her tea steeped, she wondered if this was the San Diego tournament. It must be; however, the email had apparently gone to every team from every different age group, dozens of teams, hundreds of parents. She didn't think the entire club went to the San Diego tourney. *Of course, they didn't. It was an invitation-only tournament, so only certain teams went.* The beeping microwave interrupted her thoughts. She took out her tea, settled into the chair, intentionally placed her feet flat on the floor, and took a deep breath.

Heather blew on her tea and read the next oldest email, sent via "reply-all" in response to Outraged Parent, ironically also from an anonymous email.

"WHO IS THIS? IT'S BULLSHIT TO SEND AN ANONYMOUS EMAIL. IF SOMETHING HAPPENED TO OUR KIDS, WE ARE ENTITLED TO KNOW. WHO IS THIS?"

She took a small sip as she read the next response, from a parent whose name she recognized.

"IT'S NOBODY. THIS IS A HOAX."

For over half an hour, Heather carefully read every single email. After making more tea, she went over the emails again, starting with the original Outraged Parent email. When she finished, she sat and looked out the window into the backyard. She obviously needed to talk to Steve about this development but was reluctant to pester him with drama.

She mentally categorized the responses:
First, most responders believed the Outraged Parent email was a hoax generated by a competing club that somehow got ahold of the Strikers email distribution list. These parents thought the abuse threat was nonsense, intended to disrupt the Strikers at the championship finals in two days. Why else would this be sent anonymously? This was just like that ridiculous flyer and smelled of a hoax. They called out for more support for the club, and investigation of Outraged Parent's identity.

Next, a couple of brave voices thought the club, or police, should investigate. They expressed discomfort with the behavior of some coaching staff; some might be homosexual. Old rumors still circulated that the Athletic Association for Young Americans was a bastion of pedophilia. Youth activities attract pedophiles, they said. The AAYA didn't do enough to detect and prevent, they said.

Finally, the last group of reply-alls was simply incoherent. At best, they sounded confused. This group merely repeated all the other points raised, contradicting their own points, or saying things that were completely nonsensical. Some raised wild accusations unrelated to the original email, as though Outraged Parent has invited everyone to dump every conceivable complaint on the club. Heather figured this group had nothing better to do than aggravate fear-mongering and contribute to the confusion. She disregarded those responses.

Heather reached for the phone to call Steve and as she did, it rang.

"Heather? It's Susie. Did you see the email?"

"Yes, I was trying to figure it all out. What's going on?"

"I asked about the blood. Only a couple of people, really. Only a couple. Maybe somebody jumped to conclusions. Someone said it could be rape, but it couldn't be, could it? Nobody else saw anything remotely like that."

Heather cut her off. "Wait. Slow down; are you talking about the underwear?"

"Yes, of course. I said I would figure it out, remember? Well, nobody has hemorrhoids or any other medical condition that would cause… that. And then, somebody thought it might be, well, you know… and then others started talking about that. Then it got out of control."

Heather didn't know how to respond. This was certainly out of control. Before she could think it through, Susie cut the call short.

"… be at the barn tomorrow at six o'clock for an all-hands club meeting. Gus will get it under control. We are going to get to the bottom of this and make sure all the kids are ok. Damn, I have another call coming through. See you tomorrow night." With that, Susie hung up the phone.

Heather tapped her index finger on the phone and contemplated her next move. She was going to call Steve. That still seemed like the best idea. Even though she didn't want to bother him, she yearned for comfort, for him to tell her everything would work out. Steve would not be sucked into a vortex of fear-mongering and rumors. She dialed.

"Hello?" Steve answered.

"Hi, do you have a minute to talk? Something happened."

"Only a minute, what's…"

Heather thought he asked what's up, but the connection was bad so she asked, "Can you hear me?"

"… bad connection… I can hear…"

"Steve, something happened with the Strikers. They are saying a kid was molested?"

"What?"

"The Strikers, Ace's soccer team… kid assaulted?" Heather tried to explain, but the phone buzzed erratically. She was unsure what he understood and what he didn't.

"Ace was what…"

"Someone on the coaching staff might have been molesting the kids. There is a team meeting tomorrow. Are you still coming home tomorrow?"

"… I can't hear you… this is a bad line. I have to go now anyway… call later…" His words were clipped, harsh. He may have even been shouting.

"Ok, I love you." Heather hung up the phone. The tone in his voice gave her chills. Maybe she was overreacting because of the soccer stuff, or maybe it was just the bad connection. She should've waited to talk to Steve in person. He was too busy to help her out with her own insecurities, her own uncertainty. Ace was well and safe, and the rest would get sorted out so she shouldn't distract Steve from his work. Also, some things don't translate over the phone. She scratched her temple to clear her head of the madness and turned her attention back to paying bills. *Just this last thing*, she thought, *then yoga*. Except the ringing phone kept her from both bills and yoga.

# Twenty-eight

# ALL-CLUB MEETING
# 1998

"I didn't do it, Gus," Coach Sean was pleading. "Really, you have to believe me."

"Get out! I never want to see you again." Mild-mannered, easy-going, Gus never yelled, but when he did, he yelled a lot. A stream of Portuguese profanity followed, accompanied by suggestive hand gestures.

Sean ducked. "Please talk to Robbie. He's a good boy. He'll tell you I didn't do anything. It wasn't me and it wasn't Robbie. I already told you about the problem. It was Josh and JJ."

Gus wasn't having it. "Get out now, before the parents come. Get out and never return."

Sean realized the parents would start arriving any minute for the meeting, so this wasn't the time to fight. He hoped to have a discussion later with Gus and salvage their friendship, but that wouldn't be today. "Okay, Gus. I'm leaving." Sean held his hands up in surrender. "Please talk to Robbie. He'll tell you it wasn't him and it wasn't me. You know he's a good boy. He'll tell you it's not true."

Gus swallowed hard and pointed at the door.

Sean paused after leaving Gus's office to look one last time at the weathered red barn on the Strikers fields, more than large enough to hold both the landscaping equipment and sports equipment the club needed. The club also used the barn for "all-hands" club meetings that included athletes, parents, and often siblings. The wide barn doors were swung open, showing off the central room, that had an updated floor and lighting. Club staff had spent the afternoon setting up all available folding chairs in the barn to accommodate the sizeable crowd they anticipated that night. Likely, there still wouldn't be enough.

But Sean wouldn't be there for the all-hands meeting that night. He turned his back on the old red barn and walked to his car.

*****

The parking lot and the barn were filling rapidly by the time Heather pulled up. Most kids, particularly the youngest ones and the non-soccer-playing siblings ran off to play on the soft grassy fields while the parents handled the boring meeting stuff. Heather had left Ace and Lisa at home. It was a school night. Not only that, but it would be unfair to subject the kids to this meeting. It could get ugly. Kids shouldn't see that. Still, the barn held many kids, some lazing about, some whining, and some doing homework on a small table set up in the back. Kids were everywhere.

She now wished she had spoken with Steve about the developments that led to this meeting. He texted he had to extend his trip by another day. While she admired Steve's client dedication—it's why he was an excellent lawyer—she worried about his health. Through the terrible connection, she sensed his stress. Whatever that project was, it was taking something out of him. She planned to talk to him about that this weekend when he got home. She resolved not to add to his worries if she could avoid it.

After parking her car, she walked over to the barn. She watched the children laughing and playing as she walked by and pondered the safety of their world.

*How many of you will grow up battling the hurt of your childhood? Some of you might not survive that battle*, she thought. Her abdomen tightened and turned with the *déjà vu* moment. Something about children not surviving… She stopped, shutting her eyes long enough for a couple of slow, deep breaths before heading into the meeting area.

Large groups of parents milled about inside the wide barn doors, their loud voices heated, angry. Others were quieter, sharing their conspiracy theories in whispers and with side-ways looks. She looked for a friendly face or a place to sit but, unable to find either, shuffled her feet awkwardly and considered leaving.

"Heather, Heather!" Susie called out to her. But she wasn't calling in her All-American, Soccer-Mom Barbie, Pilates Instructor sing-song voice. An unusual note in Susie's voice caught Heather's attention, and she looked up. Susie was wearing grubby workout gear, her hair disheveled. Her makeup showed minimal attention that certainly fell far short of her normal fussy grooming. Susie was waving Heather over, so Heather headed in that direction.

"I'm so glad you could make it. Everybody is upset. I can't believe it. I can't believe this is happening." Susie whispered to Heather. "Where's Steve? Is he coming?"

"No, Steve's working in Chicago. He's not coming home until this weekend," Heather answered.

"We should have a lawyer here. He'll be back for the State Cup game?"

"Absolutely. He wouldn't miss that for anything," Heather confirmed.

"Here, sit next to me, over here, before the seats are all gone."

The women found two seats together in the middle. Predictably, the prime seats in the back and along the aisles filled up first. They sat and Heather noticed Susie was holding a clump of damp tissues in her hands, wringing and twisting them into a solid glob. Susie's knees bounced up and down, her feet tapping incessantly.

"Are you ok?" Heather whispered. "You look upset."

"Oh, I am, I am," Susie replied. She looked like she couldn't contain her tears, and then she couldn't. She dabbed at her face with the damp wad of tissues. "I don't know what happened. Nobody knows what happened, but it's like nobody cares. I'm confused. Everybody is saying something different."

"That's crazy. We'll get to the bottom of it. For right now, Ace is safe. Your son Josh is safe. Maybe it's all a bunch of weirdness, with no explanation, but no harm."

"I don't know if that's true. That's the problem. I think this is bigger than we thought. We should call the police, but nobody wants to do that. It makes no sense."

"Gus will set it straight at this meeting. Then you and I are going for a girls' night out, to relax and have some fun. Everything will be fine. You'll see." Heather was unsure about the honesty of her statements, but wanted to comfort Susie.

"My husband doesn't believe any of it. He thinks it's all a hoax to hurt us at State Cup. He's furious about that. I don't know what to think—"

Before Susie could say anything more, Gus tapped loudly on the microphone. He sat at a large table in front with three other men: two coaches from upper age groups, and somebody Heather didn't recognize, maybe an administrator. Coach Sean wasn't at the table. Heather scanned the crowd but didn't spot him in attendance.

"Is this on? Can everyone hear me?" Gus asked. His voice echoed through the room and a hush dropped. "Ah hell, I don't need this." He set down the mic, stood, and walked around the table directly facing the crowd. The other men remained seated.

"Where's the faggot?" yelled an anonymous male voice from the crowd. Profanity-laced shouts erupted all around. Men stood as they yelled, with their fists in the air. A few women added their voices to the chorus. The children in the fields stopped playing to listen to the rising hostility.

Heather sat straighter, eyes wider, hands tighter, as though personally threatened. Nobody directed hostility at Heather, but it surrounded her like radiation from a nuclear detonation. She glanced at Susie, who had adopted a similar shell-shocked posture.

"Damn, looks like I'll need that mic after all," Gus muttered to himself. He turned to grab the microphone off the table before addressing the crowd again.

"All right, settle down. Settle down and we can address this thing." Gus sputtered into the microphone. "Watch the profanity. Your children are watching." The volume turned down, but the crowd was still not silent.

"Shut up, let the man speak," shouted another male voice. The shouting diminished into a few random grunts and grumbles.

Gus tapped on the mic again before he spoke. "Ok, thanks. We've heard the rumors that have been spreading and called this meeting to set the record straight," Gus began. Although the shouting had stopped, the whispering continued. Gus ignored it and continued.

"First, Coach Sean cannot attend tonight for a family emergency. He asked that I pass along his disappointment that he will also miss the state tournament. The coaches behind me have graciously agreed to coach Sean's teams this weekend. They will answer any questions that you have about the games, but I won't say anything more about Coach Sean's situation. As I said, it's a personal family situation, and he sends his apologies and regrets to everyone. That's the end of that subject."

*Sean is probably dealing with JJ*, Heather thought.

Gus continued, "The San Diego tournament was a disappointment, and I'm talking about the parents' behavior. We all need to consider the examples that we're setting for the boys. A few parents got drunk and did a crappy job taking care of the players. We allow drinking at events because most everyone is fine and is fun. But when a few people lose control, the fun ends. We may be forced to consider a drinking ban." The whispering continued, accompanied by shuffling feet. The crowd hadn't come to be lectured about excessive drinking, but Gus successfully contained the hostility, for the moment.

Heather looked around and spotted some parents she knew from Ace's team. It looked like everyone had come. She didn't recognize most other people there, parents from different teams in different age groups. Those who weren't angry seemed confused; perhaps they had missed the emails. She was sure, however, everyone on Ace's team had heard the rumors since that is where the entire mess apparently began. She saw anger on the faces she recognized.

"The Strikers are family," Gus continued. "We take care of our own. Our goal is to provide a healthy, safe environment for young athletes, to help them develop and grow into their potential. As they get older, the Club encourages athletes to pursue higher education. The Strikers have more scholarship players at university than any other club." Gus emphasized this last point. Most parents quieted at the unfailing lure of scholarship money, but a couple people made a show of walking out.

Heather had heard this before, several times. Soccer-World talk about college scholarships placated the parents, pushed the parents to push the kids. But Heather wasn't impressed with the opportunities manifested. Most players who advanced to college had ended up in academically mediocre schools with little or nothing in the way of scholarship money. Few played college soccer. She recognized the scholarship opportunity was a deception and a distraction. Clinging to that hope, some parents would tolerate any awful behavior from the club. She wasn't buying Gus's explanation.

"Keep that objective in mind here, let's keep our eye on the ball as we work through this." Gus leaned against the table. "There was an incident in San Diego. Some parents on chaperone duty over-indulged and weren't careful. The boys took advantage and misbehaved. We've spoken with the parents involved and it has been resolved. Everyone agreed parents are responsible for tournament chaperoning. The club is not responsible for kids off the field." Gus looked out over the crowd for possible opposition, but several heads were nodding, so he continued. "For now, we've decided not to ban drinking, but if something happens again, we'll have no choice. I called this meeting to reassure you we're on top of the situation and it's been resolved."

Heather looked at Susie, whose mouth was wide open above her wide-open eyes. Susie turned to look at Heather. Neither had expected this. This sounded to Heather like a bunch of mumbo-jumbo bullshit. *What about the rumors? The blood? Is Gus ignoring what happened? What did happen?* As far as Heather could tell, Susie shared her perspective, or maybe shared her confusion. Whether confusion or another emotion, Heather felt a connection with Susie.

A parent who had been fuming in the back stepped into the center aisle. "What about the fucking faggot touching the boys?" he shouted. "What are you doing about that?"

Again, the room erupted into shouts laced with profanity. Gus tapped on the microphone for quiet, which eventually came from the crowd, but not from the mic, which amplified the sound of Gus's fidgeting hands.

"There were rumors somebody on the coaching staff had touched a boy inappropriately. You remember, there was also a flyer put on people's cars a while back about Coach Geoghan. That was a lie. We've investigated it and found no proof anything happened. I've spoken to all the boys who went to San Diego, and they have said that nothing inappropriate happened." Gus let that settle with the group.

Heather switched her sight to Robbie, who shrank into the background, his face a frozen concrete mask. The childish joy, usually prominent on his face, had disappeared, along with his adorable dimples—swallowed by sunken cheeks—as though he was no longer a child. Gus and Gabi didn't seem to notice.

"We think another club has been spreading those rumors out of jealousy," Gus said. "They're trying to sidetrack us from focusing on the championship this weekend. The Strikers hold a commanding lead for state trophies. They can't compete, so they spread rumors. It won't work." Gus stood straight as he said this, his voice emphatic. "We need to come together to get through this. We have some games to win this weekend."

Heather stood to ask a question, to say "Wait, slow down. Something else is happening here. Something is wrong. You have to do something." But before she could get a word out, Susie's husband, Joe Martin, his face red and his chest puffed out, loudly shut down the parent who raised the objection. "We all know you were talking about Coach Geoghan, so why don't you say it?" he yelled. "We have the best soccer coach in the state. He's delivered championship after championship to our boys, and this is how you repay that? Where the hell is the gratitude? Sean is a hero to these boys. This is disgraceful."

Heather sat, afraid to speak, afraid of Joe Martin, afraid of his anger, afraid of the unrestrained, threatening testosterone-fest.

Gus beamed at Joe. The crowd shouted out their support for the club and for Coach Sean. Emboldened, and possibly drunk, Joe strode to the front. "Where is your loyalty?" he shouted. "Strikers has delivered championship after championship to your children. Coach Sean is the winningest coach in the state. Does that mean nothing to you?"

The group erupted into cheers. "Coach Sean! Coach Sean! Coach Sean!" they yelled.

Joe grabbed the microphone from Gus. "And Gus and Gabi have devoted their entire lives to the success of your children; does that count for nothing?" Joe smiled as he reveled in the tide's turn. "Go Strikers!"

Heather squirmed; her chair was suddenly more uncomfortable. She expected the meeting might get tense, but this direction was unexpected. What Ace had told her was substantially more serious, and it wasn't about Coach Sean; it was about JJ. She frowned as she tried to sort through the confusion. *Why are they talking about Sean?*

The momentum of team spirit filled the barn to its rafters. The children mimicked the enthusiastic support of their parents. Everyone was suddenly happy. They believed nothing had happened. Heather considered speaking up, but she refused to stand in front of that freight train. She had just seen how Joe shouted down one parent. She felt powerless to change the momentum of the mindless mob and knew better than to try. Speaking up could be dangerous when so many people were so adamant about their own "truth."

Heather and Susie looked at each other, then Susie looked down at her clumped tissues, lips pressed together. She was shaking. *What the hell is going on here? I know Susie knows what happened, I told her. I thought she would tell Joe… Surely Gus knows…*

"There is something else I need to tell you tonight. We have a little surprise for our supporters." Gus controlled the room once more. "As you leave, my wife Gabi, and my son Robbie, will pass out pennants with the Strikers logo for everyone."

Gabi, standing off to the side in her stiletto heels, waived a bit of colored cloth on a slim stick high in the air. Everyone looked at her. Her smile was infectious. "Over here, come get your flags." she called out dramatically. Children rushed up to get their swag. The room filled with excited, giggling voices.

Gus built on Gabi's enthusiasm. "I want to see Strikers' flags flying high at the tournament this weekend." Gus jumped on the table, waved one hand in the air, and shouted into the microphone. "That's right, everyone. We got this! We're gonna go out there and prove we are the champions of this state!"

The room exploded, the crowd leaped to their feet and shouted. But Gus shouted louder.

"Because—Who Are We?"

"WE ARE STRIKERS!" A boom of voices responded.

"Who Are We?" Gus yelled again.

"WE ARE STRIKERS!"

Robust cheers and multitudes of colored flags filled the old barn. But Heather noticed some weren't caught up in the *rah-rah* moment. A group of parents with serious faces congregated in the back and whispered. Disgruntled, and not so easily swayed, these parents didn't claim a flag. Heather watched them exchange slips of paper, phone numbers likely, and assumed something more would come of that budding underground resistance.

Heather turned to Susie. "We need to talk later, but this isn't the time."

Susie nodded in response. "Yes, this is weird. I'll call you," she said.

Heather stood and pushed her way to the aisle so she could leave. She watched Gabi and Robbie passing out pennants but decided against grabbing a couple. Gabi gleefully engaged with every person as she passed out the flags. Robbie stood behind his mom, looking at the ground like he wanted to disappear. Heather had never seen goofy, outgoing Robbie look so sad, so still, so quiet. Just like his parents, he was one to engage the excitement, not hide from it. Heather's observation confirmed that something bad must have happened to Robbie, just like Ace had said. But what?

*Fuck the stupid flags*, Heather thought, and she left.

On the way home, Heather tried calling Steve's cell phone, but voicemail picked up. *Is he avoiding my calls?* Then she considered he was probably exhausted, that she might add to his stress even though she needed him. *Well shit, I'm just about done being understanding. What the hell is his problem? He won't talk to me and left me to deal with all this crap by myself. When will he get home?*

*Twenty-nine*

# THE MOTION

## 2022
### TRIAL

Robbie sat alert at counsel table, resigned to the trial's rhythm and savoring the unexpected gratification of smashing JJ's face. Somebody should've done it long ago. *Josh Martin and Dad would've welcomed a few solid punches on that sorry piece of shit. But it was me, I did it.* Robbie smiled. He tried to imagine Ace hitting JJ—or anyone—but couldn't. Ace's ferocity found expression in verbal combat in court, not with fists.

Vilipend was finishing cross-examination on the plaintiff's last witness, a psychiatric expert on childhood trauma and sexual abuse. Adverse Childhood Experiences, the doc called it, ACEs. *How ironic is that?* ACEs were proven to cause various adverse health results under a bunch of studies, *blah blah.* The more ACEs a person had, the more fucked up their life would be as an adult. *Blah blah.*

Rape is an Adverse Childhood Experience.

*Ya think?*

Robbie sensed eyes, and sure enough, Ace was looking directly at him. Ace didn't need to speak. Robbie knew the look. Ace's face informed Robbie the trial was going well, exceptionally well. Vilipend was putting the jury to sleep.

*Everyone knows abuse harms children. Are they so stupid to dispute the expert's explanation?* Robbie's eyes returned the look to Ace. *I know everything's moving along. This is good for us.*

"Your Honor, that's all I have for this witness," Vilipend said.

"Mr. Elbridge?"

"Thank you, Your Honor. Nothing further," Ace replied. Robbie remembered Ace once saying that stopping when you are ahead is hard for lawyers who would naturally continue pressing forward. He trusted Ace's judgment, but he mostly was relieved the case was moving along. Glancing over at the jury, he could see the relief on their faces, too, except Juror Six who scowled.

The excused expert witness, another white doctor-looking dude, stood and left the courtroom. Robbie wondered what the bill for that testimony would total; he'd find out soon enough.

"Mr. Elbridge, do you have another witness?" Judge Moore asked.

"No, Your Honor. The plaintiff rests." Ace sat down.

"Okay. Mr. Vilipend?"

"Thanks, Your Honor. Before commencing our presentation, the Defense requests the Court hear a motion."

"Understood," Judge Moore said, as though she had expected this development. She turned to address the jurors over her spectacles and explained that they would get a brief recess so the lawyers could talk. Everyone waited while the jury exited the courtroom. "Mr. Vilipend, go ahead."

Vilipend did not stand, but his powerful voice compensated for his frail posture.

"Thank you, Your Honor. The defense moves under the California Code of Civil Procedure Section 581c for non-suit. Plaintiff has not proven his case and the Court should dismiss the lawsuit with prejudice." Vilipend held up a thin stack of papers, the written motion that his team had prepared.

*What the…* Robbie stopped the fingernail tapping and snapped his head to Ace. *They want to throw out my case? Now? In the middle of our trial?*

The judge motioned for the papers to be brought to her bench, and the bailiff accommodated her unspoken instruction.

"Proceed with argument, counsel," the judge said.

"Yes, Your Honor. As a matter of law, the plaintiff has not proved that the AAYA had any duty for his protection, and further has not proved the AAYA should be responsible for the Strikers. The Strikers were a separate, independent organization. They were in the best position to protect children under their care, not the AAYA."

Vilipend reached out for a paper passed by one of his colleagues. He scanned the note, nodded at them with a smirk, and continued.

"Moreover, the plaintiff's own father, the senior Mr. Santos, knew a predator was coaching the Strikers. He knew a child had been molested but allowed the predator to remain."

*Oh God, they're blaming Dad. Vilipend wants to throw out my case because of my dad's mistakes, as if that excuses the AAYA from their negligence.*

Vilipend straightened his jacket, sat up straight, and let his final point boom out of his atrophied body at a louder than usual volume, even for him.

"Your Honor, as a matter of *law*, as a matter of *good conscience*, Mr. Agostinho Santos is liable for harm suffered by his own son, Mr. Roberto Santos. The Court should throw out this case and require the plaintiff to pay for the AAYA's attorney's fees as sanctions."

"No!" a woman shouted from the gallery. Robbie turned to see his always dignified mother standing, palms open and raised in the air. She was shouting in Portuguese while tears flowed down her red face, leaving streaks of mascara.

The judge smacked the gavel. "Quiet! Quiet in the gallery, please."

Robbie buried his face in his hands. *Do you ever outgrow being embarrassed by your parents?*

Robbie's oldest brother stood, took Gabi by the elbow, and tried to steer her away. She yanked her arm away with another stream of Portuguese.

Lupe left counsel table to help, and together with all three brothers and Gus, they coaxed Gabi out of the courtroom.

Ace leaned in toward Robbie and asked, "What's she saying?"

"You don't want to know. Be glad nobody else here understands Portuguese," Robbie replied.

"I've never felt her get that upset before."

Judge Moore tapped the gavel with less force. "Okay. I understand these matters are upsetting, but please, if you cannot control outbursts, please do not attend the proceedings in person." She peered over her spectacles and gave the watchers a moment to settle. "Does anyone else need to leave before we begin?" Her steady voice, like her eyes, held genuine concern with no sarcastic notes.

No response.

"Fine, Mr. Vilipend, I believe you have concluded your argument, and your points are well taken with the Court. I see that the plaintiff's case may have some legal deficiencies, but I am going to allow Mr. Elbridge the opportunity to address those matters before making my ruling."

*Oh my God*, Robbie thought. *We are going to lose.* He couldn't see a path to overcoming the problems his dad's mistakes had caused. Robbie didn't fully comprehend all the legal mumbo jumbo Ace had explained, but he had always known Gus's poor decisions could be fatal to the lawsuit.

Robbie watched Ace making his way to the podium and thought about the no-look pass. He knew that somehow Ace would find and possess the ball. Ace would correctly position himself to receive the pass, even if Robbie couldn't see him. The hard part was passing on faith, but Ace always came through for Robbie. Ace was always where he was supposed to be. He always connected to the pass.

# Thirty

# CLOSING ARGUMENTS
## 2022
### TRIAL

Judge Moore found the plaintiff had shown insufficient legal support for the theory that by allowing a sexual predator to work with children, the plaintiff had created a dangerous condition in the community. Therefore, she had granted the defense's motion for non-suit but dismissed only the public nuisance claim. But, because California had extended the time limit for child sex abuse lawsuits, Robbie's claims of negligence and fraud survived. The jury would make the final decision on those claims.

It was time for closing arguments.

Ace sat ready at counsel table with one hand in his pocket, clutching the Brazilian black tourmaline. His fist opened and closed around it in pulses. The stone should have neutralized the nervous energy coming from Robbie, who was fidgeting, but it didn't.

*Maybe because I'm the nervous one, not Robbie*, Ace thought.

Later Ace would allow himself to collapse from the exhaustion of trial, fourteen-hour workdays, and late nights. Now was the time for the last push, the most important part, and he had ample energy for the task, too much energy.

Vilipend had not recalled Gus or Robbie to the stand. Their apparent strategy was to deflate the jurors' emotional responses and push forward points of logic and reason. But Ace knew better because he had surfed the waves of boredom emanating from the jury box. Deflating emotion is one thing, but putting the jury to sleep was a step too far.

At one point during Vilipend's examination, Robbie had looked to be nodding off. Ace had quickly scribbled on his yellow legal pad, ripped off the sheet, folded it in half, and passed it to Lupe, who had passed it to Robbie:

*PAY ATTENTION YOU DOLT.*

Lupe had delivered the paper with a gentle elbow jab in Robbie's gut. Robbie, good-natured as always, had nearly laughed aloud but successfully minimized his mirthful reaction to a slight smile. *Dolt?* Ace's stuffiness was unintentionally goofy sometimes.

After Vilipend concluded his defense presentation, Judge Moore had allowed a brief break for the lawyers to gather their notes, and for the jury—and judge—to take a biologically necessary respite. Ace had already written his closing argument but took a minute to consult with Lupe to add a few finishing touches. It was done. The judge and jury were seated, ready. Ace grasped his pocketed stone and breathed deeply.

"This is it, Ace, the big game. You ready to put the round thing in the square thing?" Robbie whispered.

"Damn straight," Ace whispered back.

"We are back on the record in *Santos v. The Athletic Association for Young Americans*," the judge said. "Counsel will now present their closing arguments. Mr. Elbridge?"

"Thank you, Your Honor." Ace stood and went to the podium, notes in hand. He set his notes on the podium, then stepped to the side. He wouldn't use props so stood empty-handed, with no stone, no notes, and faced the jury.

"Good afternoon. Remember at the beginning I told you a theme would develop. Now you know the theme is responsibility for protecting children. You will need to decide whether the AAYA is liable for failing to protect Robbie Santos from foreseeable, preventable sexual assault.

"First, the AAYA knew JJ Geoghan had a history of sexually abusing children. You recall his uncle, Coach Sean Geoghan, reported that to the AAYA *before* JJ joined the Strikers. That report is sitting in one of those boxes with thousands of others, untouched, unread, unattended to." Ace pointed at the stack of boxes between counsel tables that had sat unmolested and undisturbed by the defense since the first day.

"They never answered Mr. Gus Santos's email requesting instruction, begging for help. They ignored it the same way their lawyers ignored those file boxes next to their table."

"Second, despite knowing about sexual predation in their ranks, the Association never implemented policies and procedures designed to protect children. Why? Why didn't they? Taking protective action would have been easy—inform parents, call the police, inform the Association. And most of all…"

*One beat, two beats, three, here it comes.*

"Remove the predator. Protect the children." Ace turned to face Vilipend and repeated: "Remove the predator. Protect the children. But the Association failed to do that." Ace took a second to flip through his notes on the podium.

"If the AAYA had exercised due care to protect the children, we wouldn't be here. Robbie wouldn't have been raped as a child. He wouldn't have struggled with addiction, with binge eating. He wouldn't need a lifetime of counseling. What could that eleven-year-old child have been, a soccer star maybe? What other childhood dreams were sacrificed on the altar of the association's reputation?"

Ace stepped back and gestured to Robbie. "Look at Robbie. You can't see scars because the damage is on the inside. The damage is to his very soul."

Ace centered himself at the jury box and connected eyes with each of the twelve members. "No amount of money will return the talented child that could've been a college or professional soccer star. But none of us has the power to change the past. The best we can do for Robbie is compensate him for his suffering, his medical bills, his therapy. But you can do more, you can send the Association a message that they don't just get to stuff a report in a box and forget about the victimized child. The fertilizer of sexual abuse is secrecy, and the harvest is predictably tragic. We ask you to send the Association a clear message by awarding punitive damages."

He walked back to the podium and double-checked his notes before picking them up. "Whatever you decide, we thank you for serving, for listening, and for considering Robbie's claim. Thank you." Ace returned to counsel table, nodded at the judge, and sat.

"Mr. Vilipend, would you like to address the jury?" the judge asked.

"Yes, thank you, Your Honor." Vilipend took a sip from his water glass, grabbed his cane, pulled himself up, and shuffled over to the jury box. He didn't bother with notes.

"May it please the Court, counsel, ladies and gentlemen of the jury. Good afternoon. plaintiff's counsel told you this case has a theme, and it does, a theme of responsibility."

Vilipend took his turn to look every juror in the eye. They all met his gaze.

*Damn*, Ace thought. *They would've looked away from Vilipend if they favored Robbie. Then again, they all looked at me. What does that mean?* Ace quietly unfolded the note Lupe had passed to him. Not much of a note, it only contained one big question mark on the yellow-lined paper. *She's wondering the same thing. This jury seems to like Vilipend.*

"As I stated during my opening statement," Vilipend continued, "nothing is more despicable than childhood sexual abuse. But the juror's task is to separate emotion from fact. Emotions aren't facts. The *fact* is the AAYA isn't accountable for what happened to Roberto Santos." Vilipend turned his head to the gallery and several jurors followed his gaze to Gus.

"Mr. Agostinho Santos was responsible for his own son, Roberto."

A loud gasp, followed by a choking sob, gushed from the gallery. *Not again. Please don't make a scene*, Ace thought. He turned his head to see Gabi hanging her head, a tissue pressed up against her face. Tony put his arm around her shoulder. Robbie's fidgeting quickened.

"Mr. Agostinho Santos focused on how much money he could take from the FC Strikers instead of the safety of his own child." Vilipend stretched out the name—Agostinho Santos—emphasizing tones foreign to the English speaker's ear. He refused to say "Robbie," instead he continually emphasized the name "Roberto" and rolling the *r* on his tongue for added effect.

*Blame it on the black guy, predictable*, Ace thought. He snuck a glance at Juror Six who was intent on Vilipend's statement and nodding as though in agreement. *Shit.*

"We have proven that legally the AAYA was unrelated to the FC Strikers for liability reasons. They are separate entities, have separate sponsors. And, as you have seen from the financial irresponsibility of the Strikers, separate finances. Mr. Roberto Santos has sued the Association not only because the Strikers are gone, but to deflect accountability from his own father, Mr. Agostinho Santos." Vilipend sucked in a shallow breath.

"In the United States of America, we don't make anyone pay for the mistakes of someone else. No matter how serious the damage, justice doesn't work that way. We ask you today to deny the plaintiff's claims and find the Athletic Association for Young Americans blameless. Thank you." Vilipend made the slow trek back to counsel table and, after unnecessarily dramatic fussing with his papers, sat down.

"Thank you, counsel," Judge Moore said. She took off her spectacles and looked at the jury. "We'll break now, then the lawyers will return to review some additional legal points. When that's finished, the jury will return to receive instructions before retiring to the jury room for final deliberations."

The judge looked at the lawyers, asking with her eyes if there was any further matter that required her attention. With no response, she continued, "Okay then, we are in recess." She tapped her gavel and walked out.

"Okay guys, listen up," Lupe said. She had prepared the jury instructions and would submit their argument on the finer legal points.

"It's not good, is it?" Robbie asked, uninterested in more legal mumbo jumbo. Robbie and Lupe looked to Ace for a response.

"I don't know, Robbie. I don't know." Ace refused eye contact, his only attempt to conceal his fear and disappointment.

*Thirty-one*

# THE FINAL GAME
# 1998

From the back seat, Ace absorbed the colors, the sunshine, the gleeful shouts, and trembled. He struggled to sit still while his mom, Heather, drove around searching for a parking spot, any parking spot. Kids with neon flags directed her through the throng of vehicles—SUVs, trucks, and occasional sedans—many decorated with painted cheers, soccer balls, and smiley faces on the windows. Heather followed the kid waving the neon flag—not himself old enough to drive—to a spot chalked in the dirt.

The unpaved parking lot flattened the top of a small hill smack in the middle of the soccer complex. From there, you could see the surrounding game fields, dozens in every direction. Peering out the car window, Ace saw every field was full, and parking was scarce. Parent volunteers filled the brightly colored tents along the parking lot's perimeter and sold T-shirts, hot dogs, water bottles, soccer balls, and anything else that might earn a little extra money for the kids. Ace's tummy fluttered like the soccer club banners flapping in the breeze because the end of this day would see one team bring home the state championship trophy.

The second the car stopped, Ace ripped off his seatbelt and slid out the door with a hastily uttered goodbye. "Bye, Mom. Bye, Lisa. See you guys at the game."

"Good luck," Heather called out. But Ace was already bounding down the hill to his assigned field. Heather and Lisa had an hour to entertain themselves during the Strikers' warmup.

Even with the visual advantage afforded by the height of the hill, Ace had a tough time spotting his teammates through the crowd. He dodged the people and occasional golf carts that filled the paths between fields. Shouts from the sidelines of active games punctuated the steady buzz of spectators. With one hand, Ace applied soft pressure to his middle as he ran; his other hand wrapped around the strap of his bobbing backpack. While he loved being immersed in the positive vibrations, it could be overwhelming. He had to stay focused on his game. This was it. The big one. Everyone was feeling it, and of course, Ace channeled everyone's feeling it.

Ace had pressured his mom to leave early for the game, but she was accustomed to that since Ace was consistently prompt. Coach had preached: "Early is on time and on time is late." Ace took that motto to heart, just like his dad…

The thought of his dad gave him pause. Dad's meeting in Chicago had gone longer than expected, and then the flight had been canceled. Ace counted on his dad to be there but understood that sometimes the unexpected and uncontrollable happens. Dad had promised to take the next flight out, scheduled for the morning. The timing was tight, but Ace believed his dad would do everything possible to get to the game.

*****

Steve tilted his wrist to look at his watch again, but that didn't make the airplane go faster. He watched the ice cubes clink together in a soothing rhythm as he spun his whiskey glass, real glass in first class. He took a sip, allowing the smokey caramel to linger before sliding down his throat with a reassuring sting. Before he had boarded the plane, he'd had a drink or two at the airport lounge. The trip had been an unmitigated disaster. The deal fell through, and the furious client made good the threat and fired Steve and his law firm. Steve hadn't told his law partners yet but would have to deliver the bad news soon. Losing this client added significant financial pressure to his growing list of problems.

The prospect of starting his legal career again from scratch overwhelmed him. Surely the partnership would vote him out for his colossal blunder. He snorted at the conundrum; his biggest blunder was following the ethical rules. Had he behaved unethically, illegally even, there would have been no problem. But he knew his money-grubbing partners wouldn't see it that way. They would throw Steve under the bus to save the client. *How can I start a new practice when I can't pay the mortgage?*

As he stared at his whiskey, he tried to put the failed deal out of his mind and relived his discussion with Heather. He had called her back immediately but got a busy signal. Afterward, the big merger deal kept him consumed to the point of exhaustion. Between working on his client's transaction and rushing to the airport, Steve couldn't reach Heather. They hadn't connected. Steve's secretary diligently kept Heather informed about flights and hotels. So, Heather must know he was coming, *right?*

Heather had told him something happened at the Strikers. Or did she? He didn't understand her words, but he heard some urgency in her voice—or did he? Something significant had happened, not something good, maybe. Perhaps uncertainty was the ultimate source of his dread. That could be it, not knowing. Once her number popped up on his phone when he could have answered but didn't. *That was a mistake. I should have taken her call. Why did I ignore her? She needed me and I wasn't there for her.*

Sometimes knowing was worse than not knowing, at least for a minute.

Then there was the message from Gus and Sean about sexual assault at the club. Steve had had no reasonable chance to call them back. *My new friends needed my advice, and I wasn't there for them.* Another sip of whiskey failed to resolve his confusion over their incoherent messages.

He stared out the tiny oval window at the big white puffs and thought about flying among the clouds, weightless, free, as a wisp of pure spirit. With eyes closed, he imagined what that would feel like. No responsibility, no pain, no guilt, no shame.

*If I died now, I could fly away, away from everything. Or maybe I would go to hell…but would that even matter?*

"Can I get you anything else?" the flight attendant asked.

Steve tilted his head back and tossed the remaining whiskey down his throat. "Yes, please, I'd like another."

She took his empty glass with a smile and walked away.

Steve's eyelids drooped and his vision blurred when he looked out the window again. Visual focus was as elusive to him as mental focus. His thoughts turned to his only son bringing home a science award, earning a goal assist in his first competitive game. He remembered watching from a distance at the end of a game when Atticus had looked for his dad. He hadn't been there. What else had happened when he wasn't there for his son?

Steve squeezed his eyes shut and shook his head, but the next thought wouldn't go away.

*What happened to me when my dad wasn't there?* Glimmers of horror flitted about his mind like a swarm of mosquitos, but he lacked any mental strength to push them away.

*How could I forget the mosquito?*

*Where's my drink?*

*****

Through the crowd, Ace spotted a few of his Strikers' teammates and their parents. He ran to them, smiling.

"Hey guys, I'm here. Can I help set up?" Ace bounced his soccer ball between his ankles, back and forth, Tick-Tock, as he spoke to another Strikers' coach that he recognized from the under-14 age group. "Where's Coach Sean?"

"Slow down, Ace. Save some energy for the game," the U-14 coach said. "Coach Sean has a family emergency, and he can't be here. Go line up the cones for some quick drills. Then get the boys warmed up with knee raises."

Ace looked around for JJ since he usually ran those drills. But he didn't see JJ anywhere either. Maybe the family issue also involved JJ.

"Sure, Coach," he said. "Hey guys, come on, let's get warmed up." Ace gathered up the stragglers and yelled. "Who Are We?"

"WE ARE STRIKERS!" came the enthusiastic reply. The boys followed Ace onto the field where he started them on stretches and knee raises, just as Coach asked. More and more teammates joined the drill, and the sidelines filled with parents, grandparents, and siblings. Players, coaches, and staff from clubs eliminated in the qualifying matches were there. More than that, recruiters trawling for talent watched closely, clipboards in hand. The crowd pressed closer and closer to the sidelines until the referee pushed them back.

After setting the spectator boundary, the referee and line judges stood in the middle of the field and waited for the coaches to gather their teams. It was time to check for proper cleats, shin guards, player cards. After confirming both teams complied with equipment rules, the referee lined up the teams to face the crowd. A disembodied voice over the loudspeaker announced the game.

The crowd cheered.

Ace saw his mom and sister, and they waved at him. Even his little sister Lisa paid attention, with a seriousness Ace didn't think possible. Waving back would be childish, so Ace resisted the urge. But he couldn't stop the broad smile. He didn't see his dad but was confident the plane was in the air, maybe landed. Maybe Dad was already driving to the fields.

Coach gathered the team into a small huddle on the sidelines. Ace's heart raced as he stuck his hand in the middle of all the other hands. Then Robbie yelled,

"1, 2, 3, Who Are We?"

"WE ARE STRIKERS!"

The hands all flew up together, and the huddle broke. The starters ran onto the field and took their positions. Robbie was up top as forward, right up in the opposing forward's face. Josh was starting at center-back—his usual position—with the Strikers' net and goalkeeper right behind him.

"Let's go, Strikers! We got this!" Josh yelled. His voice reverberated with the power reminiscent of his dad, Joe. The Strikers' parental sideline responded to Josh with cheers.

The Arsenal players glowered, ready to reclaim victory after losing to the Strikers earlier in the year.

Ace, on wing, bounced on his toes with eyes glued to the referee. Any second the whistle would blow… and then it did. Game on.

*****

Steve stumbled down the jetway, out the door, and headed straight toward the airport pickup ramp. He had to push his way through the weekend getaway crowds but didn't have to stop for checked luggage. With his light garment bag slung over one shoulder and holding his heavy briefcase in his opposite hand, Steve tilted heavily to one side. The uneven weight exacerbated his tipsy unsteadiness.

If he hurried, he could stop by the house, change, and dash to Ace's game to get there as it started. He might miss a few minutes, but at worst he should arrive before halftime. Impeded with the dual burdens of luggage and alcohol, he pushed himself forward. There was something else deep inside, like the lure of sleep pulling him to darkness. *The forest…no, the woods.* His head spun in a way that only the darkness could fix. *Lovely, dark, and deep…* The poem twisted about his brain for some unfathomable reason. *But it was a forest…*

He pushed past a group of boys in matching olive-green collared shirts with scarves and jeans. He stopped and turned to stare at them. Sewn on each shirt was a colorful array of merit patches. Their little sunburned faces gleamed as they chattered and laughed. He looked at their shoes: waffle-stompers. After all these years, they still wore waffle-stompers.

*I used to wear waffle-stompers.*

He shivered as a memory of the forest lake's icy wetness shot through him and it all came back—the lake and everything that happened later. The waffle-stompers, the cabin, the mosquito… the Man. He looked down at his feet, confused by his shiny wingtips, but that action brought imbalance, and he lost his balance, almost falling. Jerking himself upright made his gut wrench with nausea.

*Shit.*

He couldn't go on, so he found the nearest men's room, barely reaching the toilet before vomiting. After throwing up once, he stuck his finger down his throat and made himself vomit again. He didn't have time for this. He needed to get it all out fast.

Steve washed up quickly and set off. He arrived at the taxi stand without more vomiting, and as luck would have it, there was a line of waiting taxis. He threw his garment bag into the first cab and barked his address and directions to the driver.

Seatbelt on, he could finally breathe. The cab would get home when it got home; it was out of his control now. While he had been busy rushing around, he didn't think. Now, just sitting, the thoughts came back. He thought about the merger, his best client yelling at him, degrading him for refusing to commit fraud. The words reverberated in his ears.

"I can't fucking believe you screwed us on this. You fucking loser! We'll take you to court. We'll shut down your law firm and take everything."

He covered his ears to block out the angry profanities, as though they were still being hurled at him. Steve's integrity—his adherence to ethics—had cratered the deal and with it, the relationship, a relationship that had taken years to develop.

But there was something else, too. What was Heather trying to tell him? What was the message from Gus? He trembled uncontrollably, his head pounded, and his chest tightened with pain. But images of the shining bright boys in the airport wouldn't leave him alone.

*Waffle-stompers.*

Thoughts of Atticus—of not being there for Atticus—would not leave him alone.

*They were all so little; I must have been that little, too...*
*Where was my dad?*
*What is happening to me?*

*****

At the whistle, the Arsenal forward player tapped the ball to his left where his teammate picked it up. It was an obvious start to the game, and the Strikers were ready. Robbie challenged. He pushed forward for the tackle and locked his ankle against the ball at the same time as the slower offensive player. The ball popped out at an unexpected angle to the Striker side, several yards ahead in front of Ace.

Ace's heart jumped into his throat as he sprinted forward. Out of nowhere, a large Arsenal boy leaped to the ball just ahead of him. With forward momentum on his side, the offensive player pushed past Ace and ran smack into Josh, who was ready and just as large as the Arsenal kid. The two large boys crashed, but Josh survived the scrum with the ball and kicked it to the Striker goalkeeper. The Strikers' keeper switched the field with a strong pass to the other wing.

Ace wasn't disappointed with the switch, rather, he trusted that the Strikers' keeper made the right move. The cacophony of cheering on the sidelines was silent to Ace's ears. The screaming voices blended into irrelevance behind the invisible spectator perimeter, isolating the field from the crazed swarm. Ace blocked all emotions except those he channeled from his own team, their excitement, optimism, and trust in each other. He wrapped himself into the emotions of Strikers' players to propel his own attitude as high as he could.

Ace pressed forward parallel to the opposite Strikers' winger, moving the ball upfield. With some luck, a scoring opportunity might open. But not this time. An Arsenal defender hit the ground in a slide tackle and barely got his toe on the ball. Timing the tackle perfectly, the Arsenal defender kicked the ball directly to the feet of the Arsenal star forward. The Strikers' opposite winger went down.

The Arsenal hotshot sped toward the Strikers' goal as the Strikers players who had advanced deep into Arsenal territory ran to catch up. Seeing the breakaway, Ace cut to the middle, but the hotshot saw him coming and passed to a teammate at the back door, near the Strikers' net. Josh was too deep—which allowed the Arsenal forward to get deep without an offsides call—and he was too slow to block the shot. The forward faked a shot to one side, causing the Strikers' keeper to commit to the wrong direction before sending a slow high ball into the net's upper corner. Arsenal scored first.

The Arsenal crowd erupted as the disappointed Strikers' crowd groaned.

*Something's wrong.* Ace jerked his head to the sidelines as he felt an emotional stomach punch that surely must have been his dad's distress. But Dad wasn't there. Ace couldn't find him in the crowd. He had no options but to shake off the emotion and focus on the game.

*****

Steve's hands trembled as he opened the car door after the cab had finally pulled into his driveway. With jumbled thoughts, he paid the driver but forgot the tip. He jogged to the front porch, jammed his key in the lock, and lurched through the door of his house without closing it behind him. He dumped his briefcase and garment bag in the foyer and went to the kitchen. A glass of water and aspirin might help. Maybe he'd grab drive-through coffee on the way. That would help too.

He thrust his fingers into his hair and pressed his scalp, but the throbbing in his head continued. His wedding ring caught on his hair when he pulled his hand away, yanking out several strands, but he didn't feel it. One of the kitchen cabinets held aspirin. Heather would know where, and he should know too, but he didn't. Strange that searching for aspirin in his own kitchen was confusing, like deciphering train schedules in a foreign country.

Finally, he found a glass of water and an analgesic. He sat at the breakfast table, turning the red-labeled plastic bottle in his hand. It was large, 500 caplets. That's enough to vanquish a headache. But the headache wasn't his only problem; 500 pills would be more than enough for a ride to the darkness. *The forest...*

*Lovely, dark, and deep...*

*No, not now.*

Steve opened the bottle and shook out two caplets. He tossed the pills into his mouth, followed by gulps of water. And when he stood to leave, he saw the underwear hanging off the kitchen desk. Everything was tidy, but someone had left a pair of boys' underwear on the desk by the computer.

*What the hell? Atticus knows better than that...*

Steve walked over to the underwear and saw the Strikers' telephone list, notepad, and pen. On the notepad was Heather's writing, doodles really, but two words stood out: *Why blood?* Then he saw it. Atticus's underwear was blood-stained. The moment his eyes focused on the blood, his head exploded like he'd been smacked with a sledgehammer.

Unlike Heather, Steve understood in a flash.

"No!" He screamed because he knew. With tightened lips and a shaking hand, he reached for the bloodied briefs. He knew Atticus had been assaulted. It all made sense. The messages from Heather, from Gus, the underwear.

Steve slammed his underwear-wrapped fist on the table. He screamed again. Except the pain wasn't only in his head. Pain shot through his legs and up his back. He grabbed the chair to sit, but his legs failed, and he fell to the floor. He heard the Man grunting, sweat dripping, the wetness between his thighs. The whiskey churned violently in his gut, and the pain—pounding, penetrating pain—would not stop. The room spun and everything turned green.

*Why green?*
And then it went black.

*****

The Strikers evened the score to 1-1 on a penalty kick early in the otherwise uneventful second half. All the boys on the field were red-faced and dripping; the game hadn't been boring for lack of physical effort. Each child pushed themself relentlessly toward the highly coveted State Cup trophy.

Whichever team scored in these last few minutes would most likely win. Ace dreaded the tie-breaking alternative of penalty kicks in overtime. Pushing past exhaustion, the Strikers were giving everything they had. The U-14 Strikers coach paced the sideline and even shouted once or twice before biting his fist to stop. The Arsenal coach continued nonstop, screaming in an increasingly raspy voice.

Ace took advantage of an Arsenal throw-in to check the laces on his cleats. It was a mistake. The throw-in was on his side of the field and Ace, kneeling, fussing with his shoe, gave the Arsenal an irresistible opportunity. The ball flew in as the whistle blew, right over Ace's head, straight to the receiving player's foot. Ace felt the receiving player taste victory as he pulled off a one-touch cross to his forward player, already in a full sprint.

Ace instantly grasped the gravity of his mistake. His red face turned redder. Reaching deep, he decided—the game would *not* end like that. Seeking redemption, Ace himself would channel the force of the universe, if that's what it took. But he couldn't do it alone. The Arsenal had advanced deep into Striker territory. Ace was too far behind to challenge. Resisting the urge to run after the ball, Ace got into position for the next play, like Gretzky skating not to where the puck was at the moment, but to where it was going next. On the next play, Josh would do his job and stop Arsenal's progress and get the ball back to midfield. Ace had to trust his teammates to play their own positions. He rose to this test of trust, this test of maturity. Ace didn't chase the ball, but strategized plays ahead, like a chess match. He relied on his teammates as they relied on him.

And it happened. Josh did it. He jumped higher than he ever had before, heading out the Arsenal cross. The header shot straight up, a

50-50 ball between Josh and the Arsenal player, who had materialized from nowhere. But Josh pivoted, blocking out his opponent, then executed a beautiful bicycle kick, sending the ball over his head, back into midfield. The Strikers midfielder wheeled about, caught the blind pass, faked a defender with a Rivelino *elastico*, and passed to Robbie.

This was the chance Ace needed. With the ball at Robbie's feet, Ace dashed up the sideline. Robbie couldn't see Ace, but line-of-sight was unnecessary. Robbie looked left and kicked right. Ace would be there. Ace connected to Robbie's no-look pass with precision timing. The move they'd practiced was Ace pushing forward and then returning the ball to Robbie for a backdoor shot. But Robbie was too far back. The defenders successfully delayed him. The positioning wasn't right.

*I can't do this without Robbie.*

Then Ace heard Robbie's voice above the screaming spectators, "Shoot!" And Ace saw it, the open net, the Arsenal keeper out of position. Robbie was right, it was time for Ace to trust himself. He hardened his left quadriceps and forcefully planted his left foot. He pulled back his right foot, connected with a solid thunk, and propelled the ball into a graceful arc. The world went silent as the ball soared upwards, arced, then floated like a gigantic bubble released from a dollar store bubble-maker, high into the corner of the Arsenal net. Gooooooo-aaaaAAAALL!

*****

With significant effort, Steve raised his head a couple of inches off the floor and considered more whiskey, but that thought made him shudder. With the bloodied underwear still wrapped around his fist, he pushed himself up further until he sat in a slouch. He examined the underwear twisted around his hand, turning it slowly. And he remembered. He remembered his own underwear, nearly identical, including the bloodstains. The stained white scrap of cotton shook uncontrollably in his ever-tightening fist as shame flooded through him—unbearable shame—shame that had no solution, shame that would never leave. The recovered memory smashed his life, smashed everything he thought was real, like a wrecking ball against a baby.

Steve levered himself into a cross-legged sit and stared at the underwear in his lap. An image of the Man dominated his vision, the

Man staring at the lake-wetted neck of a little boy—the Boy—Steve. The Man, the Man who called him Skeeter. He remembered the petroleum jelly dropped on the threshold of his little room, the Man stumbling, then smiling as he picked up the small jar. Steve watched as he floated above the scene, over the bed looking down. But as the Man climbed into the bed, Steve shot back into his childhood body. The safety of floating above—the safety of disassociation—evaporated as the memory returned. Steve's lungs refused their task, and he rasped as though the extra-large sleeping bags were once again smothering him. He was no longer a drunk and confused adult, but a shocked and frightened boy. And what had started as a loving hug morphed into a constrictor's embrace, the flabby thigh strong enough to pin him down. The mouthful of green flannel prevented him from screaming away the pain as his insides were shredded. Blood and ick smeared over his legs, on his underwear.

Blood on his underwear… his own underwear…

And then he heard the raspy voice, puffing blasts of air against his ear. "Never tell what we did. Nobody will believe you and I won't be your friend anymore. You will get in trouble. Your parents will hate you."

How could he forget? How could he forget his own rape, the continued abuse forced upon him? But maybe he had not completely forgotten because his body had stored the memory, his body recalled the abuse when Heather touched him, it recalled the abuse when his own children wanted hugs. His body remembered; he remembered. Buried memories ripped through the tissue of Steve's mind and found the light of knowing. The knowing metastasized like cancer throughout his being. The malignancy of every predatory touch relived was more brutal than he could bear. Steve wept.

He remembered the boys in the airport, their little, shiny, innocent faces, and the realization hit. Steve had been that little, that innocent, too. He had been just a boy, like Atticus, like his own son. His own son, somewhere out there, without his father's protection. Steve bent his head and stared at the underwear. How could he have let this happen?

Steve had failed to protect himself, failed to protect his own child. He had failed his wife because he could not be there for her either, not intimately, not physically. Her sobs from the many nights he had rejected her advances haunted him. He had let down his entire family. His law practice was on the brink of failure, and it was his own fault. He had let down his partners, his clients. Every slime covered shame swirled in the mire, blending into a quagmire of muck until each shame became indistinguishable and inseparable from the others. The disappointment, the failures, the whiskey, rocked him hard, and rocked him again. He felt as though every hit sucked him deeper into quicksand with no hope of escape, and then it occurred to him.

*Heather's notepaper....*

*****

The psychosphere slammed Ace with its emotional tsunami, followed instantly by the earsplitting roar that erupted from the Strikers' sidelines. Ten screaming Strikers on the field rushed the one Striker who had scored the winning goal. Ace could barely believe it. He stared wide-eyed at the ball resting in the net as he was surrounded by hand slaps, hugs, cheers.

"You did it, Ace! You did it!" Robbie jumped into the air and into Ace, nearly knocking him over.

Josh and Robbie lifted Ace into the air and onto their shoulders, giving Ace a panoramic view of the crowds. The colors from the waving Strikers' flags were brighter than the sun. Happiness surged into his heart, lifting his spirits as his teammates hoisted him higher. Everyone cheered the hero, high above the other children. Ace threw back his head, his face breaking into a gigantic smile, and gave himself over to pure joy.

*Thirty-two*

# THE VERDICT

## 2022

### TRIAL

"Mmmm," Robbie involuntarily exuded nom-nom sounds with each bite of his French toast drizzled with syrup and sprinkled with confectioners' sugar. He had woken up early so he could read the newspaper undisturbed over breakfast at the diner that shared a parking lot with the Superior Court. Ace and Lupe would be along any minute, but neither appreciated a hearty breakfast, so Robbie had come early to enjoy his meal alone. Tony would've been upset by Robbie's betrayal of Heather's trendy, over-priced, coffee shop-bakery where Tony worked. But Robbie favored the comfort food of an old-fashioned American diner, and weirdly, this place surrounded by the courthouse parking lot was one of the best. He sat outside where the morning sun peeking under the awning warmed his face and afforded an unobstructed view of the courthouse front door.

The jury had begun deliberations yesterday afternoon but hadn't finished. Ace believed there would be a verdict sometime the next morning, so the trio had agreed to a mid-morning meeting at the diner to review strategy options in case they lost. Robbie already knew what might happen either way, but reviewing that information was the pretense for the meeting. Robbie didn't need any reassurance, but Ace might. Ace wouldn't ask for support, but Robbie knew he was anxious. And why would he pass up a delicious meal at a fantastic diner?

Ace arrived and pulled up a chair, and immediately an attentive server poured freshly brewed coffee into his mug.

"Great service," Ace said. He blew on his coffee before taking a sip.

"Ya, I think I've found a new favorite. Now, I'll just have to convince Tony." Robbie rolled his eyes in a way that usually made Ace laugh, but Ace didn't laugh. Robbie knew Ace had given everything he had to the trial. He frequently worked late nights, with no time for friends, family, hobbies, sports, exercise, no time for anything but work. Ace had lost weight; his complexion was more pale than usual. Dark half-moons under his eyes revealed he hadn't slept well in days. Robbie wished Ace could believe in himself as much as Robbie believed in him.

"It's almost over, buddy." Robbie patted Ace on the knee. "It's almost over."

The two slurped coffee, staring out over the blacktop. Robbie wondered about the blond pony-tailed girls they had seen on the first day, absent now and forever, like soccer. The sense of impending completion drained what little energy remained after several arduous months of legal work.

"Ace, I don't have words to show my appreciation for everything you've done," Robbie said.

"You forget who you're talking to. Anyway, I've never said it, but you're the strongest person I know. If it weren't for you… I don't even know. I'd be a complete wreck. You're…" Ace stumbled for words, but Robbie saved him the effort and interrupted.

"No, you're the strong one, brother. I've always taken my strength from you."

"Bullshit."

"Hey there, lovebirds. Am I interrupting an intimate moment?" Lupe appeared from nowhere. "Mutual admiration club?" she asked.

The men, caught displaying the affection of their friendship, snickered uncomfortably, and moved the chairs apart, making space for Lupe to sit in her customary spot between them.

"No press, no demonstrators. I like the quiet," Lupe said. She stretched her arms in front of her, then without asking permission, grabbed Ace's coffee and took a sip. "So, what's on the agenda this morning, Team Santos?"

"Last minute strategic thoughts while we wait for the buzzer," Ace answered. He held up the pager given to the team by the court. The rectangular hunk of beige plastic looked like it came straight out of the

1980s, rather like the court building itself. When the jury announced it had finished or had questions, or basically if anything interesting happened, the court would buzz them for check-in.

*As always, back to business*, Robbie thought. His preference was sitting in silence, but he knew Ace needed the distraction of working, so work they would. Ace took the lead in reviewing the possibilities for an appeal if they lost, and the certainty that the AAYA would appeal if they won. The discussion between Ace and Lupe became technical, full of legalese, but with concentration, Robbie could follow.

Eventually, the pager jumped and buzzed, and the red light flashed. Their strategy session was over. It was time. Ace picked up the pager and switched it off.

"Okay, let's go," he said.

*****

Once again, Ace sat at counsel table, ready for any conceivable outcome. It was the inconceivable outcomes that worried him. Juries were notoriously unpredictable, so anything was possible. The jury may be divided, unable to reach a verdict, in which case Judge Moore would send them back to try again. She sat on her bench, looking scrubbed and starched, and not nearly as tiny as she was. On the bench, she became larger, presiding over the courtroom with unquestionable authority. She nodded to the bailiff who opened the side door for the jury.

As the jury entered, Ace tried to read their emotions but all he felt was anxiety, his, Lupe's, and Robbie's. After a long trial, the jury would be relieved it was ending, anticipating their release.

"We are back on the record in *Santos v. The Athletic Association for Young Americans*," the judge said. "I understand, Madame Foreperson, the jury has reached a verdict?"

The Foreperson stood. "Yes, Your Honor." She held out a folded piece of paper which was taken by the clerk, who passed it on to the judge.

The jurors wore blankness on their faces, except Juror Six, whose face was soft. Ace spotted a glint of light at the corner of Six's eye. *Wetness? What the hell?* Ace shook the mistake out of his head, because surely, he didn't see that.

Judge Moore unfolded the paper and read it through completely before speaking. She leaned into the microphone and read:

On COUNT ONE, was the defendant negligent in causing damages to the plaintiff?

We the Jury answer: NO

Rapid-fire camera clicks filled the courtroom.

"Who is making that sound? Stop it! Stop it now! Bailiff, please remove those photographers. As a reminder to everyone, I've ordered no cameras in the courthouse." Judge Moore banged her gavel and glared over her spectacles, refusing to read further until the bailiff returned from escorting the offending reporters out and the watchers stilled.

The following silence lingered long enough that Ace's mind swam with negative premonitions about what would come next. He hung his head and then, catching a blast of optimism from Robbie, titled his head toward Robbie.

Robbie mouthed the words, "It's okay," and then winked with a smile.

*We just lost our first count and still Robbie smiles. I don't know how he does that.* As usual, Robbie's optimism injected itself into Ace and he couldn't help but feel better, slightly. *We have one more chance with count two.*

When the bailiff returned to his station, the judge explained that because there was no liability on count one, all remaining questions about count one were irrelevant, and so she read count two. She continued:

On COUNT TWO, did the defendant Athletic Association for Young Americans commit fraud, causing damages to the plaintiff, Roberto Santos?

We the Jury answer: YES

Judge Moore ignored the resulting courtroom buzz and continued reading the verdict sheet.

If the answer to this question is yes, what are plaintiff Roberto Santos's damages on count two?

We the Jury answer: $4,000,000.00

Ace heard Gabi gasp from the gallery behind him. But the judge wasn't finished yet. She continued:

Did the defendant Athletic Association for Young Americans engage in conduct that was oppressive, malicious, or fraudulent?

We the Jury answer: YES

Multiple gasps from the gallery prompted Judge Moore to stop and wait for silence—yet again—before continuing.

What amount of punitive damages, if any, do you award to plaintiff, Roberto Santos?

We the jury answer: $18,500,000.00

Without waiting for silence, the judge looked up and addressed the jury directly.

"Madam Foreperson, is this the verdict of the jury?

"Yes, Your Honor."

"And so say you all?"

A chorus of jurors answered in the affirmative.

"Let the record reflect that all jurors consent to the verdict," the judge said. "Before dismissing you, I want personally to thank you all for your service in this matter. You worked hard, and it's appreciated. The entire justice system would fail except for good people like you. Thank you. You may leave if you like, or you may stay to speak with the attorneys and court staff."

Juror Six stared straight at Robbie and gave a slight nod. Ace felt validated that his original instinct was correct, and what he had seen was correct. Six had wet eyes. He turned to the exit and wiped his eyes with the back of his hand as he left the courtroom.

"We are in recess. Counsel, we will be back at 9:00 am tomorrow to address post-trial matters." With that, the judge exited.

Trancelike, Ace stared straight ahead without response. He had methodically carried out all the expected courtroom protocols without emotion, without even the trace of a smile. For the first time, Ace had disconnected from the psychosphere and was floating lost, trying and failing to decipher his own emotions.

Robbie stood, walked over to Ace, and gave him a hearty smack on the back. "Suck it up, Buttercup. We won."

Vilipend rose and made his way over to Ace, extended a hand and said "Congratulations, counsel. Good work, but it's not over yet. My client is likely to file an appeal, so we will be in touch." Ace appreciated Vilipend's old-fashioned professionalism, but it did nothing to assuage his anxiety. Ever professional, Ace accepted Vilipend's hand and managed to mumble something equally gracious. The Captain America lawyers said nothing, but turned their backs and walked out after snapping shut their laptops.

"Okay, boss. What now?" Robbie asked after Vilipend and his crew had left.

Lupe interrupted when Ace didn't respond. "Now we celebrate," she said.

Not that easy. There were hugs, reporters, family, well-wishers. Ace became weightless in the relief of others, the vindication of countless victims, but the heaviness of his own burden remained.

*****

It took a solid hour for the courtroom to empty. The reporters ran off to submit their stories, the watchers lost interest and left, and the court staff turned their attention to other duties. Lupe rushed back to the office to work on the next expected wave of legal maneuvers. Even the Santos clan found reasons to leave, promising a celebratory get-together later. The bailiff remained and he would start shooing away the hangers-on any minute.

Tony, who had been waiting silently for the crowd to clear, stepped past the swinging doors and stood shyly by Robbie's side. As soon as Robbie turned to him, the men pulled together like power magnets and hugged, then hugged some more. Without caring what the world might think, they shared kisses through smiling lips. Later, they would enjoy a private moment to revel in the victory. Robbie squeezed Tony's shoulders and, towering over the smaller man, whispered, "Thank you for standing by me. I love you."

Tony blushed but tilted his face upward for another smooch. "I love you too," he replied. He needed to check in at Heather's bakery after being away for so long for the trial, so after one more embrace, left the courthouse.

Robbie and Ace, the last to linger, received pointed looks from the bailiff, who was ready to lock up.

"Walk with me," Ace said to Robbie. "We've got some things to discuss."

"Why? Can't it wait?" Robbie replied.

"No."

"Ok, Boss."

As they walked away, Robbie marveled at Ace's ability to remain stern. After the late nights, the exhaustion, the emotion, Ace wouldn't let himself take so much as a breath of relief. Even though the corners of Ace's mouth turned down, Robbie didn't expect bad news. Ace was just like that, always so serious.

"What are your thoughts about the verdict?" Ace asked.

"Don't you know?"

"No. I'm no mind reader."

"I think you are going to tell me we aren't done. That there's more work."

"Of course." Ace watched Robbie's face, anticipating a negative response to what he'd say next. "So, they file bankruptcy now. You know that, right? You'll never see a dime. Did you get justice?" Ace's words released a vapor of uncharacteristic anger.

Robbie startled at the question. "Justice? No. Justice would be had if it never happened. If it never happened again. Restorative justice sounds great in theory, but true restoration can't happen. What we got wasn't justice, even if we got all the money it wouldn't be justice."

"Not to say, 'I told you so,' but…" Ace's shoulders shook, then slumped. He stopped walking.

"You of all people should understand this. It wasn't really about justice."

"Well, I don't. I don't understand. What the fuck was all this about, anyway?" Ace stood still, except for the continued shivering of his shoulders, the clench in his teeth. "He's not coming back. I can't give you justice. I can't give him justice. Nothing's changed. I've failed everything."

"No, you didn't." Robbie remained adamant, but was surprised by Ace's reaction. Ace looked like he would explode, his anger barely restrained.

"Maybe the worst part is I'm marked as Atticus. Atticus Finch. The eminent lawyer hero fighting for justice, standing by his client. But what did I get for you? I got nothing. Nothing's changed for you and Dad is still gone."

"Hey, sit for a minute," Robbie said, pulling Ace down onto the brick planter in front of the courthouse. "Your whole life you've been looking at it the wrong way."

Ace turned the Brazilian tourmaline over in his hands but said nothing. The stone felt cold and heavy, like an ordinary rock.

"Atticus Finch failed, by the way. His innocent client, Tom Robinson, was found guilty at the hands of a racist jury and then was brutally murdered by racist assholes, the same racist assholes still murdering black men in American streets without accountability," Robbie said.

"They convicted one racist asshole in Minnesota."

"Exactly, one conviction isn't justice in a country of countless dead. I know you don't believe that," Robbie said.

"Great, so I was named after a failure. Is that what you're saying? I guess that fits."

"You're still missing the point."

Ace stood, his hand clenched over the polished black stone, and his voice trembled and rose. "So, tell me, Mr. Lit Teacher, what's the point? What the fuck is the point, because I don't get it."

Robbie stood and grabbed Ace by his arms, then sat them both back down. "Breathe, you big dummy, then I'll explain." Robbie waited for Ace to calm down before continuing. "It's not about justice. It's about knowing, about accountability."

Ace bent his head to look at his hands, still fussing with the stone, thinking.

"This is the great information age. We have video. We have people speaking up. Truth is breaking through. Truth will prevail."

"Damn, Robbie. You really believe that shit?"

"I do. Evil will only succeed if good men do nothing. You're a good man, Ace. You're doing something about it."

"Oh, so now I suppose justice rolls down like waters?" Ace twisted his lips into a sneer.

"You fought for acknowledgement, accountability. You won that fight. Maybe they will never pay, but they will never again hide their misdeeds. Accountability is the first step to justice. Justice is a much longer path." Robbie elbowed Ace gently. "Besides, You—Are—No—Doctor—King! You put too much on yourself."

Ace stared straight ahead as moisture collected in the corner of his reddened eyes. "Dad's still dead."

"Trust me, I understand better than anyone why he did it. I have that battle every day with myself. But there's help now. I can work on it. I have the tools to step back, observe what I'm feeling, and move through the shame. It's still hard, really hard, but I can do it." Robbie waited for a response but continued when Ace still said nothing.

"Your dad, his generation, didn't know how to heal. If it had happened to me decades ago, I probably would've killed myself, too. Suicide happened all the time to survivors and people didn't know. But our generation, *now we know*, we understand and there's help."

Ace shook his head, still in denial. "It's my fault you were attacked… If I had spoken up earlier about what I saw in San Diego, maybe… This win isn't enough to make up for that. It isn't enough to make up for my dad."

"Fuck that, Ace. None of this is your fault. Did you forget you were just a kid? Don't put that responsibility on that little kid from 1998. You aren't being fair to yourself."

"I suppose, but it all still feels so dirty."

"It is and will always be dirty, but Ace, you did it. You drew back the curtain and exposed what's happening. It won't bring back your dad, but maybe it will help stop the pain, stop the suicides. You played an important part."

Ace gulped, and the droplets in his eyes overcame all restraint and flowed down his cheek.

"Things will never go back to how it was before, except I love you, brother. I love you exactly as our fucked-up life is right now." Robbie hoped Ace understood.

Robbie sat quietly with Ace, sharing his pain, just being there with him because that was all he could do. Ace understood what was happening; he knew and understood, so it wasn't that. There was nothing for Robbie to explain, nothing Robbie could fix, but Robbie would sit there with him anyway for as long as needed. That's what friends do.

# Thirty-three

# WHEN KNOWING COMES
# 1998

Ace burst through the already open front door before Heather and Lisa got out of the car.

"Dad! Dad, are you home? We won!"

Ace imagined the smile that would break his dad's face when he told the news. Dad would tousle his hair and give him a bear hug. He would say: *Show me your trophy!* And Ace would bask in pride when he held up the golden prize now clutched in his hand, a young soccer player mounted on a small marble square with a pasted-on plaque that stated: "STATE CHAMPION."

Silence. *He should be home by now.*

"Dad, where are you? We won!"

Dad's briefcase lay flat just inside the front door, in a crumpled heap with his black garment bag. *Dad always makes me pick up my backpack, so why would he leave his stuff here?* Ace slowed and headed toward the kitchen. Everything looked the same, just as it had when they left earlier. Mom's notepad sat prominently on the kitchen table, not where it belonged, but Ace turned his head away and walked toward the sliding door to the backyard. He peered into the backyard through the mesh screen, left open for the temperate breeze to cool the house.

"Dad?"

No answer. Ace turned and walked past the table, again noticing the notepaper, and again avoiding it. He stopped and turned back toward the notepad and then decided to ignore it yet again before turning down the hall toward his parents' bedroom. The hall was windowless and with the lights switched off, quite dark. Some illumination from his parents' bedroom door, which was ajar, lit the way. The light streamed through that crack and lit particles of floating dust, causing a yellowish gloom. He followed the diffused light but didn't peek through the crack when he got to the door. Without knocking, he nudged open the door with his fingertips, his other hand still clutching the trophy.

One step inside the threshold, Ace dropped his prize. He doubled over and nearly threw up.

His dad lay slumped like a pile of dirty laundry on the floor. His face was pale and blueish.

For a moment, Ace didn't understand the image that would haunt him every day for the rest of his life. His thoughts shut down and his burning eyes didn't see. And when the moment passed, he spurred himself to action.

"Mom! Mom!" Ace screamed.

Heather burst into the room. She choked on her scream. Nearly flying, she landed on her knees by Steve's side. She touched his face, then raced to the kitchen for the phone.

Ace kneeled by his dad's face when his eyelids quivered. *He's alive, thank God, he's alive.*

"Dad? Can you hear me? A doctor is coming." Ace stroked Steve's face, but his unfocused eyes barely fluttered open before closing again.

Steve convulsed. His eyes rolled back as his body twitched.

Ace squeezed his hand. Ace's fingers tingled as vibrations of Steve's memory flowed into him. His dad gasped again, sucking dank air through the moldy sludge that had crept over his face. Ace immediately recognized this feeling. He had felt it only once before, but he remembered. He remembered Robbie on the bathroom floor in San Diego. This was shame. Ace shivered as the swampy muck of shame saturated him, then smothered him. Darkness covered him and pulled at him. It yanked down hard. The sludge sucked him under like quicksand. Immersed, he watched light retreat from the slimy muck as he fell further away, as he plummeted into an infinite depth. As he fell, the swamp dissipated, and the light became smaller, distant, until there was only darkness. Darkness and nothing.

Nothing. The nothing swallowed up even the shame.

But another, different light appeared, and it was not falling away, it came closer. The welcoming light called to him. Ace disconnected from his hand now clutching Steve's, disconnected from his entire body.

Even through closed eyes, Ace sensed darkness turn to light because falling turned to floating. The swamp had receded; it was gone, replaced with something…

Large, gloved hands from nowhere grabbed Ace's shoulders and gently but firmly pulled him back, back out of the welcoming light, back through the darkness, and back through the dripping quagmire. Ace had not noticed the firefighters who had arrived and now surrounded his father. Ace opened his eyes and stumbled back, confused, and feeling again like he was covered in slime. None of it made any sense. Then the hands on his shoulders were different, ungloved, familiar, gentle.

Heather guided Ace further away so the EMTs could do their work saving her husband's life. Ace shook his head to clear out the remnants of sludge. He felt his feet on the floor and remembered where he was. He looked up into his mom's ashen face, her hand firm on his shoulder.

"Atticus? Atticus?"

He stared up at her, then found his voice and answered. "Mom?"

"I need you to help. Can you do something for me?"

Ace nodded.

"Take your sister to her room now. I don't want her to see. Please take care of her," she said. Although her hand felt cold and her face whitened, her voice was controlled, her reassuring mom-voice.

Ace had watched his sister plenty of times, but the burden had never been so heavy. Lisa clung to their mom, wide-eyed and silent. Ace wiped his cheeks with the sleeve of his soccer jersey and took his sister's tiny hand in his. The wide-eyed little face looked up at the big brother when she took his hand. Her face a mask of confusion screamed unspoken questions. Ace led her away. It was the best he could do to protect her from the tragic scene.

He was his sister's hero, but no longer a childhood hero, no longer a hero shark. In an instant, Atticus had become the man of his family.

# Thirty-four

# ANOTHER EVENING AT HOME

# 2022

"So, what's Robbie going to do with all that money?" Lisa asked Ace on the front porch of their mom's new house. A lover of bright colors, Lisa wore a rainbow tie-dyed tank top over jean shorts and sandals. Her long blond hair had darkened some, but was still as bright as her disposition. Yo didn't care that Lisa's fingernails were ragged and chewed because those fingers busily scratched her shaggy ears.

"We got nothing yet and may never see a cent." Ace rang the doorbell and bent down to take off his shoes.

"What? They appealed?" she asked as she kicked off her sandals.

"No. They filed bankruptcy."

Heather opened the unlooked door, welcomed them inside, and said, "You don't have to ring. Come on in. What's this about bankruptcy?"

Yo had trotted inside before Heather could finish her invitation.

Ace dumped his shoes under the bench in the foyer and hugged his mom. "Lisa asked what Robbie was going to do with his money and I told her that the Association filed bankruptcy, so he probably won't get very much of it and probably not for a while."

"That's not fair," Heather said.

"Actually, believe it or not, it's more fair for other victims. So maybe they can recover something, too. There isn't enough money for everyone. The bankruptcy courts have processes for handling that, trying to even it out."

"I guess, but still…" Lisa stammered.

"I just opened a chardonnay. Grab some glasses from the bar." Heather pointed across the room and headed to the kitchen for the bottle. The trio settled into the comfortable living area to sip their wine and chat. Yo had found an old rawhide scrap to chew while she lay quietly at Ace's feet.

An old cardboard shoebox, held together at the corners with yellowed packing tape, sat on the coffee table between a cluster of scented candles and various crystals. Ace recognized the box, but he thought about the file boxes in the courtroom, different kinds of boxes but the same story, boxes hidden all over the world in dusty file rooms, under beds, in attics, closets, the embodiment of hidden memories.

"Is that Dad's old box of stuff?" Lisa asked, gesturing toward the shoebox.

Heather nodded, and Ace just continued to stare quietly.

"I remember finding that in the closet once. Dad never let me look in it. He kept it hidden." Lisa twisted the woven friendship bracelet on her wrist.

"I should've shared this with you a while ago, but I didn't have the courage. Robbie's trial made me remember what I needed to show you." Heather opened the box, setting the lid on the coffee table, and took out an old, crumpled paper, unfolded it, and gave it to Ace. "I'll explain and answer your questions when you're done reading." Lisa scootched closer to Ace on the couch to read over his shoulder.

Ace glanced at the paper and recognized the notepaper Heather used to keep by the phone at the old house. He jerked his head up to look at his mom. "Mom…" Yo jerked her head up as well and nuzzled against Ace's leg for reassurance.

"It's okay. I'm here. You are safe. Read." She reassured them both. She gently smoothed the paper in Ace's lap, "go ahead," then leaned over to move the box of tissue closer, setting it in front of the siblings without another word.

Lisa nodded and bent her head to read her father's suicide note. The ink was faded, and she couldn't recognize the shaky, drunken handwriting. She had been too little to learn her dad's handwriting before he was gone.

*My loving family, If there is a God, maybe I'll find absolution, but I could never hope to find your forgiveness. I'm sorry that*

*I'm a failure as a provider, a protector, a husband, a father. I'm sorry... Atticus, what happened to you brought it back... my torment... I was your age. If I remembered sooner, if I had been there, maybe I could have protected you. i should have been there —*

Ace handed Lisa a handful of tissues as she sobbed openly. He held her close, absorbed in her anguish. *I wish I could take it away. I can feel her pain, but I can't stop it*, he thought. The siblings shook, cried, and clung to each other on the couch, and finally caught their breath enough to ask the inevitable questions. Disturbed by the humans' distress, Yo broke protocol and jumped on the couch to lick their faces.

"It's ok, Yo. Get off the couch. Yo, off." Ace said as he nuzzled her to the floor. "Dad said something happened to me? What's that mean? I don't understand."

"I know. It's wrong. It was Robbie, not you. I think your dad thought it was you, Ace." Heather said.

"What?"

"There's no way to really know, but from his note, and the other things in the box, that's the best explanation I can find."

"You didn't tell us." Lisa choked out the accusation.

"No, you were so little. I'm sorry. I always planned to tell you when you were older, but I was too scared. It was too painful to talk about." Heather handed Lisa fresh tissues when she dropped the slimy, shredded wad on the floor. "Time got away from me. I'm so sorry."

Lisa nodded and blew her nose. "Why now? The trial?"

"Yeah, the trial."

Ace held Lisa close and said, "I remember now that I saw the note on that day. I think that I sort of pieced things together over the years, but tried not to think about it. Still, it doesn't all make sense." Ace closed his eyes and pictured himself as a little boy, reading the note at the kitchen table while his mom had been preoccupied with the emergency medical team and everything else. He had pushed it away quickly so that little Lisa, clinging to him, wouldn't see. "You were too little, Lisa. I didn't want you to see it. I was trying to protect you."

Lisa looked up at her big brother as his words sank in.

Heather nodded. "I thought you might have seen it, Ace, but I wasn't sure. I stuffed it into this box after the police returned it because it was just too painful. We never talked about it."

"That's why, selfishly, I didn't want Robbie to do the trial, but he pushed me. He knows. I wouldn't—couldn't—have done it for anyone else, but Robbie knew and helped me through it."

"Do all the Santoses know?" Lisa asked.

"I think Gus and Gabi know, at least kind of, but they don't ask. That's why they've always been there for us. I don't know if the brothers know, probably not. It's not something we talk about," Ace said.

"I'm glad you did it, Ace," Heather said. "Robbie was right about it being good for you. The trial helped you work through a lot of stuff—me too."

"Yeah, typical Robbie, he talked me into it. I finally agreed because I thought maybe a shred of justice might redeem our tragedy, but I still don't really believe in justice, so that was a disappointment."

Heather gave the siblings a quiet minute to process and sort through the life-changing news.

A quick glint from inside the old shoebox caught Ace's eye and drew him closer. He reached inside and pulled out a small crumbly, gold rock: fool's gold. The rock's power compelled him to clutch it and as he did, he felt safe. It wasn't Brazilian tourmaline. In fact, it was rather ordinary looking, but Ace felt that this rock protected him from the psychosphere's never-ending assault. He didn't know why.

"Can I keep this rock?" He asked his mom and Lisa.

"Of, course as long as that's ok with Lisa," his mom answered.

Lisa nodded as their mom continued her story, "So, there is more to it. I think something bad happened to your dad when he was a child." She pulled out a newspaper clipping, some cloth merit patches, a Swiss army knife, tattered Polaroid pictures of Steve as a child with a creepy old man, and other various mementos of their dad's childhood. One picture showed Steve as a young boy, naked and provocatively posed.

"What is this stuff?" Lisa asked. The corners of her mouth dropped, taking part of her jaw with them.

"I think that the newspaper article is the same man in the pictures with your dad. He was accused of sexual assault, which made the paper, but no charges were ever filed. There is also a news clipping of his obituary. I think it was the man in the pictures, but I can't tell if that is some sort of scout group or religious group. It doesn't really matter anymore." Heather paused before saying the hardest thing. "I think your dad was sexually assaulted as a child and I think this man did it. His note doesn't exactly say that, but it makes sense with everything in this box. It also makes sense with how he acted in a lot of ways."

"It makes the most sense and explains the note," Ace said.

Lisa nodded before asking, "Do you think that's why he killed himself?" Her eyes searched for answers on the faces of her mom and brother. "Is that what he meant in his note about remembering sooner? Being abused…"

Ace shrugged, but Heather said nothing and sipped her wine.

"How is it possible he didn't remember that? He kept all this stuff," Lisa said.

Ace nodded. "It happens a lot," he said. "Shrinks call it dissociative amnesia. Some trauma is so overwhelming to the human brain that it shuts down, shuts everything out. Children particularly shut it out so they can emotionally survive childhood. Dad put it all in this box, then hid the box like he hid the memories." Ace could feel Lisa was confused. "The trauma returns with the memory. So, it's not just the memory, it's like going through the trauma again, like he's there back in that moment as a child. Like he's being raped again."

Heather chewed her lower lip and spoke up. "That's what the doctor expert said at Robbie's trial. When he said all that, it finally made sense to me. I think for the first time I had some understanding about what happened."

Ace snorted and shook his head. "Ya, that's what caused me to fuck up during the trial. It all hit me at the same time. At first it seems hard to believe, but think about it, people deny the pandemic, they deny the holocaust. It's human nature to deny an ugly truth. That happens all the time, too."

"You think that's what happened to Dad?" Lisa asked.

"I do. It makes the most sense," Ace said.

"We think he had post-traumatic stress," Heather added.

"Exactly. He thought it was *me* that was raped. It triggered the episode, the hidden memory of his rape came out, and…" Ace stopped, gulped hard, and bit his lower lip. "… and he couldn't handle it. He couldn't handle knowing."

Heather sat on the opposite side of Lisa and the trio hugged, and sat, and sobbed, until the shadows grew long. The mementos in the shoe box sat undisturbed, ignored. Heather went to stick the box in the coat closet, and looking at it one more time mumbled to herself,

"He couldn't face knowing."

# Epilogue
# 2022

A well-kept secret among Californians is that October is perhaps the most beautiful month of the year, sunny but cool with clear skies, a last homage to the already vanished summer before autumn's onset. Ace was at the barbeque on an October day, flipping burgers, watching young swimmers, drinking icy-cold soda, and enjoying the mood. Relaxing vibrations floated about the psychosphere, a welcome emotional shift. After the extremes of pain, fear, victory, and exhilaration, Ace savored the smooth flavors of friendship and family flowing from all the people surrounding him, all flawed and all beautiful.

Ace's mom, Heather, and Soccer-Mom Susie Martin were in the kitchen fussing. The occasion presented the perfect opportunity for Heather to share baking tips with Susie, and the gang would have made-from-scratch buns with their hamburgers. An unlikely but solid friendship had blossomed between the two very different women, both single now since Susie and Joe had divorced. Josh had been invited but was deployed to an air force base in the Middle East so couldn't be there, but he might not have showed up anyway. Gus and the three oldest Santos brothers battled it out at double's ping-pong, while the Santos brothers' wives chased the grandchildren. Robbie made the kids laugh by jumping into the pool cannonball-style and making enormous splashes.

Lupe relaxed by floating on her back in the pool, but she must have felt Ace's eyes on her because she tilted her head up and smiled, a big, stunning, radiant smile. She rested her head back in the water but kept a remnant of her smile as her eyes rested in the sun. Despite himself, Ace's heart stirred in response to her grace, but he turned his attention back to the barbeque.

Ace flipped the remaining burgers, put them all on a platter and handed it to Lisa with a smile. She walked off to set up the buffet while humming a childhood ditty to herself, and Ace walked off to find a quiet place. Set back away from the pool, Ace lowered himself into a strappy chaise lounge. Resting one hand on his stomach, he closed his eyes and tilted his head back to feel the sun on his face and enjoy the aroma of freshly baked bread wafting out from the kitchen. Instead, he felt drops of pool water on his feet and of course when he opened his eyes, there was Robbie, standing over him and staring.

"You big meanie," Robbie said. "You're making Yo work today?"

Hearing her name, Yo lifted her head and wagged her tail, but she didn't get up.

"Look what I've got, Yo," Robbie teased and held up a tennis ball. That was enough to get her up and wiggling about. "Imma throw this ball!" With that Robbie tossed the ball into the pool and Yo lost her restraint. She bounded off after the ball and jumped into the pool splashing all the swimmers.

Robbie lowered himself into an adjoining chaise lounge with a grunt just in time for Yo to return the ball, so he threw it again.

"How's it going, Ace? You got it all figured out yet?" Robbie asked.

Ace smiled. "Nah, just enjoying myself. Trying not to think too much."

"You definitely do too much thinking. It's good to see you relaxed, finally."

"Ya, I guess. Your mom and Tony are getting along well, I see." Ace nodded over at the two who were lounging on a chaise across the big suburban yard, sipping black-cherry hard ciders and chatting.

"Mom gets along with everyone, so does Tony. They are so much alike they might be twins."

"You married your mom."

"Oh my god, Ace. Don't say that! But, ok, it's true. I married my mom." Robbie laughed. "It's a relief that the family is opening up to Tony. Dad even gets along with him now."

"Your dad gets along with everyone—"

"—and so does Tony." The men said the last part at the same time and laughed.

Yo came back and dropped the ball next to Robbie, who didn't pay any attention. Not to be ignored, Yo shook herself sending sprays of water everywhere and causing more laughter mixed with reprimand.

After toweling off the sprinkled doggy water, the men sat silently for a few minutes watching their imperfect and loving family. Ace's gaze wandered back to Lupe who was still lounging in the swimming pool, this time on a blowup raft she must have found. Even though she wasn't a Santos, or an Elbridge, she was comfortable with the crazy. She possessed that special quality among many others. Ace smiled.

"Look at you, big goof ball. Gaping at Lupe like you want to eat her for lunch," Robbie said.

"I am not."

"Yes, you are. Go talk to her."

"I can't," Ace said. His smile disappeared. "She's my law partner."

"She's a big girl and nobody reads signals better than you. If she's not interested, you'll read that and respect it. Listen to your gut, but I can tell you, dude, she's interested."

"It's not professional."

"Fuck professional."

Ace looked down at his hands and frowned as he searched his mind for the right thing—the correct thing—to do, and he didn't know. Or maybe he didn't trust himself.

"It's ok, Ace. Really. She might have said something to me," Robbie said, and he jabbed Ace in the ribs.

Ace heard the sincerity in Robbie's voice which gave him just enough strength to open his heart. He let himself reach out to channel the surrounding happiness and abundant love. It was all there and embracing his emotional sponge nature, he allowed himself to soak up all of it.

Without another word, Ace rose and headed to the swimming pool.

# Acknowledgements

Reaching out for help is hard for me, but in putting together this project, I did it anyway and, to my delight, people stepped up. Thank you to everyone who said *yes* when I asked. And thank you to everyone listed in the Author's Notes for being a resource and an inspiration.

The members of the Treasure Valley Author Team volunteered hours of work reviewing my work and giving feedback. There are no words to express my gratitude to you all for the support you've given: David Rozansky, for getting us organized and his attention to detail; Elaine Lee, for her insight; Robyn McIntyre for her humor; Steve Dill for his optimism; and all of you for your encouragement. I love you all.

Russell Dick from B4U-Act reviewed multiple drafts of my writing, recommended invaluable resources for my review, and stayed with me until I got it right. I cannot thank you enough for your time. The world is a better place for your contributions.

So many others said *yes* when I reached out: Dr. Michael Seto for sharing his outstanding research papers; Rachael Denhollander, not only for her courage but also for permission to use her quote; Timothy Hale, Esq. for sharing legal documents, DC Glenn, the Brain Supreme, for permission to use his work, his enthusiasm, and his encouragement, Bob Mate for his publishing expertise, and Ethan for taking a risk by connecting with me.

My editors, Dr. M.J. VanDevere and Daniel Maurer, for your patience in helping me with the basics. You taught me much and I really enjoyed working with you. I hope to have that opportunity again.

This book could not have happened if my husband Aaron had not found me in the Emerald Dream of Azeroth and changed my life. You are my strength and inspiration, and My Love.

Finally, I acknowledge all the survivors who had the courage to speak their truth and make their claim for justice. Knowing is here because of your courage and tenacity. Thank you.

# Support And Resources

Multiple organizations exist to help survivors of childhood sexual abuse. There are few that provide support for minor attracted people. The following resources will get you started on your search for help.

National Sex Abuse Hotline, 1-800-656-4673
Rape, Abuse & Incest National Network, rainn.org
B4U-ACT, https://www.b4uact.org/
Virtuous Pedophiles, virped.org
WhatsOK.org

# Ask Yourself Or Discuss

What does justice look like for the survivor of a childhood sexual assault?

Who bears responsibility for preventing the sexual assault and molestation of children?

What are the differences between Coach Sean, JJ, and the Man from the first chapter?

How does a minor-attracted person find safe support in not acting on their attraction?

What is the collateral damage of sexual child abuse to other family members, spouses, and communities?

How many debunked assumptions about the risk of childhood sexual abuse could you identify in the novel?

How many themes can you identify from the title *When Knowing Comes?*

# Author's Notes

As a former practicing attorney and law review editor, I felt compelled to keep track of my inspirations and resources. Following is an Easter egg map of sorts, for my fellow nerds (yet some gems remain hidden):

Appelman, J. Ruben, *Children of the Snow*, Cineflix Productions, February 18, 2019, documentary mini-series.

Appelman, J. Ruben, *The Kill Jar: Obsession, Descent, and a Hunt for Detroit's Most Notorious Serial Killer*, New York, Simon & Schuster, 2018.

Bar-Lev, Amir, *Happy Valley*, A&E Indie-Films, Asylum Entertainment, January 19, 2014 ("WE ARE—" "—PEN STATE" -> "WE ARE STRIKERS").

Bass, Ellen, and Davis, Laura, *The Courage to Heal: A Guide for Women Survivors of Child Sexual Abuse*, New York, Harper & Row Publishers, 1988.

Bell, Christopher, *State of Play: Trophy Kids*, HBO, December 4, 2013, documentary film.

Boyle, Patrick, *Scout's Honor, Sexual Abuse in America's Most Trusted Institution*, Rocklin, CA, Prima Publishing, 1994.

Brown, Brené, *Listening to Shame*, TED2012, https://www.ted.com/talks/brene_brown_listening_to_shame?language=en ("Empathy is the antidote to shame.")

Brown, Patrick, *In a Town this Size, a Documentary about Child Sexual Abuse*, Cat on the Wall Productions, October 22, 2013, documentary film.

Campea, Matthew, *I, Pedophile*, CBC Television (Canada), March 10, 2016, documentary film.

Cantor, Andrés, Telemundo Deportes sportscaster ("GooooooaaaaAAAALL!")

Carr, Erin Lee, *At the Heart of Gold: Inside the USA Gymnastics Scandal*, HBO, April 26, 2019.

Chastain, Brandi, Champion, 1999 FIFA Women's World Cup Final, Pasadena (because she's awesome).

Chen, David W., *What Happens When Protectors Turn a Blind Eye?*, The New York Times, April 5, 2020.

Conroy, Pat, *The Prince of Tides*, New York, Dial Press Trade Paperbacks (an imprint of The Random House Publishing Group, a division of Random House), 2009 (First published in 1986).

Crew Janci, LLP, *A Tribute to Attorney: Kelly Clark*, crewjanci.com/tribute-to-attorney-kelly-clark/, Battle of the Lawyers (closing argument in three parts).

Denhollander, Rachael, *What is a Girl Worth? My story of breaking the silence and exposing the truth about Larry Nassar and USA Gymnastics*, Carol Stream, Illinois, Tyndale, 2019 (because she's awesome).

Dick, Kirby, *A Twist of Faith*, HBO, August 20, 2004, documentary film.

Dick, Kirby, *The Hunting Ground*, Chain Camera Pictures, January 1, 2016, documentary film.

Ellison, Keith, Minnesota Attorney General, public statement about the conviction of D. Chauvin, April 20, 2021 ("I would not call today's verdict justice, however, because justice implies true restoration. But it is accountability, which is the first step toward justice,…").

Farragher, *Thomas, Church Cloaked in Culture of Silence*, The Boston Globe, February 24, 2002.

Fedoroff, J. Paul, MD, *The Pedophilia and Orientation Debate and Its Implications for Forensic Psychiatry*, The Journal of the American Academy of Psychiatry and the Law, vol.48, Number 2, 2020.

Fisher, Aaron, and Gillum, Michael, with Daniels, Dawn, *Silent No More: Victim 1's Fight for Justice against Jerry Sandusky*, New York, Ballantine Books (an imprint of The Random House Publishing Group, a division of Random House), 2012.

Fortieth Statewide Investigating Grand Jury, *Report No. 1*, Court of Common Pleas of Allegheny, Pennsylvania, Hon. Norman A. Krumenacker, III, Pennsylvania, August 2018 (*inter.alia.*, Circle of Secrecy).

Francis, *Letter of his Holiness Pope Francis to the People of God*, Vatican City, August 20, 2018 (Not enough. Do more).

Freeh Sporkin & Sullivan, LLP, *Report of the Special Investigative Counsel Regarding the Actions of The Pennsylvania State University Related to the Child Sexual Abuse Committed by Gerald A. Sandusky*, 2012 (horsing around, showers).

Gibney, Alex, *Mea Maxima Culpa: Silence in the House of God*, HBO, February 4, 2013, documentary film.

Gregory, Sean, *How Kids' Sports Became a $15 Billion Industry*, Time Magazine, August 24, 2017.

Gretsky, Wayne (who always skates to where the puck is going to be, even if he never really said that).

Heasman, Ainslie, and Moss, Sarah, *Ethical and Clinical Issues in Treating Non-Justice-Involved People with Pedophilia and/or Hebephilia*, Association for the Treatment of Sexual Abusers, 39th Annual (virtual) Research & Treatment Conference, October 22, 2020.

Herdy, Amy, *Have You Ever Met a Monster?*, TEDxSanJuanIsland, January 13, 2016, https://www.youtube.com/watch?v=IV5jbi7otx-0&ab_channel=TEDxTalks

Herdy, Amy, *Diary of a Predator: a Memoir*, Boulder, Vincent Publishing House, 2012.

Herman, Lily, *Penn Students Hand Out Flyers to Combat Rape Culture on Campus*, TeenVogue, teenvogue.com/story/university-pennsylvania-students-hand-out-flyers-combat-rape-culture-campus, September 7, 2016 (flyers accusing rape are a thing).

Hillcourt, William, T*he Official Boy Scout Handbook*, 9th ed., Boy Scouts of America, 1979.

Hunter, Mic, *Abused Boys: The Neglected Victims of Sexual Abuse*, New York, Fawcett Columbine (an imprint of Ballantine Books), 1990.

In re Boy Scouts of America and Delaware BSA, LLC, United States Bankruptcy Court for the District of Delaware, #20-50527 (jointly administered), (multiple pleadings, over 80,000 abuse claims submitted).

Jackson, Peter, T*he Lord of the Rings: The Two Towers*, Barry Osborne, December 2002 (Based on the trilogy by J.R.R. Tolkien. Theoden: "What can men do against such reckless hate?").

Jordan, Jamal, *Queer Love in Color*, California, New York, Ten Speed Press, 2021 (<3).

King Jr., Martin Luther, I Have a Dream speech, Washington D.C., August, 28, 1963 (". . . until justice rolls down like waters and righteousness like a mighty stream." Quoting scripture).

Kohli, Diti, *'Shame on Boston University': Students post flyers, chalk messages to protest sexual violence*, The Boston Globe, February 20, 2021.

Lee, Harper, *To Kill a Mockingbird*, J.B. Lippincott & Co., Philadelphia, July 11, 1960.

Lew, Mike, *Victims No Longer: The Classic Guide for Men Recovering from Sexual Child Abuse*, 2d ed., New York, Harper Perennial (an Imprint of Harper Collins Publishers), 2004.

Loftus, Elizabeth, *How Reliable is your Memory?*, TED, https://www. youtube.com/watch?v=PB2OegI6wvI&ab_channel=TEDTED, 2013.

Los Angeles Times staff, *Inside the 'perversion files' Tracking decades of allegations in the Boy Scouts*, (database) The Los Angeles Times, October 18, 2012 (multiple horrible stories).

Lovett, Ian, *Catholic Church Offers Cash to Settle Abuse Claims—With a Catch*, Wall Street Journal, July 11, 2019.

MacGregor, Annie, *Dark Secret*, Moondance Films, July 17, 2017, documentary film.

Malone, Luke, *Episode #522: Tarred and feathered. Part II: Help Wanted*, This American Life, originally aired November 4, 2014, https:// www.thisamericanlife.org/522/tarred-and-feathered/act-two-0

Malone, Luke, *You're 16. You're a pedophile. You don't want to hurt anyone. What do you do now?*, medium.com, August 10, 2014, https://medium.com/matter/youre-16-youre-a-pedophile-you-dont-want-to-hurt-anyone-what-do-you-do-now-e11ce4b88bdb

Maltz, Wendy, *The Sexual Healing Journey: A Guide of Survivors of Sexual Abuse*, New York, Harper Perennial (a division of Harper Collins Publishers), 1991.

Markel, M.D., Howard, *Case Shined First Light on Abuse of Children*, New York Times, December 14, 2009 (attorney Elbridge).

McCarthy, Tom, *Spotlight*, Open Road Films, September 3, 2015, biographical drama film.

Morgan, Lynne, Co-Founder of Building Hope Today, presentation, Boise, Idaho, April 9, 2018 (describing the moment when husband Matt Morgan remembered as when the knowing came).

Morgan, Matt, Co-Founder of Building Hope Today, for his courage and generosity.

Morrison, Toni, *The Bluest Eye*, Plume, 1994.

Mulligan, Robert, *To Kill a Mockingbird*, Universal Pictures, December 25, 1962, dramatic film.

Murphey, Cecil, and Roe, Gary, *Not Quite Healed: 40 Truths for Male Survivors of Childhood Sexual Abuse*, Grand Rapids, 2013.

Nabokov, Vladimir, *Lolita*, New York, Vintage Books (a division of Random House), 1955, Second Vintage International Edition, June 1997.

Otto, Linda, *Unspeakable Acts*, Alan Landsburg Productions, January 15, 1990, biographical drama film.

Pelé (enough said).

Pelosi, Alexandra, *The Trials of Ted Haggard*, HBO, January 29, 2009, documentary film.

Pennington, Bill, *The Trusted Grown-Ups Who Steal Millions From Youth Sports*, The New York Times, July 7, 2016.

Perry, Bruce D., M.D., Ph.D., and Winfrey, Oprah, *What Happened to You? Conversations On Trauma, Resilience, and Healing*, Flatiron Books, New York, 2021 (I now have the tools and understanding to step back, observe what I'm feeling, and choose how to move through the fear – Oprah).

Prevention Project Dunkelfeld, various papers and media coverage, commenced in Germany, 2005 (see https://en.wikipedia.org/ wiki/Prevention_Project_Dunkelfeld).

Reed, Dan, *The Paedophile Hunter*, Amos Pictures, October 1, 2014, documentary film.

Reed, Dan, *Leaving Neverland*, HBO, March 3, 2019, documentary film.

Rezendes, Michael, Carroll, Matt, and Pfeiffer, Sacha, *Church allowed abuse by priest for years*, The Boston Globe, January 6, 2002 (part 1), and January 7, 2002 (part 2).

Rivelino, Roberto, Futebol Champion, Brazil National Team, 1970 FIFA World Cup Final, Mexico City (one touch pass to Pelé who scored opening goal on a header, Brazil won. Master of the *elastico*).

Robinson, Walter V., and Kurkjian, Stephen, *Archdiocese weighs bankruptcy filing*, The Boston Globe, December 1, 2002.

Samenow, Stanton E., *Inside the Criminal Mind*, New York, Broadway Books (an imprint of the Crown Publishing Group, a division of Random House, a Penguin Random House Company), 1984.

Sanchez, Ray, *Alleged 'rapist list' appears around Columbia University*, CNN, cnn.com/2014/05/14/us/columbia-university-flier-rapes, May 14, 2014 (again, flyers are definitely a thing).

Seto, Michael C., *Is Pedophilia a Sexual Orientation?*, Arch.Sex.Behavior, January 5, 2012.

Seto, Michael C., *Pedophilia and Sexual Offending Against Children, Theory, Assessment, and Intervention*, 2d ed., Washington DC, American Psychological Association, 2018.

Seto, Michael C., *The Puzzle of Male Chronophilias*, Arch.Sex.Behavior (2017) 46:3-22.

Simplot Fields, Boise, Idaho, the most beautiful youth soccer complex in the US. Final Game: (The unpaved parking lot flattened the top of a small hill smack in the middle of the soccer complex.)

Slade, Alzo, *The Men Who Call Themselves Non-Offending Pedophiles*, Vice News on HBO, August 27, 2019, https://www.youtube.com/watch?v=5yWklRbXDOY&ab_channel=VICENews

Sol, Albert, *Examination of Conscience*, (Spanish Examen de Conciencia), Netflix, January 25, 2019.

Tag Team, *Whoomp! (There It Is)*, Life Records, May 7, 1993, (Quoted with permission; DC Glenn is a generous soul.).

The Supreme Court of the State of Idaho, Administrative Office of the Court, *Idaho Child Protection Manual: A Practical Guide for Judges and Attorneys*, 5th ed., 2018.

Tolmach, Paige Goldberg, *What Haunts Us, Pay Attention to Who Pays Attention to Your Kids*, Artemis Rising Foundation, May 22, 2018, documentary film.

Van der Bruggen, Madeleine, *Let's Be Mature about Pedophilia*, TEDx-SittardGeleen, April 13, 2018, https://www.youtube.com/watch?v=egiBgmvv8wA&ab_channel=TEDxTalks

Van Noorden, Erik, *Desire of the Everlasting Hills*, unknown, (video) October 2015.

Vielmetti, Bruce, *2 soccer moms charged with embezzling $80,000 from club*, Journal Sentinel, Milwaukee, Wisconsin, February 24, 2014.

Vieth, Victor, *Trial Strategies in Cases of Child Abuse: Pre trial motions, jury selection, cross-examination, opening statements and closing arguments*, National Child Protection Training Center, courts.delaware.gov/childadvocate/docs/Vieth-trialstrategies.pdf

Walker, Allyn, *A Long, Dark Shadow, Minor-Attracted People and Their Pursuit of Dignity*, Oakland, California, University of California Press, 2021.

Warwick Middleton, Adah Sachs & Martin J. Dorahy, *The abused and the abuser: Victim-perpetrator dynamics, Journal of Trauma & Dissociation*, 18:3, 249-258, March 20, 2017.

Wise, Cat, and Choe, Jaywon, *Invisible Scars: America's Childhood Trauma Crisis, part 1*, PBS Newshour, December 16, 2020.

Womeldorf, Tommy, *Scout's Dishonor, A Personal Story of God, Abuse, Recovery, and Truth*, Kindle e-book, 2015.

Yoon-Hendricks, Alexandra, *New California law gives victims of childhood sexual assault more time to file lawsuits*, The Sacramento Bee, October 14, 2019.

Zabin, Amy, *Conversations With A Pedophile: In the Interest of our Children*, Fort Lee, Barricade Books, 2003.

And *Whoomp*, there it is!

www.ingramcontent.com/pod-product-compliance
Lightning Source LLC
Chambersburg PA
CBHW030623310726
48979CB00003B/852